n Creek • Ann Cave Creek • Arkansas Creek • Back Creek • ~~Bush Slough~~ • Bacon Creek • Bailey
anch • Bear Creek • Beard Branch • Beartree Fork • Beaver

Berry Run • Big Bone Island • Big Bone Creek • Big Branch
ek • Blackberry Creek • Blackberry Fork • Blackwater Creek • Blood River • Blue Run • Boone
ushy Fork • Brushy Gr... • Buckhorn Creek •
d Fork • Buzzard B... Campbell Branch •

Spring Creek • Car... eek • Cat Creek •
lay Lick Creek • Cla... Branch • Coleman
• Cope Branch • C... n • Craig Creek •
River • Cutshin Cre... Dick Branch • Dix
Dripping Springs Br... ork Branch • Dry
Creek • Emily's Run... Falls of the Ohio •
reeman Branch • Fr... • Gilmore Creek •
Creek • Graveyard... River • Greenup
Creek • Hanson's Lo... River • Hickman
• Horns River • H... anch • Houchin's
k • Hurricane Cree... acks Creek • Jake
ch • Johnson Creek... Creek • Kentucky
aurel Creek • Laure... Creek • Lefthand
k • Little Barren R... ech Creek • Little
ve Run • Little Clea... • Little Hickman
Creek • Little Mudd... stle River • Little
n Creek • Locke B... don River • Long
tts Creek • Lowe... s Creek • Lower
Creek • Marble Cr... • Maxey Creek •
th Branch • Mid... Creek Branch •
onks Creek • Mo... ck Creek • Mud
Creek • Mystic... ng Fork River •
h • Page Creek... ranch • Patton's
idge Branch • Po... • Possum Run •
amp Creek- • Pu... ys Branch • Red
ng River • Robin... ver • Rockhouse
r • Rose Creek •... d Stone Creek •
anch • Sam's Br... bgrass Branch •
Creek • Simpson... s Branch • Slate

• Sprucepine Fork • Spruce Pine Creek • Stall Creek • Stamper Fork • State Road Fork • Station
ens Branch • Stevens Creek • Stevenson's Lost River • Straight Fork • Strodes Creek • Stoner
Teays River • Teges Creek • Tennessee River • Terry Fork • Tom Fork • Town Branch • Trace
ugh Lick • Tucker Creek • Tug Fork • Turkey Branch • Turkey Creek • Turkey Pin Branch • Turkey
• Upper Teges Creek • Upper Twin Creek • Valley Creek • Vaughn Branch • Vertrees
lls Creek • West Fork Creek • White Creek • Whitehorn Creek • White Oak Creek • White's
• Wolf Branch • Wolf Creek • Wolf Pen Creek • Wooton Creek • Yellow Creek • Yost Branch

*Especially for the Flatwoods
Public Library
With all best wishes
from the authors*

Rivers of Kentucky

Nov 19, 2001

David Dick *David Dick*

and

Eulalie C. Dick *Lalie C Dick*

First Edition, March 1, 2001

Copyright 2001
By
Plum Lick Publishing, Incorporated
P. O. Box 68
North Middletown, KY 40357-0068

Dust jacket design and book production
by Stacey Freibert Design
756 South 1st Street — Suite 208
Louisville, Kentucky 40202

Dust jacket photograph (back)
By Chuck Perry

Illustrations by Lalie Dick

Other books by David Dick

The View from Plum Lick
Follow the Storm
Peace at the Center
A Conversation with Peter P. Pence
The Quiet Kentuckians
The Scourges of Heaven

Other books by David and Lalie Dick

Home Sweet Kentucky

ISBN: 0-9632886-8-7

Library of Congress Catalog Card Number
00-193422

For our daughter

Ravy Bradford Dick

in whom our rivers continue to flow

If you would know the soul of Kentucky,
visit its rivers.

C.M. Dupier Jr.

Contents

Foreword

In the late 1980s, I worked with a Kentucky Educational Television crew to make a three-part series of programs about river valleys and forest trails in Southwest Virginia and Eastern Kentucky. My role in each of these productions was to walk the trails and travel the river valleys by car and by boat, noting interesting locations and interviewing interesting people along the way.

I knew going into that work that, like regionally-identified people everywhere, Kentuckians love to talk about their state, to think about it and read about it. They love to look at photographs of scenic Kentucky landscape on postcards, in books, in family photo albums, on television and in fine arts galleries as well. In a time when our nation's media-ridden, commercialized, entertainment culture threatens to obliterate awareness of all things local and natural, Kentucky folk go on with their enduring conversation about their place, its land, its waters, its history, and its sometimes-quirky people.

The literary situation in Kentucky reflects this interest. Every year, scores of new books on life here are published, even as older books on Kentucky are brought back into print. Biographies, autobiographies, memoirs, family histories, community histories, frontier histories, political histories, children's books, collections of regional ghost stories, books by regional humorists, geographical studies, guide books on hiking, camping and canoeing, join the lists of new fiction and poetry to fill the bookstores and line the shelves of libraries.

For more than a decade, David and Lalie Dick of Bourbon County have been among the best and most prolific contributors to this phenomenal literary outpouring. Through their own Plum Lick Publishing company and other presses, David and Lalie have brought into being eight books since 1992. Their work has found an appreciative audience all across the Commonwealth and in the surrounding region. The Dicks have built a strong rapport with their readers through their many public lectures, readings and book signings. Readers at every level of society appreciate the Dicks for their personal warmth and for the vision that underlies Plum Lick Publishing, Inc.

After a full career as a journalist, David returned to his native state in 1985 with Lalie and their daughter, Ravy, to become Director of the University of Kentucky's School of Journalism. Upon his retirement from the University, David and Lalie founded their press and began through their books to shine a light of intelligence and fond appreciation on Kentucky and her people.

Several books have been written on individual rivers in the Commonwealth, but as far as I know, *Rivers of Kentucky* is the first to undertake a comprehensive study of the entire system of Kentucky's flowing streams. In making this study, the Dicks generously point readers toward the whole field of Kentucky literature as they pause to appreciate writers in the various watersheds, quoting them, discussing them, calling attention to their books. In so honoring other contributors to Kentucky's literature, they make the point that the literature of a place is not separate from the land, the water, the people. The natural world and the human culture that is lived upon it are symbiotically entwined, joined in a living web.

In its organization, *Rivers of Kentucky* follows the contours of the state's geography, beginning with the Ohio River which forms Kentucky's northern border. The first section takes the reader on a leisurely journey on a working towboat up the Ohio River from Louisville to Cattlettsburg at the Ohio's confluence with the Big Sandy River. From the Big Sandy, which marks the state's eastern boundary, succeeding chapters treat each of Kentucky's many rivers, great and small, famous and obscure. Some, like the Big Sandy, Kentucky, Cumberland, Green, and Tennessee rivers, have for centuries been historic avenues of exploration and trade. Smaller rivers such as the Licking, Red Bird, Chaplin, and Salt hold stories every bit as interesting and significant in history as the better known, larger rivers.

Fortunately for the reader, David and Lalie Dick reject the standard assumption that a stream must be at least one hundred miles long before it can be called a river. They are more inclined to let the people who live alongside a stream decide if it is a "river" or not. It is a measure of David and Lalie's intrepidity that they identified and visited thirty-eight rivers within the state, twice as many as most people would have thought. The names of these smaller rivers make a litany, pleasing to read aloud: Pond, Mud, Gasper, Logsdon, Clarks, Blood, Finns.

Rivers of Kentucky has so many different elements it is hard to hold them all in mind. It's varied contents include lists of place names that read like found poems. There are interviews with rural and small town Kentuckians in which the honest voices of local folks ring out in refreshing contrast to the tedious drone of television on which "celebrities" interview each other ad nauseum. Especially appealing are David and Lalie's own narratives about such personal adventures as canoeing on Kentucky's rivers, inevitably capsizing from time to time. Appealing also are the many local natural-born storytellers whom the authors wisely grant center stage.

Rivers of Kentucky is a treasure-trove of information and lore about this North American place called Kentucky. It is an atlas, a compendium, a guide book and a story collection all rolled into one. The book is as varied in its style and content as the Kentucky landscape itself. In less capable hands, such a mass and mixture of material could have easily spun out of control. But from the beginning, the reader is assured by the steady voices of David and Lalie Dick, who serve as confident guides through an exotic reading experience. Their writing is suffused with a spirit of generosity, humor, and good sense. It is often poetic. *Rivers of Kentucky* is one of the most interesting, original and useful contributions to Kentucky's flourishing literature to be published in many years.

Gurney Norman

Introduction

Rivers of Kentucky flows from a central concept—the great water cycle—and becomes a nonfiction narrative of the human condition. The book begins there, ends there. The everlasting hydrologic cycle includes the emergence of groundwater in the highlands where people like Terry Ratliff and James Smith labor with their hands and their natural ingenuity. The water gathers unto itself to form the tributaries of the rivers where people like towboat Captain Lonnie Ryan and Chief Mate Ron Felty navigate through the virtually zero visibility of early morning fog beneath the John F. Kennedy Bridge on the Ohio River. Below the confluence of the Ohio and the Mississippi Rivers, an elderly steel magnolia, Adrienne Stepp, watches from her window as Big River loops around her farm and washes over the Madrid fault.

Water moves down from the Kentucky Bend to the lower Mississippi, outward to the sea, where evaporation sends it upward to the atmosphere, where it condenses in clouds and returns home to the mountains as precipitation to be born again. We believe the cycle would be unfinished and meaningless if there had not been people to supply the human texture—balladeer and wood carver John Jacob Niles, hand pressman Gray Zeitz, essayist and poet Wendell Berry, novelist and poet James Still, Civil War reenactor Richard P'Poole, canoeists Ben Culbertson, Michael Hendrix, and Willie Peck, shantyboaters Mike Fletcher and Harlan and Anna Hubbard, and retired, self-proclaimed river rat Virginia Bennett. They give the water its essential character. While the rivers of Kentucky have been flowing for millions of years, the humanity called the Commonwealth has been only a drop of expectation. The best is yet to come.

C.M. Dupier Jr. has added up the numbers to support the claim that Kentucky has more miles of navigable waterways—more than 1,500 miles—than any state of the United States except Alaska. The Commonwealth has more than 13,000 miles of streams, more than 50 man-made reservoirs, and 1,500 square miles of water surface. Dr. Thomas D. Clark, Kentucky's historian laureate, has chronicled the "years of conflict," when the Ohio River separated northern and southern Indian tribes, who used as a hunting ground the land that would become Kentucky. Back then, the water was probably clearer, even drinkable. Then the river divided settlers streaming down the waters from Pittsburgh and up from New Orleans. In time, the Ohio River became the boundary separating free and slave states. Next, it delineated cultural differences between the economically-depressed Appalachian highlands and the industrial complexes of the North. The Ohio River, the part stretching from Catlettsburg, Kentucky, to Cairo, Illinois, has been a 665-mile love-hate affair. It has been a grand highway for migrating settlers and modern day commercial steerage.

There are 90,000 miles of Kentucky waterways draining twelve hydrologic basins. Depending on how the count is done, there are approximately fifty rivers in the Commonwealth (the Kentucky River counts as four rivers—North Fork, Middle Fork, South Fork, and the main stream from Beattyville to Carrollton) and hundreds of creeks, licks, branches, and wet weather runoffs. There are hundreds of unnamed streams. Rain falls from the skies above "The Chimney" and "The Towers" and "Skegg Knob" on the Cumberland Plateau (about forty-six inches annually) in eastern Kentucky and western Virginia and West Virginia, more than half of which evaporates, making this climate similar to Buenos Aires, Rio de Janeiro, and southeastern Australia. Tramping Kentucky's rivers and shorelines has worn out two and a half of our Buick Park Avenues, several pairs of shoes, capsized and roughed up two canoes, and tested our marriage of twenty-two years.

Most of us have come to trust and prefer interstate highways, intrastate parkways, jet trails, and satellite links as the main mile markers of the new millennium. The waterways of the Commonwealth are at best ignored, or taken for granted. It ought to be remembered that without its rivers, Kentucky might have been another Death Valley or Sahara Desert. Without the water there would be no place for 3.8-million people to sink their roots to grow the Kentucky experience.

Rivers of Kentucky is hardly atlas or historical textbook. *The Atlas of Kentucky, Kentucky Rivers Assessment, The Kentucky Encyclopedia,* and *A New History of Kentucky* are only four of the many fine, readily available sources of information about the Commonwealth and its waterways. So, too, is the constant reportage of the daily and weekly newspapers, from Ashland and Pikeville to Paducah and the Kentucky Bend. Their accounts should be read for the guideposts they are. Academic scholarship and responsible journalism will continue to provide citizens with the essential information they need to cope with pullution, flood, drought, soil and water conservation, ecological development, commerce, and recreation.

In Kentucky, there is a great variety of music, Bluegrass to philharmonic. There are theater, ballet studios, and art galleries. The professions are well represented. Arenas, churches, mosques, and synagogues dot the landscape. (Basketball is acknowledged to be one of the major religions.) Our passion is neither of these—our warmth is the word, written and spoken.

Life on and near the springs, licks, branches, creeks, and rivers of Kentucky has been shaped and nurtured by words and water since the days of Daniel Boone, Abraham Lincoln, and Thomas Merton. Our own purpose as rural, Plum Lick fourth-estaters is to provide an up-close, personal view of some "little people" in "little places" who make neither headlines nor the indexes of traditional textbooks. These Kentuckians have been neither pioneers nor presidents, though they might have been if they'd put their minds to it. As for spirituality, the typical Kentuckian has usually been of the cantankerous sort, devoted to the notion that one man's or one woman's soul-frosting is as good as anybody else's.

There are many professionals to thank for reading the early drafts of the manuscript, most especially Gurney Norman of the English Department of the University of Kentucky. His classic, *Kinfolks*, and his public broadcast documentaries on the Big Sandy, Kentucky, and Cumberland Rivers have been invaluable. The scholarship of Charles Dupier Jr. at Cumberland College and of Lowell H. Harrison and Carol Crowe-Carraco at Western Kentucky University has saved us from embarrassing historical mistakes. Louisville literary critic and author Wade Hall read the early drafts with the keen and practiced eye of a literary river pilot. Historian laureate Thomas D. Clark was always there, whether at the University Press of Kentucky, in his home, or in a motel room, encouraging and strengthening our will. The steadfast work of our editor, Georgiana Strickland, has been, as always, caring and crucial, a constant weathervane and a wonderful wordsmith, always helping us better to tell the stories of some of those who've made Kentucky a well-watered place in the best of ways. These encouragements and the concerted belief in the idea that there's an important place for another piece of history—a personal, current narrative of people throughout the Commonwealth—are accepted with heartfelt appreciation. We extend special thanks to Roger Brucker, who has wiggled and candlelighted his way through previously unexplored miles of Mammoth Cave. He insisted that we move beyond myths to tell the truer tale of cavers, especially the slave Stephen Bishop, who discovered Echo River.

Scholars have labored to create a faithful accounting of the historical, geographical, and sociocultural character of the Commonwealth. Without their work, the world would have known little of the intertwined importance of Boone, Clay, Lincoln, Davis, and the all but forgotten Native Americans who preceeded them. Without literature, the Kentucky experience would have been dry bones.

James Lane Allen, Harriette Arnow, Wendell Berry, Linda Scott DeRosier, Janice Holt Giles, Wade Hall, Bobbie Ann Mason, Ed McClanahan, Jim Wayne Miller, Gurney Norman, Elizabeth Madox Roberts, James Still, Jesse Stuart, and Robert Penn Warren and many, many more writers have given Kentuckians a better sense of the essence of who they are and who they might yet become. We dare to venture into their company, acknowledging that where there are errors, poor judgment, and wrongheadedness, we accept them all as our own.

David Dick
Lalie Dick
Plum Lick, Kentucky
March 1, 2001

Ohio

*My river is the Ohio, whose channel from the first has borne the
dreams of men from the old and known to the new and strange.*

Harlan Hubbard
Shantyboat: A River Way of Life

It's four o'clock on a misty mid-October morning on the west side of
Louisville. While most of the city is sleeping, towboat crews are on their
six-on, six-off watches. On the waiting *SuperAmerica*, bound upstream
to Catlettsburg, pilot John Carson and first mate Ron Felty have spoken
to their deckhands with voices muffled in vapor and mist becoming fog.

"Ready?"

"Ready."

The only other sounds are the deafening groan of the engine room,
where Bobby Burge wordlessly monitors the controls of the 4,200
horsepower twin-screw engines. Forward on the same deck, there're the
cracking of three dozen eggs, the sputtering of bacon in the galley, where
Connie Chambers from Carter County, quietly mixes batter for another
round of blueberry pancakes. There's the splash of the water at the
cutting edge of the head-tow, and the foghorn that stiffens the hair on the

1

neck of most any landlubber. For river traffic, McAlpine Lock is the only way around the Falls of the Ohio.

Rain slants through shafts of mile-long searchlight beams. Huge steel chamber-gates slowly, smoothly swing open. The *Floyd Blaskey* nudges and gathers its brood of fifteen barges carrying chemicals, mothering them downstream. Destination—New Orleans.

Marathon-Ashland Oil's multi-million-dollar towboat *SuperAmerica* has delivered its downstream cargo: three barges loaded with low-sulfur diesel, one loaded with turbine fuel, three loaded with gasoline—each one of the big barges with about twenty-five to thirty-six thousand barrels of gasoline or diesel fuel in it. *SuperAmerica* will now maneuver into the vacant chamber, where water will pour back in to raise the upbound towage to a level above the Falls. They say it's like threading the eye of a needle, but it's more like parking three football fields end-to-end in a space with twelve inches on each side and about half of a football field on either end.

"Six inches and closing," says the mate into the two-way radio microphone clipped to his life jacket. If he were to slip and fall overboard between the lead barge and the chamber wall he'd be smeared like a bucket of bright red paint.

"Hmmpff," says John Carson in the pilothouse, more than three football fields away.

"Four inches and closing," says the mate.

"Hmmpff."

"Head on the wall," meaning the front corner of the tow has touched the chamber wall.

"All right," says John, adjusting with a feather-touch the rudder stick, like a quarterback feeling the leather with the tips of his fingers. When the *SuperAmerica* and its towage are inside the lock and the deckhands have secured the temporary mooring lines, the chamber gates close and water pours in again. When the level of the surface is equal to that of the river, the gates ahead open and the *SuperAmerica* inches out, one barge loaded with twenty-five thousand barrels of gas and oil to be re-refined, and seven empty barges to be loaded again at Catlettsburg. More empties will be picked up in Cincinnati.

Connie serves breakfast at 5:30—plates of over-easy fried eggs, sausage and bacon, pancakes, toast, biscuits with gravy, hot coffee. Captain Lonnie Ryan of Princeton, Kentucky, sits at the head of the table. Other crew members come and go, but all sit together at "the table." A hot breakfast is one of the better, surer things in the life of a towboater. Thirty days on and thirty days off (a year's pay for six months' work) probably come in second. There's not a lot of talk. Maybe a joke about brussels sprouts being West Virginia cabbage. Nothing off color. Mostly voices are muted and opinions are reserved. Captain Ryan hands his empty plate to Connie and climbs up three stairways to the pilothouse to relieve Pilot Carson, who comes down for breakfast before going to sleep, the changing of the watch as well-timed as the passing of the baton in a track relay.

The moon and a single star hang over Louisville. The lights of the Galt House, the Humana building, and Joe's Crab Shack shine through the thickening mist, where, for this writer, memories return from forty years ago—the early mornings at WHAS Radio, when the only time a river barge made news was when it broke loose and ran into something. DOA (Dead On Arrival) at General Hospital was a major determining factor separating "some news" from "no news." Runaway barges were "big news." So was the building of the John F. Kennedy Bridge at Louisville.

As Captain Ryan (most of the crew call him "Lonnie") approaches the Kennedy, misty rain turns to dense fog. John F. Kennedy Memorial Bridge becomes as invisible as Camelot, heavy as a shroud. At times like these, small talk turns quickly to almost no talk, only enough to communicate without mistake.

"We're socked in pretty good," says Lonnie, as if in a whispering gallery. He checks his radar and at the same time hears the coolheaded words of first mate Ron Felty, somewhere out there in the end zone of the lead football field.

"One hundred feet from the green marker."

"O.K."

"Seventy-five feet from the green marker."

"O.K.," says Captain Ryan, standing "between the sticks," the rudder turners. He leans forward, but he knows his human eyes cannot penetrate the fog, the visibility by now almost zero. He must depend upon his radar screen and the human vision of his first mate on the razor's edge of whatever happens next.

"When you're already sliding down the hill you gotta go," says the captain, who cannot afford to waste time with hindsight or second-guessing. His fifty-one years of towboat experience, the radar, and the first mate make the crucial difference.

"Fifty feet from the bridge...forty...thirty..."

"O.K."

"Centered."

"O.K."

"You're starting under the bridge," says the first mate.

From the pilothouse vantage point, there is no Kennedy Bridge. There are only the fog and the first twenty yards of the otherwise invisible closest football field. As the pilothouse of the *SuperAmerica* slowly inches beneath the Kennedy, it looks like a silver ghost with traffic moaning over it. Cars and trucks on Interstate 65 resemble moths drawn to emerging city lights. Lonnie pushes the button unleashing a joyous blast of one long and two shorts. "Ain't no tellin' what's liabile to come loose this morning. Out here, any day's a new day to us." The captain softly murmurs aloud his praise of his first mate. "Ron can talk you in like nobody's business." Lonnie probably makes a mental note that when he retires soon he'll do everything he can to encourage Ron Felty to take the exam to become a pilot. The pilgrimage begins with being a deckhand, learning to heave a line for the first time around the kevel, learning to walk on cold, icy steel in winter, blistering heat in summer. After years of experience in all kinds of situations and with the right kind of luck, there's the climb up to mate, first mate, pilot, and finally captain.

"When was the last time you saw a lot of ice in the river?" Lalie asks Captain Ryan.

"We had some in the mid-'80s, I think it was. Wasn't as bad as it was back there in '78, '79. That was the worst that we'd had in years. Used to say, well, ever' ten years there was this cycle of ice, and the river out here would freeze up—well, it's broke that cycle."

"You can imagine what it must have been like when the pioneers came down this river," says David.

"Can't you though? Yeah."

"And later, but before technology—dams, locks, modern communications..."

"It's not been easy. You hear them talking about some of the old days. Haul coal down the river out of Pittsburgh. Start out at certain times and go so far and then wait for the river to raise a little bit, and go so far. That was before they ever built the dams. Some of the old locks weren't started to be built until the early 1900s."

"What's the worst thing that you've seen on the river?"

"I'd say that ice was. That and the high floodwaters."

"What was it like in '97?"

"Unbelievable. People didn't realize what was really going on."

"Do you want to continue doing this as long as you're able?"

"Well, I guess I'm getting to just about that point. I stayed longer than I anticipated, yes I have."

"You'll miss it, won't you?"

"I say, yes, I will, like John down there. He was retired, and now he's back out here working. But I think it's getting to the point where I need to move on and let somebody else have it."

"When you retire, where would you like to live?"

"I'm gonna live right down there where I'm at. When we moved back there we said we'd never move again. Right down there in Princeton. Going to stay right there in Princeton. It's nothing fancy, nothing overcrowded, or anything like that. We're just a good old country town."

"How would you like to spend your retirement?"

"I guess I'll just be a 'honey-do' thing. Maybe she won't make me do all the things she made up over the years," he laughs. When Captain Lonnie Ryan laughs, his throat resonates like a fog horn warming to the task.

Pilot John Carson takes over in the stretch beyond Three Mile Island, Six Mile Island, and Twelve Mile Island with the fog slowly lifting, the sun barely breaking through, bearing a tale of life on the river.

5

"When my grandpa was a little boy, he lived right where I live now, on the Ohio side of the river. There was a road that come down over the hill and he got up one morning and he looked up and there come a farmer that he knew with a wagon that was half full of shelled corn, and behind this wagon they had this big bull. I mean a big bull, probably a twenty-five to twenty-eight hundred-pound bull with horns as big around as a log chain. Pretty well the boss, I'd say. When he took a notion to go visitin' instead of going through the barbed wire, he'd go to the post, put his horns on each side of the post, jerk his head up, and pull the post out of the ground and he'd walk across. And the worst part about that was when he took a notion to come back home he'd never come back through the same hole he went out. He'd go to another post, fix his horns on both sides of it, and pull it out of the ground.

"Well, the farmer put up with him for years, and he decided he was gonna sell him. So he took him down to where the boat landing was. The bull would go along for a half a mile or so, and he'd get tired, and he'd plant down his feet and he would stop. Farmer had to wait until the bull got ready to go. They wouldn't let the farmers bring the cows and hogs, chickens, and stuff into town. So they got down to the pens on the edge of town, and the guy who either owned or run the place told the farmer he could wait there for the steamboat but he couldn't put the bull in the pens because he was afraid he'd tear 'em up. Now this bull was big. So, along outside the pens was this great big tall grass, nice lush grass, and the bull, he just started eating. And he eat and he eat. And there was a building there and alongside of it was this old No. 3 washtub, where water ran off, and it was full of water, and the bull drank it all.

"Well, along about two o'clock the packet boat pulled in and the first thing they did was to blow the landing whistle. *Whaaaaa! Whaaaaa!* And that old bull had never seen or heard anything like that before and he was just sure that there was another bull on that boat, and he wanted to fight him. Anything he liked to do, he liked to fight. He got to pawing the ground and snorting and bellerin' and carrying on. So they come on in there and they loaded the other animals and took the corn. But they decided they weren't gonna take that bull, because he was a pretty big bull and he might tear something up. Mate said, 'Captain, you think we

6

ought to take this bull?' Captain said, 'Why yeah, we'll make seventy-five cents.' Mate said, 'Well, he's big and he might tear something up.' 'Nah, we'll handle him.'

"Well, they got the temporary fences all set up on the boat and went back for the bull. That bull wheeled around and down over the hill he went just as hard as he could and he went right up that gangplank and right into the pen. Well, he looked all around and there was nobody to fight, so he just walked up to the pen fence and shoved it on out and he was loose. On the boat.

"In the meantime, they'd backed away from the landing and that bull could hear that steam hissing around in the engine room, and he just knew it was another bull. So he walked up to the bulkhead that was made out of one-inch tongue-and-groove board, and he just run his horns through there and jerked his head back and he had him a hole. Well, he jumped into that engine room, and he looked around for that other bull and he couldn't find him. In the meantime, they had backed out into the river and they'd begun to shift the engine up, and the bull looked around and everthing got pretty quiet and he kinda relaxed a little bit and just about that time all the grass he had eaten decided to leave. He throwed his tail over his back and just when he'd got started real good he turned around real quick and he just kept turning around and around and painted the whole engine room. Well, he got done and he thought he might just as well urinate while we're here and he let go with about fifteen gallons. Well, about that time he jumped into the river and swum over to the shore.

"Well, the boat went on to where it was going and in a few days it come back and the farmer came down to get his money. Well, the captain, he was still mad. They got out on the bank there and the captain broke the poor old farmer's arm. The farmer cut the captain across the back of the leg several which ways. Required about sixty-seven stitches. Now, the moral of this story is, don't lose an arm and a leg over a whole bunch of bullshit."

We have ourselves some good laughs as we move on up the river, about seven or eight miles an hour, past Eighteen Mile Island, Westport, and Patton's Creek, which marks the Oldham-Trimble County line. Little by little we're becoming more serious, because we want for the first time to see Harlan and Anna Hubbard's Payne Hollow. He was a writer and artist, and she was a musician and gourmet cook. They were not in favor of electricity and had a contrary view of progress.

Anyone looking for Payne Hollow will have considerable difficulty finding it on twenty-first century maps. The remote place where two of the most unusual of Kentuckians spent their splendid days, almost four decades of quiet, inspired years apart from the mainstream of modern technology, is in Trimble County, downstream from the sweeping bend of the Ohio and the Milton community. About eight miles south and across the river from Madison, Indiana, the location of Payne Hollow is north of Corn Creek, just south of the mouth of Moreland Creek, which is downstream from the mouth of Spring Creek, south of the confluence of Gilmore, Cooper, and Page Creeks with the Ohio.

Harlan Hubbard's *Payne Hollow Journal* completes a trilogy that includes *Journals, 1924-1944*, and *Shantyboat Journal*. On March 9, 1954, he wrote: "I would be unhappy and frustrated, living with college people, with intellectuals as friends and neighbors exclusively. I need the touch of earth in my society. That is why we enjoy our farm friends and neighbors. They are the sanest people, they keep society strong and healthy."

Wendell Berry has remembered the extraordinary and simple lives of the Hubbards in *Harlan Hubbard: Life and Work*: "The paramount historical significance of the Hubbards' life is that they lived and thrived in a place in which, by the conventional assumptions of our time, all human possibilities were exhausted."

Anna's and Harlan's ashes are buried beneath a canoe in front of the house where they lived at Payne Hollow. There's a headstone with the etching of a heart and an arrow through it. Paul Hassfurder, an artist who oversees the house given to him by Harlan, has told the *Courier-Journal*: "It was not meant to be a museum or display place. It is a place where I shall live my life with great respect for the foundation that they laid."

In *Harlan Hubbard and the River: A Visionary Life*, Don Wallis recalls Harlan's gift: "I think of myself as one apart, one who has had a revelation beyond the ken of ordinary people, and ecstasy surges up unbidden....I must give people what they ask of me. And yet: I must be true to myself."

After Wises Landing, we're slowly coming to the realization that what we're experiencing at this moment are autumn leaves in great color and profusion. And we should be satisfied with that. The mouth of Corn Creek and Preston Hollow flow into the Ohio, and the shoreline from there to Payne Hollow is strewn with the kind of driftwood Harlan would have loved. Many a tall tree has fallen. The house where he and Anna lived is barely and briefly visible with binoculars. Then it's gone. We've heard that Harlan's goat shed has all but fallen into the river. High water has eroded the foundation. The greater truth is that a time has passed. Pinpointing exactly where something fine once happened is like priests of several religions claiming to know exactly where their prophet ascended.

We see the mouth of the Little Kentucky River, then the Kentucky and Wendell Berry's Port William, renamed Carrollton in 1838. The shoreline has now been stripped—for seeding, we hope. The hands on the courthouse clock say 4:25. A church steeple gleams in the October afternoon. Wendell is away for a while, teaching in England. Port William lives in his books. Carrollton lives in the reality of approaching winter. We live, one mile marker at a time, one river of Kentucky at a time.

We witness the parking of the three football fields in the Markland Lock, then head on upstream aboard the *SuperAmerica* toward Cincinnati. The pilot and the captain, in their turn, steer to the Kentucky side to miss Craig Bar, to the Indiana side to escape Vevey Bar. We pass directly over what used to be Big Bone Island, swept away by an upended barge in an ice storm, past the mouth of Big Bone Creek dividing Trimble and Boone Counties. The town of Rabbit Hash lies in darkness. In the distance are the lights of the Queen City and northern Kentucky, with seven bridges spanning the Ohio River, connecting North and South. The lights stretching from Ludlow to Fort Thomas, from the Mississippi Barge Line Terminal to the Little Miami River, are spectacular. Before turning in at 3:30 a.m. to our bunks we request that the searchlight be spotted on the entrance to Coney Island, where the Big Bands came to play at Moonlight Gardens. The arched entrance and the lighthouse replica stand like sentinels, guarding the memory of the crowds that once passed through. It is done. Coney is another mile marker. Nothing more.

We love. We sleep.

The river from Coney Island to the Meldahl Locks and Dam at the 434.1 mile marker fills our dreams. We want to believe that we are the water and the water is us. We want to believe that all the water that's here now was here in the beginning, and all the water that's here now is all the water there'll ever be. We have loved and fancied within the water cycle, therefore we do not expect to die. Such is the dream game we play with death. Elementally, we'll be present as long as rivers flow to the sea, as long as the sea gives us up in order for us to return in clouds to begin again.

We witness for pioneer, present, and future Kentuckians. The early settlements and modern metropolitan communities have had at least one important thing in common. Most of them have been built and developed on, or relatively near, waterways. Our home of homes is a tiny place on Plum Lick Creek in Bourbon County, where we flow to Boone Creek, to Hinkston Creek, to the South Fork of Licking, to the Ohio. We are haunted by the countless voices who continue to ghost the Ohio, a stream *within* the northern boundary of Kentucky, a distance of 665 miles from Catlettsburg to Cairo, Illinois.

"Howdy folks, I'm Captain Mary Miller. Welcome aboard the *Saline*, one of the finest little working steamers on the Western Waters. We usually work the bayou country of Louisiana—around the Red River— but right now we're on a special trip home to Portland at the Falls of the Ohio in Kentucky." The representation of the voice of Mary Millicent Garretson Miller (1846-1894) brings her to life in the Portland Museum in Louisville, the audiotape recalling the woman who, with her husband, built steamboats in their front yard. Mary Miller obtained her license and was captain of a sternwheeler at the same time her husband, George

"Old Natural" Miller, was the pilot. Mary said: "When I married George Miller, I married the river. And the river's been good to us."

Today at the entrance to the Portland Museum, we read the words of Father John Lyons, who in 1939 saw and felt the bad as well as the good: "Perhaps the river which has brought so much sorrow and distress, has bound these people to one another and to the very land which it has tried to take away from them."

During the Pleistocene Epoch—about 1,600,000 to 10,000 years ago—the channel of what Captain Miller and we now call the Ohio River was located farther north. Waters of the ancient Ohio and Teays Rivers flowed across the center of what would become Ohio, Indiana, and Illinois. Water from the land that one day would be the Commonwealth of Kentucky flowed into the Teays. After the glaciers came and retreated, the Ohio River began to trace its present course— pathway for pioneers, main artery today for barges filled with commerce in both directions, diesel engines churning the brown water, interstate semis battling bumper-to-bumper for position on bridges connecting shores, jet trails webbing the dawn in a new millennium, lovers slowly awakening on a towboat called *SuperAmerica*.

"My world begins, then, here in W-Hollow, the little core of my Kentucky, of my big United States of America, and then of the six continents of my bigger world," Jesse Stuart wrote in *My World*. In silence, we remember Jesse as we pass beneath the Jesse Stuart Bridge above the Lock and Dam downstream from Greenup. We head on up to Catlettsburg, where we dock for what's left of the third night on the *SuperAmerica*. We say our goodbyes, including a hug for Connie the cook, and we reluctantly disembark.

On the drive back to Plum Lick, we wonder about what we've seen from the river, coming to understand the meaning of the saying, "You've never seen a town until you've seen it from the river." We remember the Old World charm of Maysville in Mason County, the beauty of Augusta in Bracken County, and the financial power of metropolitan Cincinnati. But to know any city, especially a river city, they must be tramped.

The old Cincinnati of the Great Depression decade, with its

waterfront despair—Hoovertown encampments of Appalachian misery—and before that the Newport ("Little Chicago") of the prohibition-crazed 1920s with succeeding decades of deep-seated immorality and sociological upheaval, bear little resemblance to the Cincinnati, Newport, and Covington of today. There is no Prohibition, probably the most important improvement of all. Telling people they can't drink something is like telling the Ohio River it ought to behave like recycled water at Disney World.

Newport, Kentucky: A Bicentennial History edited by Thomas L. Purvis, recounts the days of organized crime—gambling and graft, prostitution and extortion—that bred the Sodom on the eastern edge of the mouth of Licking in mid-twentieth century. Reform came to Newport, the sinful "stepchild of Cincinnati," in the 1960s, the fundamental change due in no small part to the Committee of 500, formed in 1961 with the encouragement of Governor Bert T. Combs, child of the eastern Kentucky mountains.

In the heat of summer, we stand beneath the World Peace Bell in Newport at high noon to hear and feel the vibrations of the three-ton clacker tolling the hour. "Honoring our past, celebrating our present, and inspiring our future," is the way the promoters have described the bell's purpose. Maybe. "Past" is debatable, "present" is dubious, and "future" is doubtful.

Some memories won't go away, won't die so easily. After all, this was Vegas East. Beverly Hills only one mile down the road. Tommy Dorsey. "Deep River" and "Dry Bones." Show girls. Big Daddy. Big Momma. Bingo! Ed McClanahan had it right in *Natural Man*: Newport was "Kentucky's own sinkhole of sin...."

We saunter over and have lunch at Captain's Cove Bar and Grill at the corner of 5th and Monmouth, next door to the Syndicate Restaurant (formerly the "Playtorium"), near the spot where former Newport Police Chief George Gugel's official car is on display. He was one of the city's public officials indicted on September 13, 1961, for conspiracy to "pervert, corrupt, or obstruct public justice." He resigned and was not found guilty.

Sitting on high barstools on the old battleground, we talk softly, thumbing through the pages of the bicentennial history of a city where, one hundred years ago, rural families were arriving in mule-drawn wagons. "During 1895...a collapse in tobacco prices left eighty-seven of the state's one hundred and twenty counties unable to pay the expenses of local government, and led most of them to lock up their classrooms at least once for lack of money to pay their faculty." The illusion of gold at the end of the rainbow vanished. A community of promise lost its way. "Given the city's degree of complicity with organized crime, it was small consolation that the gambling clubs drew virtually all their business from out of state. Newport lay within 400 miles of 40% of the nation's population by 1959, and was a major tourist destination, in large part because it had long enjoyed a regional reputation as an easy and inexpensive place to get married. Few conventioneers meeting in Cincinnati could resist the temptation to see just what a wide-open city looked like. So heavy was the demand for taxis to shuttle persons across the Central and L&N Bridges from downtown Cincinnati, that it supported seven cab companies in Newport."

The young woman behind the counter gratefully disengages from small talk with a regular. She brings us beer. We look at the pictures of the flood of 1937. My God. Immaculate Conception church looks like a lighthouse. Like a cerement, the crest of the flood wrapped around most of Newport. The death toll throughout Kentucky in the 1937 flood was two hundred and twenty-seven, approximately two-thirds of the national number. Property damage in Newport and Dayton, Kentucky, was devastating. After the record-breaking crest at eighty feet (flood stage at Cincinnati is fifty-two feet), and after the unusually slow fall of the river, the damage estimate in Newport alone was placed at $5 million, more than $47 million in today's value. Statewide damage was estimated to be $250 million.

Before 1937, on the Ohio there had been the disastrous flood of 1913, when more than seven hundred died. Other major floods on the Ohio occurred in 1763, 1772-73, 1847, 1884, 1927, and 1997. A primary reason for persistent flooding of the Ohio is the hydrologic cycle's iniquitous cyclonic patterns, churning northeastwardly up the Ohio Valley. Coupled with the extraordinary runoffs from the Appalachian plateau, the regularity of Ohio River torrents historically has been a virtual certainty. Flood control measures have helped, but history proves there are no guarantees.

After the debacle of water and human corruption, there have been flood control measures and reform movements in an effort to keep the city of Newport safe from the dangers of deluge and depravity. Today, a walk down Monmouth Street is like a stroll through a scorched city after the enemy has been driven to the sea. It's not easy to know whether the seeds of corruption once sown on such fertile ground will sprout again in the hearts of Puritans. The forces of good and evil have formally withdrawn from the battleground. Monmouth seems lonely, with a tired wistfulness for the days when sin was less hypocritical.

Today, stretching south from the Peace Bell and a new, acclaimed Aquarium is a strip unlikely to attract highrollers: "Discount Outlet," "Donate your Plasma," "E-Z Cash Power," "Rental-Purchase," "Spaghetti Dinner for Two, $4.10," tanning beds, pawn shops. Frances Peluso, years etched in her aging face, stands behind the hand-worn counter of her small grocery on the east side of Monmouth Street. She sells us cauliflower and broccoli seedlings, a little something to take back to Plum Lick to plant in our kitchen garden. She grew up on a farm near Butler in Pendleton County, and she was one of those who migrated to the big city. Despite the turmoil at mid-century and "the noise at night," which persists even now, Frances Peluso is a survivor.

Covington, its old-worldliness, church steeples and slender houses competing for space, sits on the western lip of the mouth of the Licking, presiding over it like a mother coveting play. The corner of the mouth is dirty with jagged pieces of coal, reminders of barge traffic bringing fuel down the Ohio from the highlands of Kentucky, water descending from as far away as Magoffin County.

James Bradley sits on a River Park bench in Covington, a small book in his hands, a benevolent look on a face with its own special creases. We go and sit with him. Cast in bronze, Mr. Bradley looks as real as life. The plaque in the sidewalk reads: "The life of this one man summarizes the experiences of millions of African Americans. Born in Africa in the early 19th Century, slave traders brought Bradley to America as an infant. By the time he was 18 years old, Bradley managed his master's Arkansas plantation. Over a 5-year period he earned enough money to purchase his freedom. As a free man Bradley crossed the Ohio River, here at Covington, the legal and symbolic divide between slavery and freedom. He enrolled at Lane Seminary in Cincinnati in 1834. Bradley was the only ex-slave who participated in the famous Lane Seminary debates on slavery and abolitionism. Bradley's participation stood as an eloquent witness to the equality of all. His speech declared that the great desire of the slaves was 'liberty and education.'"

A small van slows down and a black man leans from the window and asks: "Who is the gentleman?"

"James Bradley from Africa," we reply with pride in our newfound knowledge.

"Not a slave?" the stranger hurts to know.

"Yes, he was," we answer with a mixture of guilt and deep-rooted shame. "He was in Arkansas, bought his freedom, and had a great deal to do with emancipation and education."

"That's interesting. Thank you very much," says the black man, driving away, peacefully accepting our complicity.

The shoreline, pounded smooth by the lapping water, makes us want to live the life of a shantyboater, if only for a day, maybe a night, so that we can be more natural with the river. At the water's brown edge are pieces of coal, chipped relics, a small tattoo on the ankle of a girl lying by the side of a fishing friend. We marvel that in this day and time people still find pleasure in coming here to fish and reflect. It's as if they can't even see the city. Here we sit and at the same time over there at Riverfront Stadium is the "25th Anniversary of the 1975 Cincinnati Reds." (They won the first of two consecutive World Series. All the cogs in the wheel of the "Big Red Machine" are there, the whole team—except the hub, Pete Rose.) What has become of us that in twilight time we stay on this side of the Ohio and sit with sad statues on the River Walk, we silently wonder.

"You promised more," Lalie muses with a whither-thou-goest glance of blue-green eyes.

Warrened in the downward turn of the river at milemarker 506 in Boone County, where Parks Branch comes in, Rabbit Hash is made to order for good old boys, good old girls, and good old dogs.

Goofy, the mayor of Rabbit Hash—a duly elected, big old black unclassifiable kind of dog—narrowly beat out Junior, the Labrador retriever, in a heated election two years ago. Goofy did not deign to participate in this year's Labor Day weekend parade—Rabbit Hash 2000. He may have been out of town at a mayor's convention, or he may have been across the river at the Rising Sun casino boat. Who knows? (More than likely he was lying in the road on Upper River Road, bemoaning his testicular cancer that some say has left him a balless politician.)

This year's parade was led by Dakota, a splotchily colored, grandly configurated dog suggesting Australian shepherd genealogy with a possible dash of Catahoula, maybe a pinch of blue heeler. Before and after the parade, Dakota artfully high-steps through the picnic table area on the off chance of food dropping from plates or the fingers of sweating, yapping human babies. Dakota commands more panache than bedraggled, dishwater Millie, known locally as Millie the Moocher, considered by some human beings as "the worst begger stray, but nonetheless the spirit of Rabbit Hash, because she's nobody's dog."

There's Sheila, "a horrible little red mutt." Then there are Junior, son of Herb, son of Barker. Herb, who until the day he died "barked all the time," is buried up on the hill. He has a small monument. There are two other Labs, Belle and Polly, and a Llewellyn setter, Lou. There are many more self-respecting, gnat-attracting dog citizens of Rabbit Hash, but an accurate census has not been a requirement and any list claiming to be complete would be suspect.

Steinbeck's Charlie would heist his leg on the whole damn thing, but the superdog in Rabbit Hash is Sam, the Akita belonging to Terrie, who operates the Rabbit Hash General Store. Sam is the "fun police," the top dog. His critics say he does not like it when the other dogs are having too much fun. He's prepared to break it up, especially public fornication. Sam has a deep, practiced growl and a most serious look on his face, cool and confident. Dakota makes wide, prideful circles around Sam. Hell, Charlie might not have gotten out of the truck.

The Labor Day weekend festival at Rabbit Hash also includes raffle tickets, lemonade, and pure-pork-bbq sandwiches at the "Hard Times Country Cookin" booth set up outside the General Store, which dates back to 1831. (Rabbit Hash may have earned its name from a long-ago occasion when the area was short on food and long on gnats and rabbits.)

Mike Fletcher, who for the past ten years has been building a shantyboat about a half-mile up from the mouth of Big Bone Creek, stopped by our Plum Lick Publishing tent, and he proceeded to *lasseiz le bon temps roulette* ("let the good times roll"). He whipped out the fixings for Sazerac cocktails, a little something he learned at the old Roosevelt Hotel in New Orleans.

In a separate glass, put:
1 cube sugar
1 shot Angostura bitters
1 shot Peychaud bitters
Just 'nuff water to muddle (about 1 to 2 Tbsp.)
Swirl to dissolve sugar
Throw in double shot of rye (Old Overholt is Mike's favorite, but
    Henry McKenna bourbon will do)
Coat inside of a brandy snifter with Pernod (liqueur)
(Some shake this over ice and pour into the glass. Some don't.)
Mike says, if you put all ingredients in the freezer without ice, the
    drink will be ice cold
Rim a glass (an old-fashioned glass is preferable) with a cut lemon,
    then squeeze the lemon slice into the drink

John Steinbeck is smiling, and Charlie, his giant poodle, is sympathetic. They, like Sazerac, are different. Not sweet. Not sour. Rye gives it a kick. Bitters give it an unusual taste. Hmmmmm. Nothing like it. It was born at the Sazerac bar in New Orleans, Lalie's hometown. She was born in the Baptist Hospital there. David was born in Good Sam in Cincinnati. Hot damn.

We should have said it was damn hot in Rabbit Hash at the end of the first summer of the new millennium. Sweltering. Shade in short supply. Gnats and mosquitoes and probably chiggers everywhere. Randy Cochran, retired Scripps Howard journalist, who has found his home of homes in Rabbit Hash, wipes his brow and barkers home-ground cornmeal. He has come up from his "rollover" boat, an ingenious strategy for hunting ducks, the boat deliberately unbalanced so that one gunwale nearly dips into the water. Makes it possible to scrunch down beneath the higher gunwale and peep out with a gun. Usually the plan is to drift downstream, closing the gap with unsuspecting, newsworthy ducks. How Randy manages to do this with a Labrador retriever on board is something we've not witnessed.

We turn to talking shantyboats with Mike Fletcher, whose noble *Jennie Lynn* has a sixty- by twenty-foot hull with a forty- by twenty-foot cabin. There's also *Elizabeth*, a rusty thirty- by twelve-foot pusherboat with a one hundred Detroit Diesel. *Jennie Lynn's* and *Elizabeth's* home port is about one-half mile up Big Bone Creek at the 516.5 mile marker on the Ohio, close to the junctures of Big Bone, Mud Lick, and Big South Fork Creeks.

Walking up the ramp of Mike Fletcher's *Jennie Lynn* is the beginning of an urge to be back in coon-ass country. ("Coon Ass," a corruption of "Cajun," a derivative of "Acadian.") Mike is torn between love of Boone County land in Kentucky, where he was born, and spiritual connections with the bayous of Louisiana, especially the French Quarter of New Orleans. But, like Harlan Hubbard before him, Mike Fletcher is drawn to the Ohio and the Mississippi Rivers. Unlike Harlan and Anna Hubbard, Mike has a yen for electricity.

Mike remembers the one time he visited Harlan. "He was roasting soybeans outside in an iron skillet," says Mike, arranging bratwurst on a cajun cooker on the forward deck of the *Jennie Lynn*. Inside, electrical wiring stretches fore and aft to supply the needs of a combination refrigerator-freezer and a CD player. Here's a shantyboat with certain amenities. But the underlying idea is the same: no property taxes to pay, the sunsets and sunrises are for the taking, and the river is the landlord.

When "Ginnie" looks out on her river, the Ohio, she spreads her arms and her heart and recalls a lifetime of sweet memories because the river washes away the painful times, the hurts, disappointments, even slavery. For the past eighteen years, she's been there in the mornings when the sun rises over Fort Thomas, Newport, and Covington, and she's been there in the evenings when the sun sets beyond the bend at Ludlow.

Virginia "Ginny" Bennett, seventy-six years young, lives out the rest of her days in a tiny apartment with a balcony overlooking the stream the French named "La Belle Rivière"—the Beautiful River—and Indian tribes called "O-he-zhu," "O-he-yo," and "Spay-lay-we-thepi"—the Great River, the stream that classifies, collects, and conveys all the rivers of Kentucky. The Ohio is "the Great Mother" welcoming home her children, forgiving them their transgressions, giving them a place to come to.

Ginny spent sixteen years with the Greene Line Steamers, six years with Columbia Marine Service, eight years with BB Riverboats. She's been purser, harbor manager, gift shops cashier, and crew cook from Pittsburgh to Cincinnati, Cairo to New Orleans, St. Louis to the Upper Mississippi. Ginny's great-grandfather would be proud that the navigational light beneath her balcony—the 471.7 mile marker—was named this year for his descendant. "I wish I could talk to my great-grandpa. He was a master pilot, but he didn't have lights, locks, or dams. He could read the river."

"What does the river mean to you?"

"If you take a trip on any boat, like the *Delta Queen*, once you get your [regular] clothes off, the scenery is different all the time. You don't know what's around the bend. I just love the whole tranquillity about the river."

"Storms?"

"I've been through some pretty good storms. Got stuck for a couple of days on the river."

The *Belle of Cincinnati* heaves into view, passes beneath the north- and southbound hum of cars and trucks on the I-75 bridge and commands the middle of the river alongside Ginny's balcony. The night air of early June is cool, simply one of those fine moments. A good life has both the fine and the not so fine. The trick is to savor the good and learn a lesson from the bad.

"V-B mobile to the *Belle of Cincinnati*," says Ginny into her microphone.

"Be right back," says the voice on the *Belle of Cincinnati*.

"Switch over to ten, please."

"Gone to ten."

"Kerry, blow me a little whistle and make my visitors feel at home on the Ohio River," says Ginny.

"Be happy to," says Captain Kerry Snowden as the *Belle of Cincinnati* slides by with one long and two shorts—then another—one long and two shorts. The passengers probably don't know that the steam whistle is for an elderly Kentucky lady watching from her little apartment on the southern bank of the river. Animosities between North and South have another chance for reconciliation. Battlements of despair stretching from the highlands to the lowlands, baked by the sun like bison bones of collective memory, are slowly passing downstream.

As the sun drops down, spreading its glory, and darkness closes in, the 471.7 navigational light begins to blink bright red. The drivers of the speedboats darting up and down the river like fireflies probably don't know that the warning signal has a name—Virginia Bennett—but the towboat captains and pilots and the paddlewheel captains and pilots, they know. "For a number of years they've seen many accidents, especially when we have high water. The Coast Guard installed this light. Since I'm such a river rat, they named it after me," says Ginny. "They can hold on that until they get lined up to miss all these bridges. This one down here is the most dangerous of all. If you don't get lined up with the first one, you're in trouble."

Ginny says she wants her ashes placed inside a sturdy urn and sunk as far down as possible into the sediment at mile marker 471.7. She says she doesn't want to be washed away to the Mississippi and the Gulf of Mexico. Can't say as we blame her. Everybody is entitled to make such a decision without debate with interlopers. We don't tell her that we've fussed with our own ideas about cremation, and that we've rejected them all. It does make a lot of practical sense—cleaner, more efficient, less expensive. The world is running out of space, no question about it, but we disrespectfully tend toward the lustfully impractical, and we intend to keep the marrow of our bones as long as possible in the hope of one more kiss.

Ginny's apartment is small, some might say a shoebox for memories. We like the sign on the front door: "Home Port." The eagle on the balcony railing came from the engine room of the *Chris Greene* steamer. Red and green lights are hung at the corners of Ginny's pilothouse. "Running lights have burned in my home since 1936. They took the cabins off the *Tom Greene* and the *Chris Greene* and the captain said, 'You can have these.' I used to [climb] up and change the bulbs. Now I have a friend come and change the bulbs. I wouldn't take a million dollars for them."

The walls of the two-room apartment (not counting the narrow mess deck) are lined with pictures of steamboats and packets. They include the *Island Queen* and the *Betsy Ann*. Memories of the *Island Queen* flow back from sixty years ago: the screech of the calliope, the raising of the stage, the pushing back from the shore on the Cincinnati side, the ten-mile voyage to Coney Island, the strong, fetid smell of the river; the red-headed boy pawing at the young girl's freckled breasts—wishing he could fondle them—the leer in his eyes, not caring if anybody or God himself saw what he was doing, the oily smell of the engine room, the long arms of the pistons turning the big paddlewheel, the spray of the water coming up to dampen the stern rail, the cage called the jail where the rowdy were placed for safekeeping, the Kentucky hills sliding by, and finally the calliope playing wildly as the splendid boat noses into Coney Island landing.

"Tell us about river people."

"The river has a mystique about it," says Ginny as the lights of Greater Cincinnati cast red, green, and yellow reflections on the surface of the water. "River people are all very friendly and if anyone is ever in trouble there'll be a boat there as quick as they can. I've got river water in my veins...My mother used to say I could smell the steam from the riverboats even before they blew their whistles."

Virginia Bennett has a good friend with whom she worked for many

21

years. Clarke "Doc" Hawley is pretty much retired now. He's been the captain and pilot of the *Delta Queen*, the *Belle of Cincinnati*, the *Belle of Louisville* (formerly the *Avalon*), the *President*, the *American Queen*, the *Mississippi Queen*, and the *Natchez*. He began his career more than forty years ago as deck hand and popcorn cooker on the *Avalon*.

At Galatoire's on Bourbon Street in New Orleans, Doc's favorite restaurant, during a summer side trip, we dine on oysters, shrimp, soft shell crabs, red fish, hot garlic bread, baked caramel custard, and bread pudding. The wine is superb and the coffee is *au lait*, the feast almost as good as the stories told.

"If Mark Twain came back today he would be comfortable on the *Belle of Louisville*," says Doc, remembering the day when Jefferson County Judge Marlow Cook bought the *Avalon* for $34,000 and renamed it the *Belle of Louisville*.

"Tell me something, Doc—those Derby Week races between the *Belle of Louisville* and the *Delta Queen*. They were staged weren't they?"

He smiles.

Should've known. Fact is, we all knew. "I remember we reporters were sent out there to do live reports for WHAS Radio, and we were expected to act as if it were a real race. Hell, the *Delta Queen* could've run off and left the *Belle of Louisville* any day in the week."

Doc smiles again. The look begins in his strong hands, moves to his shoulders, and from there gives his mouth its etched texture. "If she wasn't loaded down with polititians or it wasn't a windy day, we could make it good and close."

Doc Hawley was alternate master on the *Delta Queen*, serving with the legendary Captain Ernest E. Wagner, considered by many to be "the ultimate riverboat captain." It was he who gave Doc his first job as popcorn cooker and calliope player on the *Avalon*. Capt. Wagner's career began in the Great Depression as coal passer and ice cream vendor on the second *Island Queen* (the first *Island Queen* was the nation's first strictly excursion boat, built in 1896 and destroyed by fire in 1922). Wagner rose steadily up the hierarchy of riverboat command.

On September 9, 1947, the second and last *Island Queen* was tied up at the wharf in Pittsburgh. First Mate Ernest E. Wagner was asleep in his quarters. An engineer drilled into a fuel tank, and the resulting explosion was horrendous. Wagner leaped from his bed, ran aft, looked toward the bow, and saw it enveloped in flames. According to the account in John H. White and Robert J. White Sr.'s *The Island Queen: Cincinnati's Excursion Steamer*, Wagner "had to walk six feet through flames" before jumping into the river. He was severely burned, but he swam to shore and survived. Nineteen crewmates died when the last of the *Island Queens* went down.

Ernest Wagner's next duty was as captain aboard the *Avalon*. Three years later he spotted Clarke C. "Doc" Hawley and saw in him the makings of a riverboat captain. They left the *Avalon* together in 1961 and went to the *Delta Queen*, and it was there that they and so many other river rats would find their home of homes.

Captain Wagner died of cancer on October 11, 1979, and at his funeral at New Richmond, Ohio, a young, vivacious woman paid a tribute. She, like so many others before her, had fallen in love with the river.

Her name was Betty Blake.

She was a popular coed at the University of Kentucky in the late 1940s, the daughter of State Senator Stanley "Step-and-a-Half" Blake of Carlisle in Nicholas County. (Friends affectionately attached the nickname because of the senator's serious limp.) No matter what anybody thought of his politics, it was so easy to fall in love with his daughter's smile. She'd stop you dead in your tracks. Make you turn around and look. Make you want to be in her presence. Make you dare believe that she might be yours. Some women are just that way.

Betty's warmth and personality and energy took her into salesmanship, and eventually she became president of Greene Line Steamers, Inc. But the intervening years were marked by miles of relentless knocking on doors, up and down the Ohio and Mississippi Rivers. Betty called on beauty shops and barbershops, excursion passes in hand. She knew where the heartbeat of America was most likely to be. "It was the time before Milton Berle and the living room," says Doc, as we sing "Happy Birthday" two times to strangers in the Galatoire tradition. "Tramping the rivers was the cooling off of America," says Doc, who in 1994 co-authored *Moonlite at 8:30: The Excursion Boat Story*.

It's the story too of a young girl from Carlisle, Kentucky, who loved the river as much as she loved life itself, and whose heart never left it. Not ever. It was fun. It was forever without beginning or ending. Sometimes, especially in Greenville, Mississippi, it was exasperating. Some towns are that way. Just downright tough to sell. You'd think they'd be happy to see the riverboat coming around the bend, you'd think they'd be happy to receive a call from Betty Blake. But every town is different as every day is different. Betty accepted it as a special challenge. She worked harder and smarter because she wanted as many people as possible to go for a boat ride and make it "moonlite at 8:30."

Doc remembered getting the call from Betty's sister in Georgetown, Kentucky, in April of 1982. Betty had finally gone in for a checkup, and the doctor had sent her right away to Sloan-Kettering. Stomach cancer. But, no, she shouldn't have had that. No, it's not possible. It's crazy. "Betty wants to see you, Doc," said her sister, Helen Shu. "She has only days left."

"I caught the first plane," says Doc, "And when I walked into the room in Georgetown, Betty was propped up in bed and there was so little left of her. But she took my hand and she said, 'I'm going to lick this, Doc.'"

"If anybody can, you can," Doc remembers saying. "Her last words to me were, 'How are ticket sales in Greenville?'"

"I turned away, went into the other room, and I cried."

Betty Blake died at 12:30 a.m., Tuesday, April 13, 1982, at the home of her sister. The evening before she'd helped to celebrate her aging father's birthday. Virginia Bennett remembers the memorial service in Cincinnati at Christ Church Episcopal, overflowing with friends. They played a Johnny Cash tape from a program he'd dedicated to the saving of the *Delta Queen*, which was back in the time when the boat's future was in doubt. The service ended with the whistle of the wonderful *Queen* shrilling one more time for "the final landing," and there weren't many dry eyes after that.

There was a reception aboard the excursion boat the *Betty Blake*. Friends threw a wreath upon the Ohio. There was music—"Good Ship Lollypop"—and memories of the '40s and '50s came rolling back: "Satin Doll," "Ole Buttermilk Sky," and "Got a Date with an Angel."

Betty is buried in the Carlisle cemetery, along with other members of her family: Senator Blake, Betty's mother, Analaura, Lizzie, Luther, William H., Pickett, Cody, Dixie, and Edward. When we went to pay our respects in the summer of 2000, too long in the passage of riverboat tramping time, we were not ready for the epitaph on Betty's small marble monument:

Hi there!
I'm Betty Blake
Sept. 20, 1930
April 13, 1982

With the coming of the steamboat (the first was the *New Orleans* in 1811) Louisville grew steadily toward 1830, when it became the largest city in the Commonwealth, situated at the Falls of the Ohio, approximately midway between Catlettsburg and Cairo. Economic and political growth was joined by an outpouring of books, making Louisville a Mecca for writers.

The memoirs of Pauline Autenreith Tafel, a German immigrant who moved with her husband to Louisville in 1848, illustrate the importance of personal diaries. He was a farmer and a pharmacist. She was the mother of eight sons and two daughters. She died in 1907. Mrs. Tafel's story is recounted in Eugenia K. Potter's 1997 book *Kentucky Women*. "Nobody can imagine how much work there is on a farm....The sun rises and the earth revolves as if nothing had happened. Somehow, we don't die of grief. Instead, we must remember our duties, we must go on with our lives accepting the inevitable. These reasons gave me the strength to let reason prevail."

A justification for farming as a "reasonable" human activity is found in the connection between the topsoil of agriculture and the taproots of literature. Kentucky authors draw sustaining moisture from the peace at the center of their awareness. The number of nationally prominent poets in Louisville during the period Dr. William Ward calls the "Coming of Age, 1860-1930," is unusual for any river town in America. They include Madison Julius Cawein (1865-1914), "perhaps the best nature

25

poet in the nation," and Joseph Seamon Cotter (1861-1949), considered to be "Kentucky's first African American poet."

The literary outpouring at Kentucky's largest city has included patrons of St. James Court and members of the Authors Club of Louisville: Annie Fellows Johnston (1863-1931) of the *Little Colonel* series, and Alice Caldwell Hegan Rice (1870-1942), who wrote the best-selling *Mrs. Wiggs of the Cabbage Patch*. Another group of Louisville-area authors in a new century of literature is Green Rivers Writers, based in Jefferson County, the passion of Mary "Ernie" O'Dell.

Louisville has been the home of the legendary Bingham family: Robert Worth Bingham, publisher of the Louisville *Courier-Journal* and the *Louisville Times*, and his successors, Barry and Mary Bingham, Worth Bingham, Barry Bingham Jr., and Sarah ("Salley") Montague Bingham, each contributing to the printed word in the city named for Louis XVI.

Barry Sr. (1906-1988), in his introduction of Queen Elizabeth II in New York on July 9, 1976, said: "It is a time to celebrate our common heritage of the dignity of man, rooted in the deep soil of the Magna Carta. It is a time to rejoice in our common use of a rich and noble language. It is a time to treasure the knowledge that English is indeed the language of liberty....It is in that spirit, Ma'am, that we see your visit to America today. Ours is, we believe, a 'permanent union' in the sense of enduring good faith between proud and independent peoples."

Mary Caperton Bingham, wife of Barry Sr., was passionate about the rivers of Kentucky. She fought for them. She took on the stripminers, whose by-product was the contamination of waterways. She was also passionate about the large percentage of Kentuckians who lacked access to free public libraries. By 1955, through her efforts, there were more than one hundred bookmobiles. She was earnest about the quality of words, too; for a quarter of a century she was the book editor of the *Courier-Journal*. Mrs. Bingham's daughter Eleanor spoke of her mother the day she died: "My tiny little giant of a mother has, more than anyone else in my life, been an example of strict and lofty standards. She was always a parent of whom you could truly say you knew where you stood because she always made it crystal clear where she stood—on any issue from eye makeup to between meal snacks to literacy, civil rights and the value of the 1928 Book of Common Prayer over any mediocre Episcopal texts."

After the Ohio River curves past Louisville, it takes a southwesterly direction to West Point, where the Salt River enters. From there the Ohio shapes the northern boundary of Meade County, giving it more miles of Ohio River shoreline than any of the other Kentucky counties along the northern border of the Commonwealth. It's not that Meade County is so large (305 square miles compared to Jefferson County's 386 square miles), it's the way the Ohio River makes a triple loop around Meade, named for Captain James Meade, who was killed in Michigan at the 1813 Battle of the River Raisin. Each September, Meade Countians stage the "Down by the Riverside Festival."

Downstream from the county seat, Brandenburg, there're Big Bend, Oxbow Bend, and Little Bend, the Ohio River flowing now like a grand ribbon, wreathing woodlands of cedar and white oak and long bottomlands with names like "Paradise." The beauty and majesty of the panorama are a portrayal of Shangri-La.

Mt. Hope Methodist Church and its cemetery sit atop Big Bend, where family names live on—Noble, Garver, and Crawford—recalling nineteenth-century pioneers. Some sandstone markers have no inscriptions, an indication that prosperity was often elusive. The church—red roof and tiny steeple—is presently vacant. The six pews on one side, eight pews on the opposite side, and the facing four choir pews in front are places where people have sought spiritual release from earthly heartaches.

A short distance down the road, seventy-four-year-old James "Buck" Terry wonders aloud if he should go up there and mow a little grass because he has family buried at Mt. Hope cemetery. His wife's mother and stepfather, the Robinsons, are among those who've been laid to rest on top of Big Bend. Buck is one of those quiet Kentuckians who speaks slow but when the words come out, they're clear as drops of water falling softly on his garden.

"Just growed tomatoes all my life."

"What's the secret to growing tomatoes?"

"Stake 'em, tie 'em, and sucker 'em."

"How many do you set out?"

"Eight-thousand, ready on the first of July. Seventy-two days from time of setting."

"I thought May 10 was the safest time in Kentucky to set out tomatoes."

"Set mine out April 14."

"What about late frost?"

"Burn old hay rolls. Smoke takes care of the frost."

"Go by the moon?"

"Yessir. Sign of Cancer best time. Pisces good too. Some signs won't grow."

Walking into Buck Terry's seeding shed is a trip into a Promised Land of ingenuity. His father was a good carpenter, but Buck's friends accuse the son of "shimming" everything. Piece of wood here, extended board there, homemade stove with an old iron barrel for the working part, staves of dogwood and sassafras for more experiments with tomatoes, tomatoes, tomatoes. There are corn, beans, onions, and lettuce, but tomatoes reign supreme at Buck Terry's Elysian Fields up there where the Ohio River makes its grand loops.

In a conversation about agriculture and how people may have a fighting chance to relate to it, Buck begins by saying, "I don't owe nobody nothing."

He acknowledges that he might have missed out on some opportunities along the way, but you can sense a nice clean smell to the idea of not being in debt, especially when you're in your mid-seventies and have been through two heart attacks. The conversation comes around to "family farm" and "alternative crop," and Buck is of a mind that whatever anybody chooses to call it, the secret is in individual sun-up to sun-down work, a passion for the crop, and the ability to find somebody willing to pay for quality. Anything else is whistling past the cemetery.

Buck and his wife, Rosalyn, have raised five children, three boys and two girls. A son is a policeman, another works in chemicals, another in construction, a daughter is a teacher, and the other daughter is a housewife married to a banker. Rosalyn says "Farming is a lot of hard work."

"Do you take tomatoes to the Riverside Festival?"

"By the time you work in the field all day, you don't feel like going in to set up a table," Rosalyn explains.

Some might call her husband the tomato king, but he'd probably prefer a simpler title—the tomato man, most likely.

Buck says, "I want you to have these eight 'super steak' tomato plants. They'll weigh two to three pounds, and they eat real good."

It's nice to be remembered by something as noble as a mortal Kentuckian, an American with a strong hoe, a willing back, and a desire to use it to make things grow and become both beautiful and mouth-watering.

After Big Bend, there's Oxbow Bend. Wolf Creek empties into the Ohio across from Bulls Point on the Indiana side, and the water seems to eddy toward the little Kentucky community of Wolf Creek, the county's first permanent settlement, prosperous with river trade. Today the town has slowed to a sleepy sigh, a shadow of its former self. A lone woman resting on her front porch watches occasional motorists passing through.

The Commonwealth's northern boundary has for almost two hundred years perplexed and aggravated the states of Ohio, Indiana, and Illinois. Downstream from the triple loop, a controversial tract of land, Green River Island, lies across the Ohio from the mouth of the Green River. It's the present location of Ellis Park Racetrack. The main channel of the Ohio changed course, moving south from Evansville, leaving about two thousand acres attached to the Indiana side. The Supreme Court ruled that the land belongs to Kentucky because the Kentucky boundary is the 1792 low-water mark on the north bank of the river. The issue is murky because each state has a minimum of one hundred feet of the river from the legally established boundary. Casino "riverboats" have a narrow channel within which to operate and sometimes barely navigate.

Owensboro, called "Yellow Banks" by early pioneers, is the next major city south of Louisville. The breadth of the Ohio River at

Owensboro—439 miles downstream from Cattlettsburg—bulges to accommodate Yellow Bank Island and Owensboro Bend Bar. The river is beginning to seem as big as the Mississippi, even though its marriage with it is still 223 miles away. The Ohio River serves a population larger than that of Canada, hauls more freight than the Panama Canal, and moves more water than the upper Mississippi. An argument is sometimes made that it's not the Ohio that empties into the Mississippi but the Mississippi that finds its way to the Ohio. It's not the Mississippi River that empties into the Gulf of Mexico, it is the Ohio. David and Lalie fuss about this, but the nice part about fussing is that it leads to peacemaking.

We two lovers lean against the balcony railing of the seventh-floor suite in the hotel overlooking the Ohio River at Owensboro. It is June, the traditional month of marriages, but the joining of hands occurred when we were much younger. Many times, even in the beginning, we wondered how physical love would be in the ending years of our marriage. Now we know. Some October mornings are cold, but the nice part about that is that after October comes November, and after November comes December, and the increasing cold drives feet to touching, and memories from twenty-two years before become fretful warmth, recollections almost always encased in water.

We're standing together on the balcony overlooking the Ohio River at Owensboro, and we watch with deepening pleasure the towboat *Edwin A. Lewis* pushing fifteen barges of coal upstream. That's how we see life in these twilight hours. Hasn't all been flood. Hasn't all been spring water trickling down green valleys. For us, in the half-light, it's sheer willpower requiring intelligence and the instincts born of towboat pilots reading the river.

When the *Miss Nari* pushes upstream the *River Explorer* with its broad passenger top deck and its oval exercise track, we stare in wonderment that anybody would purchase tickets on a vessel to spend time running around in circles. There they are, logging their exercise miles, headphones attached, counting their calories and their carbohydrates. We're at peace with their right to do so, but we hope they'll understand our obsession to stand still and behold the flow of the water and the people who love and dream along the way. River tramping has always had its imperfections—

calamities and monstrosities—and Belle Rivière is no exception. The Ohio receives the Tradewater River at Caseyville. The Cumberland River empties into the Ohio at Smithland and the immense volume of water from the Tennessee River empties in at Paducah.

On July 4-5, 1778, Lieutenant Colonel George Rogers Clark befriended a small hunting party and from its members he received information crucial to victory over the British at Kaskaskia. The campaign "saved" the Illinois country for the United States. It also resulted in "Clark's Land," an original patent of almost 74,000 acres, which became the site for present-day Paducah, forty-seven miles upstream from the confluence of the Ohio and the Mississippi.

General William Clark, of Lewis and Clark fame, subsequently was deeded a portion of the land. It was William, the younger brother, who developed the site of the town kindly named for Chief Paduke and his tribe of Chickasaw Indians. General Clark had the location platted on June 18, 1830, and by 1990 the population had grown to 27,256. Judging from one of the legends, Clark's befriending of Paduke may have borne some resemblance to the Dutch befriending the Manhattan Indians, exchanging twenty-four dollars in trinkets for the slender piece of real estate that would become New York City. At least Chief Paduke's name lives on in the twenty-first century, and there's a likeness of him in the middle of Jefferson Street in Paducah. In the 1909 statue of the handsome chief sculpted by Laredo Taft, Paduke is looking heavenward, long hair flowing, Grecian in grandeur, as if wondering, Good God, what happened?

The floodwaters of 1937 reached all the way to the statue of the great chief Paduke. The Ohio Valley flood of that year has been recorded as "the greatest natural disaster in the history of the U.S." It drove more than one million citizens from their homes. Over 90 percent of Paducah was inundated. Damage was more than $22 million. In the new millennium, there's an $8 million floodwall. Upstream on the Tennessee, there's a chain of TVA dams and reservoirs. Chief Paduke may be thinking, How much is enough? His is likely a troubled spirit.

Irvin Shrewsbury Cobb (1876-1944) is Paducah's main claim to international literary fame. His humorous writing endeared him to

31

journalists, editors, and publishers across the nation and in several parts of the rest of the world. His 1941 autobiography is titled *Exit Laughing*, and he may have thought Chief Paduke should have done the same. In 1912 Cobb wrote a collection of short stories called *Back Home*. His best-seller, *Speaking of Operations*, appeared in 1915. In Hollywood, in 1935, Cobb played the Mississippi riverboat captain in the movie *Steamboat Round the Bend*. *In Kentucky: The Proud State*, Cobb, wearing the hat of the humorist, cigar thrust upward, wrote with pride and joy: "The Tennesseean is more a Southerner than he is a Tennesseean, the Kentuckian is more a Kentuckian than he is a Southerner—more a Kentuckian, indeed, than he is anything else whatsover. From center to circumference, from crupper to hame, from pit to dome, he's all Kentuckian." Possibly Cobb is correct, but he died before the homogenization of North and South, East and West.

Paducah's famous adopted son, Alben William Barkley (1877-1956), was born in Graves County, south of McCracken County, of which Paducah is the county seat. Barkley was vice-president of the United States (1949-1953) in the Truman Administration. The "Veep" and Irvin S. Cobb are buried in Paducah. Barkley was revered as one possessing considerable common sense. "Alben" became a household word with a nice, firm ring to it, one most Kentuckians believed could be trusted. But that may have been due also to the fact that most households in Kentucky were traditionally overgrown with Democrats, and having Alben the "Veep" tended to make up for a wide assortment of embarrassing rascals.

One history of Paducah, originally called Pekin, is John E.L. Robertson's *Paducah, 1830-1980*. It was published in 1980 and is a useful guide to an understanding of Kentucky's last major city on the Ohio before it empties into the Mississippi. Another account is *The Story of Paducah* by Fred G. Neuman with an introduction by Irvin S. Cobb. Paducah is the last Kentucky port of call on the Ohio River, a region of sloughs, bottoms, small lakes, and ponds. The headwaters of Mayfield Creek include Little Brushy Creek, which begins at the community of Lowes, birthplace of Vice-President Barkley.

Mary Wheeler (1892-1979) was born in Paducah and is buried in

Oakgrove Cemetery there. She taught music at the Hindman Settlement School and Paducah Junior College. She collected folk songs of the mountains of eastern Kentucky and the Ohio River. *Steamboatin' Days: Folksongs of the River Packet Era* was her final work (1944). She wrote: "One of the great periods of this nation is associated with the river packet era. The search for songs of the packet boat days leads away from broad city streets...into cabins along the river bank or on a hill with the broad stream below."

From the window of Room 316 of the Paducah Executive Inn, at 6 o'clock on a March morning, the sky is gray over the Ohio River. Sky and water merge in oneness and silence. A towboat nurses its barges slowly upstream. On the other side, a piece of Illinois separates the water and the sky. There seem to be no people out there besides the towboat captain and crew.

"Make a pencil point here," Retired Colonel Arthur Kelly of Springfield, Kentucky, once told us as he drew a circle around the meeting of the Ohio and Mississippi Rivers, indicating a radius of about fifty miles. "Consider," he said "In this tiny area is the collection of all the water of the Ohio, Tennessee, Cumberland, Wabash, Green, Salt, Kentucky, Licking, Miami, and Big Sandy."

He could have added the Kanawha, Muskingum, Allegheny, Monongahela. He might have added the tributaries of the upper Mississippi: the Missouri, Illinois, Des Moines, Skunk (Iowa), the Iowa, Wapsipinicon, Maquoketa, Plum, Apple, Turkey, Wisconsin, Yellow, Upper Iowa, Root, Black, Zumbro, Saint Croix, Elk, Platte, Skunk (Minnesota), Long Prairie, Willow, and Swan, and the waters of Lake Itasca, where the Mississippi officially begins.

To cross the bridges over the Ohio and the Mississippi at the Confluence of America is to witness the great end and the great beginning, a union at the heartland of the nation, closure reopening like a night-blooming cereus. The combined waters roll on, barging human thought, bound for New Orleans.

It's time to tramp the tributaries.

Big Sandy and Little Sandy

I used to lie on my belly on the faded wooden bridge that crossed the creek by my house and stare at the water until it seemed that the bridge was moving instead of the creek. As the water streamed past me, I would imagine that I was going on a big ship to someplace exciting.

Linda Scott DeRosier
Creeker

It's raining the first day of September as we cross the little bridge over Island Creek and help each other, hand-in-hand, to climb up the rock-slick path on the side of the mountain to the Hatfield Cemetery. Thunder is bellowing—*bum-bum-bumpbumpbump-bum-bum*—on the West Virginia side of Tug Fork of Big Sandy River, lightning obscured by the sun shaffffting, cracccccking through puffs of clouds scudddding along the mountaintops. When we finally arrive and for the first time see the marbled likeness of "Devil Anse," looking defiantly toward the north, we stop to catch our breaths. We are left speechless by the steepness of the assent, then the presence of the hatless, bearded face blackened by years of storm, eyes deeply set beneath heavy brows, nose grandly hooked, shoulders broad, arms coming down at sobering attention. Seven-buttoned spatterdashes hold the pants neatly in place, as if the old Confederate guerrilla were answering General Lee's roll call one more time.

William Anderson "Devil Anse" Hatfield feuded, farmed, and sired thirteen children on the east side of Tug Fork upstream from the site of the Battle of Grapevine Creek, January 19, 1888. In life, he stood tall and sometimes felt called upon to crouch low to draw a deadly bead for family. He was a generous, truthful man who saw no purpose in suffering kindly any troublesome Kentuckians or other firebrands, *"quire"* flatlanders included. It was his habit to insist that peaceful passersby stop for supper and spend the night in this dark corner of Appalachia, where panthers, bears, and rattlesnakes carved out and secured their homes in the highlands and the hollers. Whenever night closed in, critters could be especially dangerous.

When a commercial photographer appeared to capture the quintessential feudist, Devil Anse and his boys posed with proud, earnest looks on their faces. With dark and doubting casts of eye, cradling their weapons as bravely as lionhearted warriors, they displayed what the world had come to expect, satisfying morbid curiosity about the most famous of all the Applachian feudists. This celebrated picture of the Hatfield clan is usually cropped to leave out the vainglorious photographer who set the camera's timer, then positioned himself on the left of the Hatfield family. Only after they had eaten their supper did Devil Anse agree to sit for a portrait. The photographer is said to have asked, "Where are your guns?" The Hatfields politely obliged with their props, and the picture was staged to specification for Seaboard newspapers.

To a New York reporter, Devil Anse once allowed as how "I belong to no Church unless you say that I belong to the one great Church of the world. If you like you can say it is the devil's Church that I belong to." He may have actually used those words, but one thing for certain—Devil Anse was a straight shooting Tug Fork man whose family tree today includes doctors, lawyers, teachers, and a governor of West Virginia.

We look up in awe at the Italian marble statue of the old patriarch in Logan County, West Virginia, where he was laid to rest January 6, 1921. All but two of his children are buried here, along with their mother, Levicy Chafin. And further up the mountainside are the unmarked graves of immigrant workers—Czechoslovakians, Yugoslavians, and Italians—who came to America seeking jobs in the coal and timber industries and died here in obscurity without ever once being involved in a feud.

We visit with Jean, the widow of one of the grandsons of Devil Anse and Levicy—Tennis Jr., son of the youngest son of the Hatfield clan, Tennyson. Jean sits in a catch-as-catch-can trailer at Crystal Block and Sarah Ann on Island Creek, a short distance downstream from the Hatfield cemetery. She sells tombstones, which had been her husband's occupation. A sad looking man comes in to make a payment on a marker for his girlfriend's departed husband. Jean receives the money, and her receipt is a knowing look.

The walls of the trailer are filled with priceless Hatfield pictures. We ask Jean the predictable questions: What does she believe led to the Hatfield-McCoy feud? Was it the Civil War? The McCoy who fought on the Union side? Or the argument about who owned the pig?

"Never knew a Hatfield or a McCoy that could hold their liquor," says Jean, finishing her sandwich, which she has offered to share with us. "No road until the '30s, traveled the creek. Had to fight to live. No plumbing. Hatfields were gentle people, generous people, but don't try to take something from them. Either raised it or killed it." She dabs her mouth with a paper napkin. "Devil Anse had two bears. Killed the mama and brought the babies home and raised them. Family loyalty, not like now."

"What was Levicy like?"

"Went to the creek, washed clothes in the creek. Very sweet little old lady."

"The Tug Fork, what kind of river is it?"

"Rises fast. Pigeon Creek, Island Creek. Four times Williamson's been flooded. Course they've got the floodwall now. You are welcome to stay for supper and spend the night," says Jean, in the way Devil Anse might have said it.

We have to be on our way, we explain, but we purchase some Devil Anse cards and Altina L. Waller's *Feud: Hatfields, McCoys, and Social Change in Appalachia, 1860-1900*. Jean signs it: "Mrs. Henry Hatfield, grandson of Wm. Anderson Devil Anse Hatfield." Now we know where we can go to get an honest deal on our family monument complete with headstones, if "Old Blue," our pickup truck, can make it that far up into

37

the mountains. Shoot, we'll just drive over in the springtime, load 'em up, and bring 'em home.

Pigeon Creek pours out of West Virginia into Tug Fork at Naugatuck, bringing the waters of Big Branch, Laurel Fork, Conley Branch, Hell Creek, Elk Creek, Millstone Branch, Rockhouse Fork, Rover Branch, and Nighway Branch, all the way back to half-mile-high Horsepen Mountain. Island Creek flows to the north and empties into the Guyandotte River at Logan. The easternmost point of the Commonwealth is located approximately where Ben Creek empties into the Tug Fork at the juncture of Virginia, West Virginia, and Kentucky. The Tug continues northwesterly, forming the boundary between Pike County, Kentucky, and Mingo County, West Virginia.

Wolf Creek and Coldwater Creek are among the many streams draining Martin County, Kentucky, site of the 250-million-gallon "slurry" spill of October 11, 2000. An abandoned underground mine collapsed, sending the black goo to the Tug Fork and as far downstream as the mouth of Big Sandy. It was estimated that it would take as long as six months and tens of millions of dollars to clean it up. The ecological consequences could not be immediately calculated, but the incident led to protests sponsored by the Ohio Valley Environmental Coalition.

The roiling, churning waters of Tug, Levisa, and Russell Forks of Big Sandy arise in a frightful fever, twisting and tumbling through towering mountains, cascading down 1,600-foot canyons, where the beauty and fragrance of the laurel and yellow lady's slipper are delicate and beguiling.

Breaks of Big Sandy, created 250-million years ago in the late Paleozoic period, has cut the channels deep with tides, where imperfect, thirsting human beings have staked their claims to "home." Some, like Devil Anse Hatfield and Ran'l McCoy, remained isolated, stubborn, proud, emotional, and political, and, when occasion dictated, downright mean and murderous.

Randolph "Ran'l" McCoy feuded, farmed, and sired sixteen children on Blackberry Fork, a tributary of the Tug on the Kentucky side, in Pike County. His wife, Sally, was his first cousin. He died March 28, 1914. In the McCoy Cemetery on Blackberry Fork are the graves of four of

Randolph and Sally McCoy's sons, Tolbert, Pharmer, Randolph Jr., and Calvin, and a daughter, Alifair—all victims of the Hatfield-McCoy feud of the troubled late nineteenth century.

When we try to visit the McCoy cemetery on Blackberry Fork, down the way from South Williamson, Leckieville, Toler, and Hardy, we find a sign on the side of the road: "This is not public access to the McCoy cemetary. Private property. No trespassing." We park the car, grit our teeth, and walk up the steep, gravel road to a house. A basset hound greets us. If it had been a pit bull, we would have been in a heap of trouble, and not on a bet would we have opened the chain link gate. Polite knocks on the door go unanswered. Maybe nobody's at home. Maybe somebody hopes that two more Hatfield-McCoy curiosity seekers will take a hint and go away. We do.

Before leaving Blackberry Fork, we visit the place where Randolph McCoy's cabin was burned on New Year's Day 1888, the date of the infamous retaliatory raid when the Hatfields killed Alifair and Calvin and pistol-whipped their mama, Sarah. We drive deeper into McCoy country to the meeting of Blackberry Fork and Blackberry Creek, then to the left and northeast toward Matewan. On the Kentucky side of Tug Fork is the spot where, on August 9, 1882, the Hatfields tied the three McCoy boys—Tolbert, Pharmer, and Randolph Jr.—to pawpaw trees, then pumped about fifty shells into their bodies. This was in retaliation for the election-day murder of Ellison Hatfield.

There are at least two good scholarly books on the Hatfield-McCoy feud: Otis K. Rice's *The Hatfields and the McCoys*, and Altina L. Waller's *Feud: Hatfields, McCoys, and Social Change in Appalachia, 1860-1900*. Either of the books is infinitely more valuable than the Hollywood versions and the journalistic accounts of a story that has stuck in the craw and consciousness of the nation and won't go away.

There was a Hatfield-McCoy reunion and reconciliation breakfast in the summer of 2000. We were scheduled to attend but became too busy at the other end of the state. The event made news nationally, so we read about it in USA Today. There was a picture of a Hatfield-McCoy softball game, which the McCoy's won (15-1), and a tug of war also won by the McCoys, speaking a book or two about the relative level of violence

39

today in Appalachia. There's been a thundercloud of words written about the blood feuds of Kentucky, especially eastern Kentucky. John Ed Pearce, in *Days of Darkness: The Feuds of Eastern Kentucky*, dismisses Devil Anse as "an illiterate, selfish killer and a rather cowardly one at that, a frontier Godfather who sent his minions out to kill off his enemies, and who let them go to prison and the gallows for it while he sat back and profited from the killings."

The Kentucky feuds happened, for real they did, but they weren't any bloodier than the Al "Scarface" Capone-James "Big Jim" Colosimo days of Chicago's prohibition-era savagery. True, it's dubious tomfoolery to immortalize either the Hatfields and McCoys or the Capones and the Colosimos, but it's dishonest and unforgivable to broad-brush an entire culture, whether of eastern Kentucky or the south side of Chicago.

The Levisa Fork joins the Tug Fork at Louisa to form Big Sandy, and it continues the next twenty-seven miles to mark the boundary of Kentucky and West Virginia. Big Sandy reluctantly empties into the Ohio at Catlettsburg, as if put out by its loss of individual identity. The trip down from the Breaks includes white-water sections, rock-strewn ripples, and lazy pools where the water seems too tired to move on downstream. Everything depends on flood time, ebb tide, drought, and the destructions wrought by the commercial forces of an energy-craving civilization.

We drive to the point on the West Virginia side at the mouth of Big Sandy, where we make deep footprints in the mud on a wet, blustery day in late winter. Woebegone, we stand there to feel what Billy C. Clark portrayed in his book *A Long Row To Hoe*. He chronicled the feelings of many Kentuckians, young and old, who've stood at the beginning of the wide, deep, muddy, and polluted water separating Kentucky and Ohio, the southern culture from the northern. Perhaps Kentuckians are obsessed with feelings of persecution, as if they believe Ohioans must think the only civilization that matters begins on the northern side of the river.

"I watched my brothers stand here under the willows on the Kentucky shore and holler across the Ohio at boys on the far bank. 'Buckeye knockers!' they yelled over and shook their fists.

"'Corn crackers!' the Ohioans yelled back, their voices rolling over the water like waves." That's Billy Clark talking, about 1940.

The voices aren't usually as strident sixty years later, but undercurrents are subtle and surprising, and the water is no less muddy, no less smelly with the castaways of an aluminum-can culture. Traffic on the Ohio and over its many bridges has had, maybe, a democratizing effect (though never known for tidiness). "Buckeye Knockers" and "Corn Crackers" don't have the punch on the end of the nose they once did. But old grievances based on past misunderstandings and persistent cultural differences don't necessarily disappear with the passage of a generation.

The main stream of Big Sandy from Louisa to Catlettsburg lays to bed traditional belief that in order for a "river" to be a "river" it must have a length of at least a hundred miles. Maybe to appease tradition, the Kentucky General Assembly in 1954 declared that Big Sandy included the Levisa Fork as far south as Millard in Pike County, where Russell Fork empties in, a declaration conveniently making Big Sandy a hundred miles long. Levisa's headwaters gather further to the east of Fishtrap Lake, deep in the mountains separating Kentucky and Virginia.

Near the top of a mountain three miles from Martin, up Stephens Branch in Floyd County, there's a steeper climb to the real world of Terry and Deborah Ratliff. Sit still and stay awhile. Breathe the cool, minted air. Don't be in a hurry to run to the telephone to call the *CBS Evening News* with Walter Cronkite, or his successor, Dan Rather, or the heir apparent, John Roberts, and say, "There's no story here, damn it, send me someplace where there's something happening." Or call Revlon Chain Drug Division and moan, "Hell's bells and blossoms' butts, they don't wear cosmetics up here. Whose idea was it to send me to this neck of the woods in the first place?"

Terry and Deborah's twenty acres, "steep as a mule's face," trace back to a Revolutionary War land grant. Their two-and-a-half-floor cantilevered tulip poplar log cabin grew from Terry's own hands. He made some of his tools. He's mainly a chairmaker, but when he needs to be, when he wants to be, he's a toolmaker too. He is both, because he relies on dependable native intelligence. There's a plentiful supply of this inventive, renewable resource along the streams of the Appalachian Mountains.

"There was nothing here but a path. My dream was to set our house here and not change it. My grandfather, Beverly, was a coal miner. He raised pigs, corn, sold eggs, and he grew what the family ate. He sold railroad ties for twenty five-cents apiece. My father, James, worked for twenty-two years in the mines. In '67 when the mines quit we moved to Indiana."

Terry—born down the mountain in Beaver Valley Hospital—returned home to Kentucky and graduated in 1977 from the University of Kentucky. He majored in psychology. He and his wife Deborah have two teenage children, Carlie and Joseph.

Terry's career took a turn to chairs and tables and mantles for fireplaces and thingamabobs like a hand-carved wooden ball that when you pull it in the WC, the commode flushes. Where's the leaning outhouse with a half moon cut in the door? Where's a bearded, barefooted moutaineer wearing a black stovepipe hat and sucking on a corncob pipe, with a finger crooked through the handle of a jug marked with three X's on the side? There'd be nothing wrong with a well-built outhouse on a power outage night, whether it's in Kentucky or in New York City. The trouble is that outhouses in Manhattan borough would be as unnatural as springhouses, icehouses, and meat houses—too many people, 1.5-million in a space of only twenty-two square miles, without the freedom to relieve and refresh themselves as they damn well please.

"I try to visualize what I want in a piece of wood, see the grain, let the wood, the log determine....I'm at my best when I'm not worrying about anything....On a good day I'm working with wood and wood is working with me," says Terry.

When he receives an order for a cherry dining room table with four chairs for a couple in Pikeville, Terry goes out into the woods and selects the tree. Sometimes it's a neighbor or a stripminer that calls and says, "There's a log over here, you can have it if you come and get it."

Terry was twenty-six years old when he made his first hickory bottom for a chair. For a couple of years he made "smurf" furniture: "half a log, smooth it up, put legs on it and call it furniture."

At forty-four, well past the years when he was a professional in community mental health, Terry Ratliff is a self-taught chairmaker. "I'm not a carpenter," he smiles, "...no formal classes...[but I learned by] listening to and watching Buck Justice of Floyd County and Irving Messer of Knott County, and Woodrow Burchett, the Sage of Cow Creek."

It was the late, legendary Woodrow who gave Terry a valuable lesson in self-esteem and the pricing of the wood that goes in raw and comes out smooth, ready to sit on and push back from the table after a good meal of homegrown meat and vegetables. "At the Squirrel Festival, Woodrow came by with some friends who laughed at my rocking chair with a price tag of $1,600. I was red-faced. But Woodrow came back and he said that chair is worth it. He said, 'If you don't value your work nobody else will.'"

Terry considers his work to be folk art. "Heritage is involved... quality...the way it was done one hundred years ago." He has taught chairmaking at the Hindman Settlement School at the forks of Troublesome Creek. We first met him at the 1999 festival at Old Fort Harrod in Harrodsburg, but the best way to get to know a chairmaker is to sit in one of his chairs on his own front porch, then go out on the ridgeline to the place where he works. That's reason enough to drive up Stephens Branch to listen and hear Terry Ratliff's words flow.

"Start with a log...bring [it] back...split wood out with wedges into quarters, and bolts ...use a board break, a froe, and a shaving horse....Cherry is more difficult than hickory...tulip poplar grows fast and works easy....White oak is a favorite for furniture building, it has a dense grain pattern and will take a lot of compression....Some people wouldn't call it making a living....This twenty acres is my garden, surrounded by a hillside of hickory, oak and walnut, facing east for the morning sun...poplar, maple, southern pine, black gum, sweet gum, sassafras, five or six kinds of oaks."

Terry sums up his passion for chairmaking: "The Temple is right here within us."

That pretty much sums up how we feel about being middle-of-the-road Episcopalians. Priests are fine and bishops are handy, but individuals comprise the laity without which priests and bishops wouldn't have a chair to sit on or an outhouse to call their own in the event of spiritual emergency.

Stephens Branch flows into Right Fork of Beaver Creek, which joins Left Fork of Beaver between Hite and Alphoretta. Beaver Creek gathers Arkansas Creek and rolls on northeastward, where it empties into Levisa Fork of Big Sandy at Allen City in Floyd County. Jim's his name. He's found his niche, and he's sharpening it. James Smith was born on Marrowbone Creek at Lookout in Pike County. Marrowbone is at the headwaters of Russell Fork. Jim was seventy-six years old in April 2000.

"We lived so far up the holler, we got to use the water first," says Jim, who has moved down from the mountains to the foothills. The "retired" lumberjack, carpenter, writer and reader of verse still arises at four o'clock in the morning because, he says, that's when it's the quietest.

He's become one of those rare breeds: he's a sharpener. Chain saws to scissors, knives to pinking shears, James Smith turns "dull" into razor-sharp. He can build teeth on a steel surface where there weren't any before. In the satellited, throwaway society rollercoastering through the Information Age, most consumers equate dullness with "done in," "done for" and "dead for certain." James Smith acts on the belief that anything that ever had a cutting edge deserves a second chance and therefore is a likely candidate for repair.

In his tiny ten- by fourteen-foot shop behind the house he built with his own hands in Montgomery County, Mr. Smith has presence amid equipment seldom seen by a public that prefers newness to buffed-up and restored. There's the clipper hone for sharpening the tools of barbers, beauticians, and sheepshearers. Then come the scissors vice and the pinking shears sharpener. There're the handsaw filer, the handsaw retoothing machine, the band sander for limb trimmers, the machine for coating carbide saw teeth, the tote welder, and the knife grinder (any size up to three feet).

"I make things to make things work," says Jim with the satisfaction that comes from knowing his passion, understanding it, and living it as if it were the most important thing under the sun. Over the door, inside his postage stamp-sized shop, hangs James Smith's father's old crosscut saw from Pike County, hanging there as a stern, simple reminder of the days before rural electric. Beside the door the hard steel ax remains upright from the '30s and '40s, when Jim left home to go west with the Civilian

Conservation Corps. Back then he was only sixteen years old. His father and mother, Fred and Mae Bartley Smith, had moved from Pike to Floyd to Montgomery County, a mini-way west.

In the CCC, Jim was sent to logging camps in Idaho and Washington. He earned a dollar a day. Once a month, the government sent fifteen dollars to Jim's parents, held out six dollars for a savings account, and presented Jim with ten dollars—if there were thirty-one days in the month. After his tour of duty with the CCC, Jim was a natural as a "rigging slinger" in the logging industry in the Pacific Northwest, and he moved up to a whopping six dollars a day. When World War II began, Jim headed home to Kentucky and joined the army. When that was behind him, he proved the value of vocational training. Jim predated Vocational Industrial Clubs of America, founded on the principle that trade skills have respectability.

Universities of the liberal arts would be helpless without construction crafts. In his time as a carpenter, James Smith helped to erect the Singletary Center for the Arts at the University of Kentucky. He oversaw the installation of the foldaway bleachers at Rupp Arena, and he helped build the IBM facility in Lexington. Jim has built thirty-five houses, including the one where he shares a fifty-five year marriage with Blanche Harvey Smith, a native of Magoffin County.

Nowadays, while Jim sharpens tools, Blanche designs "chicken scratch" quilts. She looks up from the work in her hands to remind Jim to tell his visitor about the verse he's written. The sharpener smiles and begins to recite "Just How Tall Is a Tree."

> *Look around you*
> *and you can see*
> *That nearly everything you touch,*
> *Nearly everything you see,*
> *Is in someway built or constructed*
> *from a tree.*

People usually say to Jim: "Can you sharpen this?" He usually replies: "I'll have to study it." His vocation today is a culmination of a lifetime of looking at tasks, sizing them up, and going to work to make them right. From the days of his youth when he shod mine ponies in the coalfields of eastern Kentucky, to this time of his seniority, James Smith stays keen on the pleasurable edge of achievement.

Carol Crowe-Carraco has written *The Big Sandy River*, a history that includes the frolicsome story of how fate almost fingered Kentucky's eastern boundary as the Levisa Fork instead of the Tug Fork. The Virginia government sent commissioners and surveyors to the western territory to establish the state boundary. Their instructions were to determine the larger of the two streams, Levisa (one hundred and sixty-four miles long) or Tug (one hundred and fifty-four miles long). The surveyors were commissioned to designate as the new state line the more significant of the two waterways.

As the story goes, the team selected the Tug Fork and promptly celebrated by getting drunk. During the night, there was a deluge, and the following morning it was clear that the Levisa was the stream with the greater capacity. The team of surveyors decided, however, to confirm while sober what they had determined while drunk.

If the Levisa Fork had been selected as the border, Kentucky would have lost a large piece of Lawrence County, a portion of Floyd and Johnson Counties, and all of Martin and Pike Counties. John Ed Pearce, journalist and author, has been accused of rejoicing at such a possibility, of saying in public that somebody ought to dam up the Kentucky River or do something to get rid of eastern Kentucky. "No," says John Ed, "I did not say it. Somebody in the Chandler administration said it, but he didn't mean it." Tracking down such things is tricky business.

Pike County alone, the largest of Kentucky's 120 counties, is 786 square miles. Lawrence County is no small area—425 square miles. Johnson County is 264 square miles, Martin is 231, and Floyd is 399. Add these together and it becomes a grand total of 2,105 square miles, an area larger than the state of Delaware. The number of streams in this area defies arithmetic.

Big Sandy has a tragically rich and, at the same time, deeply impoverished history. A sense of this is evident in Harry Caudill's classic,

Night Comes to the Cumberlands. It's not everybody's favorite book. As controversial as Steinbeck's *Grapes of Wrath*, Caudill's first book (1963) threw a relentless, searing light upon the land where he was born, Letcher County, on May 3, 1922. Among his other books are *My Land is Dying* (1971), *The Mountain, the Miner, and the Lord* (1980), and *Slender Is the Thread* (1992). Twenty years after the publication of *Night Comes to the Cumberlands*, the University of Illinois Press published Caudill's *Theirs Be the Power: The Moguls of Eastern Kentucky*, a stinging rebuke of politicians and coal and timber industry leaders.

Catesby Clay of Bourbon County, one of the keelhauled, has compared Caudill to an abolitionist like John Brown, as compared to an emancipationist like Abraham Lincoln. At lunch in Lexington with Mr. Clay, president emeritus of Kentucky River Coal Company, and Dave Zegeer, retired Bethlehem Steel manager for eastern Kentucky, they make the case for a market demand for cheap energy and responsible restoration of stripmined land. It is an argument that understandably does not immediately please the activists working in the tradition of Harry Caudill. Yet the question is asked: When the population quadruples and there's a demand for fuel, what do you do? "I must tell you, whatever the arguments advanced, we find stripmining to be *ugly*," says David.

"Do you feel the same way about cutting open a mountain to build a highway?" Mr. Zegeer asks. "Or what about shaving off a mountainside for commercial development?"

"As in U.S. 23 through Pike County?"

"Exactly."

The U.S. 119 cut through Coburn Mountain in Pike County, costing $41.6 million, is another example. If this kind of amputation of a mountain can be rationalized in the name of shorter driving time, why the outrage about stripmining?

And the superhighway, such as Interstate 75, is that not commercial? Profits for trucking companies, pleasure for Florida-bound tourists? Are not "strip malls" aptly named?

Thirty-six years after the publication of *Night Comes to the Cumberlands*, after a Kentucky Humanities Council talk on *Rivers of*

Kentucky, which we presented to the Filson Club in Louisville, a woman and her son introduced themselves. She was Anne, widow of Harry Caudill, and their oldest son, James. He said that *Night Comes to the Cumberlands* was his father's most important book, but that the best from an artistic sense was *The Senator from Slaughter County*.

"Did your husband talk very much about water?" we asked. "Especially headwaters?"

"He was so obsessed with saving mountains and the streams," said Anne. "Harry wrote because he had things to say. He wasn't concerned about how well he sold. He had an incredible correspondence with people. He wrote articles for the *Mountain Eagle* [the Whitesburg, Kentucky, muckraking newspaper]. He talked all the time. His mother came from brilliant minds."

Harry Caudill died November 29, 1990. He is buried in Cynthiana near the Licking River, the hometown of Anne Frye Caudill. She acknowledges that the eastern Kentucky described by her husband in *Night Comes to the Cumberlands* is not the same highlands today. "On the surface, great changes have been made in the whole country. It's less isolated because there are better roads. There are sewer systems and medical care. The medical profession is the biggest employer but industries have not come in and there is large unemployment. Basic problems remain."

A basic American problem is an elitist perception that overshadows grassroots reality. Perhaps if he were alive today, Harry Caudill would agree that the valley of Big Sandy represents a major possibility, another Kentucky beginning. But if it is a story to be ignored by the mass media in favor of a steady diet of entertaining character flaws, then America stands to lose, and to lose greatly. To trace the Levisa Fork of the Big Sandy from Louisa to Paintsville to Prestonsburg to Pikeville and beyond Fishtrap Lake to Fedscreek and Mouthcard is to follow a trail that speaks volumes at every turn.

One such volume is Caudill's *Dark Hills to Westward: The Saga of Jenny Wiley*. One of the strongest and bravest women who ever set foot on Kentucky soil, Jenny Wiley saw five of her children killed by Indians. During her captivity (1789-90), she was taken north to the mouth of Big Sandy. Then, unable to cross the Ohio, her captors traveled up Little Sandy, where she finally escaped. Jenny knew the streams as well as she did the backs of her hardened hands. Caudill has retold the true story for readers and travelers to the eastern Kentucky mountains.

> *Her grave was dug beside her husband's and may still be found by patient searchers who rake away the leaves on a little point near the town of Paintsville—a name derived from the Painted Licks. The legend of Jenny Wiley has set her name, too, upon the land. The great sycamore, where Dull Knife killed her baby, survived to 1850 and was called "Jenny's tree" by two generations of mountaineers. The little stream by which it stood was called—as it still is—Jenny's Creek. And beyond the Tug and Levisa in Kentucky is another stream—the one Jenny followed on that long-gone day when she obeyed the omen of the hopping bird. It, too, was given her name by settlers who had heard her story and Jenny's Creek still tumbles into Big Paint Lick, honoring to our own time the first white woman ever to wade its waters.*

Today there is Jenny Wiley State Resort Park, named for a woman remembered for raw courage and rare intelligence. With the passage of two centuries, her saga needs no fictionalization. The Appalachian women who have followed her are worthy of an audience non-addicted to television. In her 1999 best-selling autobiography, *Creeker*, Linda Scott DeRosier takes her readers to one of the myriad places to be seen, smelled, touched, heard, and felt in the Jenny Wiley highlands: Left Fork of Greasy Creek. There are also Middle Fork and Right Fork, Otter Branch, Yost Branch, and Pigeonroost Branch. All coming together at Boons Camp, they form the beginning of Greasy Creek, which empties into Levisa Fork between the communities of Thelma and River.

In each of these places, women have not just survived. They have loved their families and their land. Linda DeRosier makes an observation seldom understood by those who would attempt to understand the mountain people of eastern Kentucky: "The prototypical hillbilly stereotype, while exaggerating the profile of rural residents, is not at all representative of those Appalachians who were brought up in the cities and small towns of that region."

DeRosier, who now lives in Montana and is married to a university president, is proud of her heritage. She's loyal to it. "Perhaps the place Two-Mile shows up most in my life today is in my notion of kin and how that concept is defined. I have never sought liberation from my people, however far I may have strayed from the homeplace. I have left no one behind. Instead, my sense of family has simply expanded to include a lot of folks I have met along life's way, some of whom were just not lucky enough to have been born in eastern Kentucky."

Verna Mae Slone's 1979 book *What My Heart Wants to Tell* is another piece of plain honest writing. Verna Mae grew up on Caney Fork, which flows northeastwardly from Alice Lloyd College at Pippa Passes past Hollybush and Raven. She has written about sacrifice, about her proud ancestors surviving in the mountains of eastern Kentucky despite overwhelming odds. "It was so cold that February morning in 1863 [when her father was born], the wind almost bounced off the sides of the hills as it roared its way up Caney Creek and up the mouth of Trace, whirling the icy snow around the log cabin."

In the preface Verna Mae speaks to a problem:

> *So many lies and half-truths have been written about us, the mountain people, that folks from other states have formed an image of a gun-totin', 'baccer-' spitting, whiskey-drinking, barefooted, foolish hillbilly, who never existed, but was conceived and born in the minds of the people who have written such things as* Stay on Stranger *and the* Beverly Hillbillies....*No matter what we do, we can't make folks believe we are any different. These lies and half-truths have done our children more damage than anything else. They have taken more from us than the large coal and gas companies did by cheating our forefathers out of their minerals, for that was just*

money. These writers have taken our pride and dignity and
have disgraced us in the eyes of the outside world.

The headwaters of the Little Sandy River gather in Poplar Hollow in sparsely populated Elliott County (6,455 persons in the 1990 census). Near the community of Little Sandy, Turkey Branch and Howard Creek form the main stream. Doctor's Branch feeds in at the Faye community, and shortly thereafter Wells Creek makes its entrance. The waters of the Little Sandy form Grayson Lake. The tributaries include Fighting Fork and Upper Stinson Creek.

Little Sandy flows alongside Kentucky highways 1 and 2 through Jesse Stuart country to Greenup, where the waters empty themselves into the Ohio River opposite Haverhill in southeastern Scioto County, Ohio. The East Fork of the Little Sandy joins the main stream north of Argillite, which thereafter cuts east to Kentucky 2, looping around the Jesse Stuart State Nature Preserve and Trails. Jesse's daughter, Jane, his and Naomi's only child, still lives in the one hundred and fifty-year-old house Jesse made famous through his many books: *Head o' W-Hollow, Trees of Heaven, The Thread that Runs So True*, and *Man with a Bull-Tongued Plow*. It has not been easy for Jane, anguish coming like the heaviest of dark clouds undulating above and dipping into the valleys of the Sandys. She has written of her father's protracted suffering before his death on February 17, 1984. In her book *Transparencies*, Jane Stuart has worked to understand her father's and mother's beginnings and endings. In solitude Jane has found fulfillment and freedom.

Jesse Stuart should be remembered most of all because he was a teacher. When we visited his gravesite in the Plum Grove Cemetery in the country of the Little Sandy, we read the words on his monument, and we saved them:

No one can ever tell me that education,
rightly directed without propaganda,
cannot change the individual, community,
county, state, and the world
for the better. It can...

51

and I am firm in my belief
that a teacher lives on and on
through his students...
Good teaching is Forever
and the teacher is immortal.

Jim Wayne Miller has said of Jesse: "He was instinctively positive, an affirmer....Because he was both a dreamer and a doer, he turned his dreams into deeds and words. He did not tear down. He was a builder—of barns, fences, land. And he was a builder with words."

The author of *Taps for Private Tussy* also had a rich, sharp, ribald sense of humor. He'd probably feel right at home to the west of Little Sandy, high on a hill overlooking Licking River—on Scrabble Ridge. Jesse might claim "Radio" as a distant cousin, else a member of the brotherhood.

Licking

*A Kentuckian is a man who insists on telling you a funny story,
usually about Kentucky.*

Eslie Asbury
Both Sides of the River

"Radio" Stewart rousted himself—oh, about five o'clock—on a wet
Scrabble Ridge morning in late February of the new century, the twenty-
first. He pulled on his khaki pants, smoothly swooshed in his shirttail,
sensed his way from the bedroom past his easy chair in the living room
where foxhound trophies were stacked floor to ceiling, ambled through
the kitchen where the syrup bottle still had some sticky sweetness left on
the sides of it, and, with his walking stick helping to pick the way,
perambulated out the back door to do proper justice to the celebration of
George Washington's birthday. Radio is a patriot.

Oyez! Oyez! Oyez!

His nickname, "Radio," stuck a long time ago when somebody
thought that if Nicholas, Fleming, and Menifee Counties could each
have a "Radio," Bath County ought to have one too. Heck *far*, Kenneth
Stewart figured, it might as well be him as somebody else less deserving.

It's important to answer the call to duty. With the good grace befitting a card-carrying Scrabble Ridger, he accepted the nomination and agreed to serve without pay or promise. After all, how many "Radios" do you have in a county? Any county? Anywhere?

"Radio" is one of those nice names that's easy to remember. Radio Stewart is somebody not easily forgotten, not easily confused with "Bill" or "Bob," "Ben" or "Bo," and definitely not to be taken for granted.

Radio is a fox hound patriot. That means his dogs are his passion. He lives, quivers, sleeps, and breathes dogs. Not just any kind of dogs. He fancies *fox* hounds. He cares as much for them as George Washington did for his country. Think about it. Radio's hounds run like the golden juice of Old Glory when it started out with just the first out-of-the-box thirteen stripes and thirteen stars, nothing complicated like Ohio and four-dozen other afterthoughts.

At Scrabble Ridge, high above a loop of the Licking River between Turkey Run and Locust Creek, Radio's lean, strong hounds live for the rising of the sun the way George Washington prayed for warmth and something to eat at Valley Forge. In both places—Valley Forge and Scrabble Ridge—it's the basic survival thing, plus a little bit more. Grit and guts come in several shapes and sizes.

With Radio's dogs, every day is a new day with all kinds of fox possibilities. Winter or summer, it doesn't make a Jack Russell bit of difference. Full-throated "ba-roooing," leading the pack after the red menace, "wa-woop-wooping," feeling the cold February air sweep deep down inside swelling canine lungs, the hunt is not the closest thing to heaven—hell *far*, the hunt *is* Heaven.

The chase, with its sudden turns, its intoxicating smells, soaks through to the innermost depths of dog DNA, swelling like a sponge left out in a dadgum cloudburst. It tracks back to the werewolf in us all, from Shelley's "bold only to pursue" to Service's "huskies howled and the wind began to blow." Man and woman *wish* they could be dogs, if only for the first headlong plunge down the hill. Catching the fox, getting a mouthful of fine underfur, is nothing to compare with the smooth-as-silk rhythm of leg, shoulder, and hindquarter muscles moving lickety-split like Licking River flash floods.

54

George crossed the Delaware River in the winter of 1776, and he treed Cornwallis and the gotdamned Redcoats at Yorktown in '81. Radio crosses Little Flat Creek close to the Bath-Nicholas County line in Kentucky in the winter of 2000, and his dogs chase the bejesus out of Reynard and just about anything else that moves on four legs, up and down, backwards and forwards, in the Clay Wildlife Management Area (WMA), embracing almost five thousand acres of loblolly pines, sycamores, and cedar woods, bordered on the north by the overflowing Licking River and on the south by Cassidy Creek, roaring after four inches of rain. It's a frog-strangler kind of morning. A fox that can't swim is a fox that's looking for a hole to get into. Groundhog mothers and daddys stay at home. They don't have to tell their chillun earthquake stories. Deer hightail. Squirrels scramble upstairs as far as they can git. Wild turkeys fly. Hog-nosed polecats stamp their feet and pucker their anal glands.

The dogs answering Radio's call on a cold February morning are Digger, Bad Eye, Bonnie, Little Yeller, Granny, Big Jump ("He's the man"), Patty, and Little Miss Priss. (Cassie has a cough and has to be left at home.) They're unpenned at the gates of their ramshackle plywood shelters, leashed, and led to a crate in the back of the pickup truck. If they don't go in just right, Radio taps them on the backside with his walking stick and snaps, "Git in there." They're as crowded as chickens that should be so lucky. While the roosters in Radio's and his wife Mary's backyard prance around in the dawn's early light, *ker-rrr-uuupping* like somebodies other than parts floured and fried for Saturday night or dumplinged for Sunday afternoon, Radio's hounds know they're on the downhill slope of the twice-a-week holy crusade. The dog theology is to take no prisoners and leave the souls of foxes to the Great Creator who slipped up and put 'em here in the first place.

A dog saunters up the road toward Radio's place, looking for the entire world like a dog above it all. Looks like he's been out all night, up and down the Licking River, maybe had a bitch to see about. Maybe had some new ground to lift his leg on. He has a big, insulting number "26" painted on his side, and there's no way he can lick it off. He looks guilty and strange.

"What's *that* dog?"

"Number 26."

"Branded?"

"Painted."

"What's he doing out here, walking up this way, all by himself?"

"Won't let you catch him," says Radio, adding, "I'll straighten him up or else." Doesn't sound too good for Old 26. Other less sensitive, less forgiving hunters might've dropped Old 26 on the spot. There's that old saying about old dogs and new tricks, and several principles are involved—two being the price of bullets and wasting time at the start of another ride down the pike to fields of foxhound dreams.

The roads along East Fork Flat Creek, Flat Creek, and Little Flat Creek to Sprout, Kentucky, are generously sprinkled with plastic bottles, aluminum cans, pieces of fence, water gap gates, broken Burley tobacco sticks, supermarket plastic bags, oil cans, and all sorts of valuable things swept down during the night. It looks like the recycling plant has exploded. Clothing waves from tree limbs like closets turned on their heads. *Brown*, everywhere. The accumulation of swirling, sometimes ponding water is heading downstream toward Falmouth, where a crest of fourteen feet over flood stage is expected. Bad, but not as bad as '97 by about ten feet.

"That backwater over there?"

"Yip. Backwater."

"Looks bad."

"Seen it higher than that," says Radio, who remembers the floods of '38 and '97.

"Cassidy Creek is not over the road."

"When it is, Mister, you better look out," says Radio.

The pickup truck loaded with dog patriots turns into the Clay WMA, heads up the hill, then eases out on the ridge where, at 5:30, two ladies have started a nice bonfire for the Nicholas County Hunt Club's "Washington Birthday Hunt." Nothing fancy. Bonfire probably too nice a word. Just plain *far*, roaring *far*, probably a better way of putting it. Everybody who has wood to burn has brought it by the pickup truckload and, as Robert Service says in *The Cremation of Sam McGee*, "heaped the fuel higher." There's a rusty, moon-shaped piece of tin around one side to reflect the heat and keep from scorching ankles. Like the man says, nuttin' fancy.

"Thought we'd have to swim to get here," says one of the ladies.

"Hmm, hmmp," says another.

Anybody who wants a picture of what's about to happen next needs to be sure the batteries are up and the film is in the camera. Dog revolutionaries wait for no man, especially royalty. They don't pose for second chances. "Kiss her again, Mister" won't work here. Cell phones and thingamabob dot com won't connect.

At 7:41 a.m., the door of the rocking wooden box on the back of the pickup truck is unlatched. Eight hounds shoot out of their confinement like prisoners untied from a Cherokee stake. No warriors in gauntlet would have been fast enough to matter. Radio's dogs have the get-up and go of Washington's ragtag crew at the Battle of Monmouth. George's men understood the weakness of British General Clinton, and Radio's modern Kentucky hounds know a thing or two about the eternal world of foxes, coyotes, and other assorted red- and yellow-coated villains.

Big Jump and Little Miss Priss and the other six dogs go down that Nicholas County hill like they've known for two hundred and twenty-two years where they're going and why they're bothering to do it. They have the pop and fizz of a bottle of hot Ale-8, shook up and foaming down the green glass sides.

"There they go!"

"Where?"

"Right there!"

"Can't see 'em."

"See? Their tails are turning."

"Where?"

"Right there, damn it. Through the trees."

"Can't see 'em."

"Gone, now. Son of a bitch."

You might say, one way of looking at it, the day has begun for dogs and more or less come to a standstill for human beings. Nothing to do now but stand around the *far* and discuss important things like a nearly 50 percent cut in tobacco production and the price of gasoline creeping up to two-dollars a gallon. There's some have-on and back-and-forth about alternative crops—asparagus, brussels sprouts, artichokes, and those gotdamned peppers—but these city-started, doomed-from-the-start, half-assed notions don't last longer than another piece of wood in the *far*. And all that talk about gunless societies. Next thing you know a military hero or an assassinated president can't be properly sent off with a twenty-one gun salute. Won't even be able to stop a groundhog dead in its tracks or a fox raping and scattering hot, wet feathers in a hapless hen house.

Nobody whips out a cell phone and checks in or out with anybody. Nobody huddles around a radio to hear Ralph Hacker and Sam Bowie take turns lamenting and rationalizing, jawing up one side and down the other about one more disappointing University of Kentucky basketball game. The fact that Tubby Smith's Wildcats are clawing around with the University of Georgia Bulldogs at Rupp Arena is not mentioned around the *far*. Either of these varmints—bob-tailed wildcats or wrinkle-faced bulldogs, especially the English breed with their troubled, deep-set eyes—pales in comparison to the atomic fusion of foxes and hounds. Tubby could announce he's following Rick Pitino to the NBA. It wouldn't be big news out here on this day. There are more important matters to tend to. More interesting things to discuss. Shit *far*.

Radio, who played high school basketball at Bethel and once was told by Adolph Rupp to "come see me when you get to college" (it didn't work out that way), sits on the tailgate of his pickup and proudly explains the difference between a Walker hound and an English fox dog. It has something to say about why George Washington carried the day and there was a new country to become the father of, while, at the same time, the British Empire gave up custody of its scruffy, misbehaving, orphan child.

"Walker hounds don't take commands. They're faster than English dogs. By God, Walker hounds go the way they want to. Now, the English hound is used to an organized hunt. There's a master that controls 'em. Cracks his whip twice, and they come around by his horse and wait for the horn to blow. Faster he blows the horn, faster they run. 'Tally Ho' and all that there. Then he *fars* a pistol and they come back in a hurry and get behind the horse. Funniest thing ever was. Never go to running until he blows that horn. You don't 'see the fox,' you 'spy the quarry,'" says Radio with a sly, side smile, indicating that he does have outside knowledge to be called upon from time to time. But not too much. Might be judged to be a blabbermouth or the biggest toad in the puddle. And who in hell wants to be that?

"Man called up and wanted some Walkers. I said, 'Bill, you can't handle my dogs. They ain't bred that a-way.' My dogs broke and they gone," says Radio.

Radio favors neither bottle bills nor assembly-line production quotas. The former amounts to a variation of taxation without representation deep in the inscrutableness of every man's perceived right to throw anything where he by God pleases. The latter is a case of taking a perfectly good critter and stripping him of his body and soul. Might as well take a Walker hound and turn him into a greyhound with no more sense than to confuse a mechanical rabbit with the real thing. It's all right to train greyhounds to run themselves until their bones give out so people can bet on them until they're not fit for anything but fish meal, but it's not all right for Ale-8 bottles to catch rain in the backyard. Speed is important, but if all that's wanted is "do this *this* way and no other way," somebody's barking up the wrong loblolly pine. Radio's critics would say he's dead wrong on both the bottle bill issue and the assembly line philosophy, but he stands his ground. Some things take time. He paces himself. It may not look pretty, but pretty is as pretty does.

"You got to breed these old slow bitches to old slow dogs," says Radio, profoundly, when asked how the Walker genes work. It's clear that Radio is neither master, nor horn blower, nor time—nor grounds-keeper. He's not put together that way. He knows when to shut up and listen, but he does love to talk, mainly about dogs, sometimes about people. When a man standing next to the *far* is asked if Radio ever stretches the truth, the man replies: "I've never caught him in a lie, but I never did pin him down that close."

Radio is the kind of feller who doesn't cave in to flattery. A man says, "Radio, that's a good hound."

Radio replies, "Son, you don't know him like I do."

Amen.

Radio recalls a fight in a bar, awhile back, involving a man named Lauder who liked to walk into a place and declare, "I'm going to whip the biggest son of a bitch in here." Now, Homer Shepherd was sitting in this bar up around *Far* Tower Ridge up about Bainsbridge, Ohio, and "Lauder, he went in, looked ever'body over, and he walked over to Shep, and looked at him and said, 'Mister, you're the biggest man that I've seen in here.' He said, 'I guess, goddamn, you're the man I'm going to have to whip.' Shep said, 'Well, man, you don't want to whip me, I don't even damn know you.' And Lauder blazed loose and hit him up the side of the head with his fist. I damn, the fight was on, and they tore up this bar all to pieces. They throwed 'em out, and we took 'em on to *Far* Tower Ridge, hunting, and they fit all night long. They'd fight awhile and set down and rest awhile. And they'd get up and fight again. And the next day about nine o'clock, Lauder said, 'Shep, I can't whip you.' Shep looked at him, and he said, 'Lauder, I can't whip you neither.' Lauder said, 'Well, I'll tell you what let's do, by God, let's just go get drunk together.' And they went and got drunk, and Homer Shepherd said, until the day he died he'd never had a better friend in his life from that day on, than Lauder was. I guarantee it, by damn," says Radio.

Radio has put on some weight, needs his cane to navigate, and every once in a while owns up to needing cataract surgery so he can see a feller better when he's eye-to-eye talking to him. But Radio doesn't need to see well enough to read what's been written about the Walker hound. Hell *far*, he could have written the book himself.

"The form of the hound should be harmonious throughout. He should show his blood quality and hound characteristics in every respect and movement. If he scores high in other properties, symmetry is bound to follow." That's what it says in *The Foxhound Stud Book*, which includes dogs from Ada to Zula.

"Ada, whelped May, 1899, was owned and bred by Woods Walker of Paint Lick, Kentucky." Ada was "by Hardy, out of Alice, by Tray out of Bess by Brute out of Molly. Tray by Steele out of Vanish, Hardy by Squealer, out of Lucy, by Tramp—Squealer, by Raider, out of Fan."

The hounds are running hard, their voices coming back in varying qualities of tone and thrust, floating back over the tops of dense woods and undergrowth—"wo-uff," and an occasional "wo, wo," or a "wup, wup." They're in full cry. Oh, Glory be and God Almighty.

"They done hit. Big coyote must'a jumped up in front of them," says Radio. A good foxhound patriot can tell these things by the sounds coming from the dogs, even though they're well out of sight. If an owner can't recognize the voice of his own dogs, there be something missing in his training.

"Can't believe these fox hunters, sometimes," says a man warming his hands above the curved piece of tin.

"Snowed a little bit here this morning," says one of the women, studying the flames.

"Everybody likes to talk about Radio."

"Yeah, they do, Honey. As long as they're talking about me, they're not talking about you," says Radio with kindness.

Radio observes a couple of Jack Russells making life feisty for older, worn out, down-on-their-luck, *far* dogs waiting for handouts—a blue heeler, and a Labrador retriever. It's a lazy, Jonathan Livingston Seagull breakfast flock uninterested in winning battles with king's or anybody else's foxes. The pair of Jack Russells come in low, which is the only way they can come in at all, what with their tense dewclaws, short legs, and shorter tempers. They run around in tight circles, a constant worry to older, aching dewclaws

"What's a Jack Russell good for, Radio?"

"Pissin' on truck *tars*," says Radio with remarkably restrained disgust.

The *far* was getting hotter with the addition of several sizable tree stumps, but it takes off for sure when the wooden pallet, which has been a dry place for the ladies' feet, is thrown in. It makes everybody move back. Even the Jack Russells take notice and go off to look for another truck *tar* to piss on. There's a plate of beans at midday, sliced bread to mop up the sauce, and cold Ale-8 to wash it down, which at Valley Forge would have been considered a feast.

While Radio and his friends savor the first foxhunt of the new century, the dogs make up their own minds. They decide when enough is enough. In such a situation, an edict from Parliament would have had no effect on comings and goings. The King or Queen of Whatever could string up a Walker hound by his pecker or her woose. All the King's men could torture him or her at their pleasure. But unless they're disemboweled, drawn and quartered, and decapitated, good American Walker hounds, like Big Jump or Little Miss Priss, will be out there putting the royal fear of God into the foxes. Nothing for Radio and all Great Hunters to do but bide their time and wait for the dogs to wear down and finally head back in the direction of the pickup truck.

"They have to come back to me or just stay gone. I've got a bitch that's been here three months," says Radio.

Forget who's master and who's the whipper-in. Save your horses, your creased jodphurs, and your saucy hats. And, good God A-mighty, don't let any red-blooded Scrabble Ridger hear you blurt out anything as silly as "Tally Ho!" There's nothing fancy about taking in dogs worn down to a nub, and there's nothing so fine as a bright *far* at the end of another day of a good, long life.

Licking gathers unto itself in the southeastern corner of Magoffin County south of Gunlock. The headwaters, near the convergence of Magoffin, Floyd, and Knott Counties, include Straight Fork, Sprucepine Fork, Howard Fork, and Ann Cave Creek. The Magoffin-Floyd County line wiggles along the mountain ridge from Poplar Gap north to a point near the Gypsy community. Streams to the east of the line head eastward toward Levisa Fork of Big Sandy. Streams to the west of the watershed run toward the main branch of Licking, often mistakenly called the North Fork.

In Magoffin County the many streams feeding the Middle Fork, or main channel, include Grassy Creek, Left Fork, Will Branch, Brushy Fork, Big Branch, Molly Branch, Howard Branch, Bear Branch, Whitley Branch, Long Branch, Salt Lick Branch, Puncheon Camp Creek, Pigpen Branch, Lick Branch, Jake Fork, Meredith Branch, Brushy Fork, Gun Creek, Middle Creek, Rocklick Fork, Beartree Fork, Rockhouse Fork, Burton Fork, Mash Fork, State Road Fork, and Burning Fork.

Each stream has an individual reason for its name, but it's too often lost in time passing. Preservation becomes the responsibility of those who still remember life by riverside and who are willing to write it down so that generations to come will have a richer inheritance—good company on a winter night when they stretch their feet toward the inside *far*.

J.C. is buried alongside Burning Fork on the edge of Salyersville, where the main fork of Licking is normally little and lazy. J.C. wasn't little and he wasn't lazy. Anybody calling J.C. May a hillbilly might had better smile. Anybody trying to belittle him would be somebody who never sat down with J.C. when he sharpened his chainsaw, then followed him when he snaked a tulip poplar down a hill, offered a nip of 'shine, or laughed and told stories about honest-to-God people in Licking River Valley. Sometimes the river is peaceful and sometimes it's violent. When the rainfall is heavy and the runoff loses its senses, the tide rolls down from Little Half Mountain, Big Half Mountain, Fredville, Duco, Royalton, Galdia, and Arthurmable, coming at you, roaring like seventeen prides of lions.

The 1960s tide came suddenly during the night, sweeping through Salyersville, blocking roads and threatening lives. It was the time when J.C.'s friend, "Big John" Blankenship plodded through the town, water to his chest, single-handedly towing a boat with a rope, using only the strength of his arms and his legs. He rescued men, women, and children who had no other way to escape from their drowning homes. The National Guard and the Red Cross had their parts to play, but when the tide first rolled, it was men like "Big John" Blankenship who made the first difference.

J.C. knew Big John, knew him well. In their day, they were the stuff of which good mountain men have naturally been made: full of life, full of basic caring, overflowing with instinctive behavior, strong as Rough and Tough Creek. They've known their way around chainsaws and hunting dogs, white lightning, pickled eggs, and pure apple cider, rattlesnakes, revenuers, and reverends. J.C. May was a patriarch who, in the twilight of his years, tended his garden on Burning Fork and gave good food to good people. J.C. May married Ruth and she birthed Janee and she birthed Deon.

Real people at the headwaters of Licking may talk with an "accent," but that hardly has anything to do with their fundamental value systems.

For instance, there'll always be differences of opinion about proper waste disposal. Who's to say it's a sin to fill an old car with junk and park it in your yard but it's all right to haul it off and dump it someplace else? Who's to say that squeeky clean conditions add up to crystal clear thinking and honest dealings?

Take the story of the Appalachian family living during the Depression, sharing their home with pigs and chickens, buying flour in quantity, storing it in a tub in the middle of the room. Naturally, the chickens roosted at night on the rim of the tub, and just as faithfully and good-naturedly the woman of the house arose several times during the night to make sure the chickens were all pointed in the right direction—heads in, tails out. No cause for ridicule. So stop laughing. Neither the chickens nor the human beings in the house were on welfare. They were looking out for one another so as not to make the mess any worse than it already was.

Continuing northwesterly through West Liberty, the 320-mile-long Licking River is the principal source of water for Cave Run Lake in the Daniel Boone National Forest. The first main tributary of the Licking River downstream from the Cave Run Dam in Rowan County is Triplett Creek. Its headwaters are near Haldeman, close up to the Carter County line. Haldeman is the birthplace of Kentucky writer Chris Offutt, author of *The Same River Twice.* "The river flows beside us and touching it means touching the sea," he writes. That pretty much sums up how many Kentuckians feel, especially eastern Kentuckians, when outsiders go to talking about them being landlocked and stupid.

Licking forms the boundaries of Bath and Rowan, Fleming and Nicholas, Bracken and Nicholas, and Bracken and Harrison Counties. In Cynthiana, a normally small stream empties into South Fork of Licking. Gray's Run arises between Lees Lick and Leesburg in southeastern Harrison County. It flows to the northeast, past Connersville Mill and Co., which isn't as big an outfit as it sounds. There are three employees. They don't need job descriptions and evaluation reports. They take their time and do things to suit themselves. They smile like they're having a hellava lot of fun.

If you didn't get behind the business card you'd think that Bill and Billy Kelly are the whole thing there on the southern edge of Cynthiana. Behind every Bill and Billy there's probably a Sue. Sue Kelly is the wife of Bill and the mother of Billy, and they are Connersville Mill and Co. of Harrison County.

"Well, it all started with this old blue crock," says Sue, giving it a pat as she hefts the stoneware piece down from the 1842 cabinet.

Nearby, the 640-pound Home Comfort wood cookstove is one of a houseful of antiques. Look in almost any direction and there'll be something old looking back at you. Everything appears to be exactly where it ought to be. The fire in the fireplace is real, no imitation gas logs. The bearskin rug in front of the fireplace is real. It didn't come from one of those super stores, one of those dragons that has gobbled up Main Streets about everywhere you look. Some people have a knack for finding treasures beyond the bypasses and the inner and outer loops. While Radio Stewart looks for strength in foxhounds, Sue Kelly looks for possibilities in little out-of-the-way places.

"I went looking for a crock and came home with an engine," laughs Sue. "I collect farm machinery." Sue, known to her family as "Jack," grew up as the tomboy in a family of nine girls and two boys. After bringing home the first little engine with the crock three years ago, Sue didn't stop there. "Before long we bought a little mill, then another little engine and mill, and then another engine and mill from Tennessee. I run the little mill and do all the sacking. We ground over three thousand pounds of corn last year."

That translates into more than a ton and a half of two-pound paper sacks full of white or yellow cornmeal or grits. Each sack of meal is tied with string and has a "Mother's Cornbread" recipe attached.

2 cups plain corn meal	1/2 cup plain flour
3/4 tsp. salt	1/2 tsp. baking soda
3 tsp. baking powder	2 cups buttermilk
1 egg, beaten	3 tbsp. shortening or bacon drippings

Heat oven to 400 degrees. Put shortening in 10-inch iron skillet (or

9x9 inch baking pan or corn stick pans) and heat while mixing batter. Mix remaining ingredients well. Pour batter into hot skillet. Bake 20-25 minutes or until beginning to brown on top. Turn over to broil for a few minutes to brown evenly. Remove from oven and turn onto a plate. Serve hot. (Corn sticks should bake 10-15 minutes.)

What started out as a hobby for the Kellys has wound up being not only work but also a way of giving back. They believe it's important to remember how things began. "We grew up dirt poor. Daddy was a poor tenant farmer and we had to scratch and dig to make a living. People were awful good to us, and I always said that if I got to work that I'd give back to my community." Sue and Bill have lived up to their promise. They don't try to define what the word "community" means, they don't measure cornmeal to commercial exactness, but they're apt to give you more for your money rather than less.

For forty-three years, Bill has driven a church bus and chauffeured handicapped people to and from worship. Sue quietly smiles at Bill's telling of it. She tastes his words, measuring their correctness before taking hold of the strand of conversation. "I like doing charity work for my hometown," she says as she stirs a pot of beans and checks the cornbread in the skillet on the south side of Cynthiana, cradled in the double-crescent embrace of South Fork of Licking. It may not be New Orleans, with its culinary fragrances and carnal delights on Bourbon and Royal streets, but the rich aroma of Sue's Mountain Pie is seeping from the oven door in her home sweet Kentucky, just up from Gray's Run. Lordy.

Time is a delicious ingredient. It's not necessary, therefore, to wait any longer for the second of the only three recipes in *Rivers of Kentucky*. With cornbread taking its place alongside the finest Louisiana French bread, Sue's Mountain Pie is the equal of the best French Quarter desserts, be they Paul Prudhomme's Bread Pudding with Lemon Sauce and Chantilly Cream, or the Baton Rouge Junior League's River Road Banana Flambée.

After you've died and *almost* gone to Heaven, walk on in for a dish of Sue's Mountain Pie:

1 cup butter or margarine
1 tsp. baking powder
1 cup milk
1 cup sugar
1 cup plain, unsifted floor
2 cans sweetened fruit (NOT pie filling), any kind, undrained

Heat oven to 350. Melt butter in 10-inch iron skillet. Mix baking powder, milk, sugar, and flour and pour into butter. Stir well to mix. Add undrained, canned fruit. Bake about 45 to 60 minutes. Serve with whipped topping or ice cream.
Amen!

At the top of the Kellys' list of giving is the May benefit for the Cynthiana Museum. They co-sponsor the event with their friends Bob and Helen Hyatt, and together they feature "duelling gristmills." If only "Devil Anse" Hatfield and Ran'l McCoy had turned their six-shooters into plowshares. If only pride had become patience. If only better schools, teachers, students, and parents had come together sooner along the rivers of Kentucky.

Bill, Billy, and Sue also fire up the mills for the benefit of the new Maysville Community College, Cynthiana branch, all proceeds going to the college. Come fall, you're likely to find the Kellys grinding away at the Covered Bridge Festival in Falmouth, Frontier Days in old Washington, the regatta in Augusta, the Corn Festival in Stanton, the Wooley Worm Festival in Beattyville, the Steam Engine shows in Paris and Germantown. "We set up the mills for the whole month of October at Double Stink Hog Farm," says Sue.

Next time you're at an outdoor festival and hear the putt-putt and the pop-pop of three engines, don't think of it as the sound of a piece of machinery. Think of it as the dinner bell calling you to some of the best cornbread or grits you'll ever enjoy.

There are two things as good as food. One is making love, the other is canoeing on Licking. The three combined make an afternoon in June seem like heaven on earth, mindful that around each bend there can be a message from hell, when gravity and flow get together on the proposition. All the food on the most sumptious of Tom Jones table spreads, all the love in the most feathery of beds, or buck naked beneath the pawpaw trees, cannot match the thrill of floating from slack water into rapids on Middle Fork of Licking.

We turn onto MouthofCedar Road and put in downstream from the mouth of Cedar Creek southwest of Mt. Olivet, eight of us in four canoes. Michael and Miranda lead the way, followed by Barry and Lalie, Willie and Ravy, and Bill and David. In each canoe, more experienced river rats paddle aft of the unschooled, untried first-timers, finetuning the direction of the needle bow with pinpoint precision, canoes being as willowy and vain as they are vulnerable. The authors of *Rivers of Kentucky* and their daughter ride separately on the slicing edge where the water curls back with a pleasant, deceptively innocent, rippling sound. Bringing up the rear, seventy-year-old David and eighty-six-year-old Bill are wise and noble, somber chieftains content to allow younger braves to read the river.

With each sound of approaching rapids, Michael, Barry, and Willie stand upright, perfectly balanced in the cool breeze. They calmly study the unpredictable current ahead, looking for the deepest "V" on the water's surface, deciding whether to take the port or starboard side, lay in close to the bank or shoot down the middle where rocks the size of cannonballs lie beneath the surface. Submerged boulders, slick as deer gut on a doorknob, are primed to capsize canoes and disgorge their human contents, young or old, fed or unfed, loved or unloved. The slippery, larger rocks usually don't move. They wait for the moment when the bow of the canoe strikes, lifts, and pivots. The current is constant, pressure insistent.

No two rapids, as no two days, are alike. The fallen tree trunk that was not here yesterday could be a threat today, could be swept away tomorrow. Even a slender limb of a fallen silver maple or sycamore acts like a lowered limbo bar.

Miranda, Lalie, and Ravy drop their heads as Michael, Barry, and Willie maneuver their canoes through the narrow passage. They come about in the new slack water and look back to watch Bill and David make their approach. David's hand goes up to take the small limb and push it up as he ducks under, as if he were on a riding mower on a lazy Sunday afternoon. This limb on this day does not move. The canoe responds by tipping, water pouring in, David and Bill pouring out. They arc like pieces of moon sliding beyond the horizon. Not a pretty sight.

Feet seek the bottom of the shallow rapids. Lungs hold on tightly, windpipes automatically slam to the off-position. Knees strike rocks worn as smooth as the Western Wall by millions of kisses. When faces reappear they are drawn, peevish, wrinkled with amazement. Hands claw for the nearest thing to cling to. Swimming is a redundancy. The upsidedown canoe is jammed. David's new tape recorder squeeks pitifully as it drowns, the elements of oral history as lost as baby ducks fluttering and failing to follow their warning mother. The reporter's notebook is waterlogged, pages melded, words wiped away as if nothing had ever been written. Wrist watch ticking? It is. John Cameron Swayze'd be proud. (Old time newsman who saw nothing wrong with selling waterproof watches at the same time he was commentating.) Billfold in hip pocket? Yes. Hen and Rooster whittler's knife? Yes, but rust is on the way and fused blades can't be far behind. And how is Bill? He's standing in the rapids, water dripping from his face, wondering how in hell he ever got hooked up with a feller who doesn't know a canoe from a riding mower. For a moment the octogenarian seems dazed, but then he speaks, clearly: "I'm all right. A little excitement is good!" Bill is the Chief Sitting Bull of Licking.

The braves come back to help their senior Hunkpapas empty water from their canoe, steady it while gingerly they regain their seats, and grandly push them off again for the rest of the seventeen-mile, five-hour trip from mouth of Cedar, past the mouths of Beaver Creek and Greasy Creek, under the Claysville Bridge to Bill's getaway in Harrison County. His wife, Martha, is waiting there with real food and knowing looks.

"How many more rapids are there?" frets David.

"Several," says Bill, remorsefully.

Canoeing on lower Licking is like being in a primitive world, devoid of menacing civilization. Trees rise up, roots exposed by natural erosion, limbs extended toward the center of the winding stream. Overhead, parallel jet trails are wispy reminders of the other sphere of commerce and urgency. The river is as silent as the jet trails except for the distant reverberation of the turbulence in the next rapids.

The sound begins as a whisper, a murmur, a susurration increasing in intensity until whiteness appears, water bubbling like a rapid boil in a stovetop pan. The intensity is not as great as white water in a "wild river," but the rapids on lower Licking are a training ground where injuries do occur. Solo treks involving anything fewer than two canoes can spell disaster. To be thrown and dashed against a large rock, to be trapped beneath a canoe, to be tumbled through a rapids, can be fatal if there's no immediate help. The river stretches ahead, pressured by the current, a ceaseless, demanding force. Human life sits astride the narrow spine of the canoe wherein balance is precariously paramount. Paddles provide a measure of control, but the will of the water will not be denied. It need not be flood time to see such a fundamental truth.

Even in the calmest of times, hunger enters the picture of aching shoulders and soiled, sticky underwear. It's time for a midday rest stop on the Robertson County side of Licking, where there are several large flat boulders upon which to spread picnic lunches. The only sounds are the occasional pileated woodpeckers at work on a tall sycamore, the hum of insects on the young leaves of approaching summer. Miranda, Lalie, and Ravy have water-splashed, sunbaked faces where cosmetics are swept away like words in a reporter's drowned notebook. Femininity has been brought to a new reckoning in shoulders, arms, hands, legs, ankles, and feet, coordinating strength to countervail the river. The power of the hydrologic cycle has dulled eroticism.

Michael, Barry, and Willie are confident in their competence to shoot most any rapids, but at every bend of the river their manhood has been sounded out and carried to a sobering brink. In the depths of their testosterone they know there are certain limits imposed by the flow of the river. There's neither dread nor paranoia about helplessness, only quiet acceptance that the day will come when no amount of potency or ingenuity will satisfy or compromise the Water Carrier.

Bill and David look like old beavers emerging from underwater dwellings. They rub the backs of their wrists against their mouths as if to confirm that their lips have not been sacrificed to the clever rocks in the rapids. The septuagenarian and the octogenarian reach out for younger hands to help with the first and trickiest step from the canoe to the riverbank. Age has its uncertainties as well as its prerogatives. When seated or stretched upon the ground there's an illusion of youth with remembrances of pleasurable tumbles in stinkweeds along the water's edge. The remembrance of fantasies fullfilled on hot summer days before the indulgence of canoes was in a time when it was blood-pumping joyful to walk through ripened clover to the water's edge, sit and stare at the muddy water for a time, strip down and take a plunge to the bottom where the water was cooler and sweeter.

The conversation turns to the most recent tumble from the canoe. "You've been baptized," says Barry.

"Didn't hear a blessing," replies David, glumly.

After sandwiches, cookies, and lemonade, it's time to push off again. There's no hurry, but nobody wants to be in darkness on the river. Nor would a storm be a welcomed event. Lightning searching for a home, wind bending eroded tree giants, and flash floods descending from upstream would be hellish. The canoe represents stability spinning on the head of a pin.

The rapids come and are left behind until there's a widening expanse of frothing spray where the stream is dotted with so many rocks the "deepest V" is difficult to discern. Michael and Miranda shoot through at midstream, the canoe rising and falling as if it were designed especially for them. Barry and Lalie follow more to the port side, and Willie and Ravy traverse slightly closer to the Harrison County side. They wait in the slack water to watch the descent of Bill and David.

"We're going in closer to the bank," says Bill. The water seems a little quieter there. David places his paddle alongside his right leg and takes a firm grip on the opposite edges of the canoe. He sees the partially submerged tree trunk and watches the narrowing gap as plummeting speed becomes a new factor. A clean hit might be tolerable. Then again, might not. Thoughts come in microseconds. To those watching in slack water it may seem like hideous slow motion.

71

The bow strikes the tree trunk. The sound is a hard thud. The canoe rises, twists, and spins. David is thrown like a weather-worn rodeo clown on a penis-pinched maverick. Bill, too. The water is slightly deeper but both Hunkpapas bounce from the rocky bottom and burst through the surface as grinning warriors appear to help and comment. "Baptized again," shouts Barry.

"Still no blessing," mutters David, sourly.

The safe arrival at Bill's camp comes none too soon. Bodies ache for dry clothes, but spirits address the possibility of more outings on the rivers of Kentucky. "How about Red next time? How about Green? Hell *far*, how about a trip all the way down to New Orleans?"

North Fork of Licking joins Middle Fork at the juncture of the Bracken, Harrison, and Pendleton County lines southeast of McKinneysburg. The headwaters of North Fork include Willow Branch, which provides the reservoir on the south side of Brooksville. South Fork of Licking makes a final loop, passes under U.S. 27, and joins the main stream at "the point" just upstream from the Blue Bridge on the west side of downtown Falmouth where the flooding in 1997 was devastating.

In February of 2000, high water revisited Falmouth, and bad dreams of '97 resurfaced. A small town bordered on three sides by rivers is a town simply vulnerable, exposed, and insecure. So is a town with a Town Branch. Flemingsburg was taken by surprise. At Harmon's Pool Hall the water came through the front door so fast the pool sharks climbed up onto the tables and waited to be rescued.

The beginning of South Fork of Licking is at Ruddles Mills in Bourbon County at the juncture of Hinkston and Stoner Creeks. About one mile from the eastern edge of North Middletown, near the spot where Indian Creek empties into Stoner Creek, upstream from the old dam and waterworks, there used to be a good place to go swimming. You had to be careful you didn't dive in and bury your head in the mud. It was also wise to stay away from the dam because of the possibility of being sucked down by an undertow, where logs were whirled over and over. You just might drown or have your young brains growing with moss on the rocks (it was long before "911").

On a recent visit, the stinkweeds are too tall to see anything, and the abandoned waterworks have reverted to private ownership. What's left of the playground for boys and girls of summer is—well—just a good memory. That's all. All it is and all it ever will be for those of us who don't skinny-dip the way we once did. So stand and look for a while, like William Least Heat Moon, to let faded images of good old boys and good old girls filter one more time through aching hearts and minds. Who knows? The knotted swing rope may still be there. The boards nailed to the tree for a launching pad may still be in place. New young people may drop by in July and August to cool off and cavort in the stinkweeds, but we wouldn't know any of them. They probably wouldn't want to know us.

Back up the car, but don't leave without checking on a schoolmate who still lives six hundred yards downstream. Edward "Buck" Carter and David started out in the first grade together. Buck had always been a good sort. He's remembered as somebody who loved to do things with his hands—anything—good stuff, like carpentering, welding, backhoe digging, and his real passion: discovering new veins of groundwater or old forgotten water lines.

At the end of the drive up the lane alongside Old Stoner, Buck and his wife, Sara Louise Martin, are waiting outside the cottage where they've chosen to live out their years in their home of homes in the bottomland just off Stoney Point Road. As simple as that. We go inside, sit, talk for a while, and then we get down to the purpose of the visit. "Buck, when did you first realize you were a water witch?"

"When I was eighteen to twenty years old," raggedly breathes seventy-year-old Buck, who has come to the time in his life when he depends on his green oxygen tank.

"Or, do you prefer to be called a dowser?"

"Water witch is fine."

"Does it run in your family?"

"My daddy used to say 'There's usually one in every family.' You might be one and not know it."

"I guess they are a lot of disbelievers about water witching. So what do you say to *them*?"

"I've proved to a lot of them that it does work. I can take one side of the switch and take your hand and make a believer out of you."

"Let's go outside and give it a try."

Two small, freshly-cut apple tree forks, about eighteen inches long, lie by the doorstep. Buck and Sara Louise have cut them earlier and left them there. He takes one and his schoolmate takes one. He explains that any green switch will do—cherry, peach, apple, or plum. We walk to the side of the house where Sara Louise turns on the spigot to simulate a vein of running water. "Water has to be moving," Buck explains, weary and short of breath without the oxygen tank.

Do just as you're told. Shut up and listen. Grasp the limber ends of the fork, the divining rod, letting old, tired fingers wrap around toward yourself. Extend thumbs as if hitchhiking in both directions on a blue highway. Buck does the same thing, and he lets his classmate walk a couple of steps in front to provide the opportunity to be the first to say, "Look a-here, look a-here!"

Either it's a case of trying too hard or not hard enough, or it can be that what we have here is not the member of the family who has the witch's touch. When Buck reaches the waterline the base of the fork pivots down and, with a low groan, he says he can't hold it back. We do this several times still with no results. So he takes one end of the switch in his right hand, takes his friend's right hand in his left hand, and let's him hold the other end of the switch, and they walk the walk together, which is good for brotherhood. Sure enough, the apple switch turns down like it's diving for home plate.

"I felt it then! That's unreal!" (A younger student would have said, "Cool!")

Buck is asked how much he charges for finding water veins and lines and such, and he says, "Nothing." When asked why, he says, "It's a gift," which sounds fair enough. (Buck's father was a wart-remover back when warts were more prevalent than they are today. He'd tighten a string just right around the wart, say a few magic words, then bury the string in a secret place. When the string rotted, the wart dropped off.)

Nature is not fair. It doesn't understand the meaning of the word. In

1997, water must have used a huge divining rod to find Buck, Sara, and Rex, their fifteen-year-old Rhodesian ridgeback/Australian shepherd guarddog. He's so old, it pains to look at him. He struggles to rise, but mainly he just watches every step Sara Louise takes. He may be old, but nobody in their right mind would want Rex to think they were up to no good.

Stoner Creek dowsed the Carters, Rex too, with four feet of water in their house. They're still cleaning up after the flood that caused havoc throughout Kentucky. With approximately equal disdain, Old Stoner barely tolerates witchers, ridgebacks, and disbelievers of the gift of dowsing.

Sara says people wonder why they didn't move to higher ground after the flood. "We love this place here, it's so nice and peaceful, nobody's close to us."

The day we visited Edward "Buck" Carter was the last time he ever witched. On Tuesday, October 17, 2000, he breathed his last. He had everything planned, including the placement of his ashes out in the driveway oval. There would be no memorial service until Sara passed on, and then there might be one for the two of them because, Buck said, he wanted them to be together.

It's surprising and possibly uncharitable that there's no Boone River in Kentucky, only two Boone Creeks and just a few Boone Forks. One of the Boone Creeks is in eastern Bourbon County. (The other is in Garrard County.) It was on the Bourbon Boone that Indians scalped Daniel's brother Edward. While Daniel has been immortalized, poor Edward molders in virtual obscurity. Daniel deserves praise, and others have written about his bravery and accomplishments up one side and down the other. Some siblings have a knack for immortality.

Only a rock enclosure and an ancient buckeye tree on See Pike commemorate the spot where Edward Boone, hunter and hunted, went down in flashing fury in October of 1780. The buckeye grew from that bloody piece of ground alongside the stream that today still carries the name Boone Creek. With the passage of two hundred and twenty years, there have been lots of curious ins and outs and carryings on—some puzzling, others pleasing. In another two hundred and twenty years, there may be no way of knowing what has gone before that caused such commotions, unless somebody stops by and writes it down.

Nowadays, on the other side of See Pike, which runs parallel to Boone Creek, there's a sight to behold. It's a little huckleberry above a persimmon, as the old timers used to say. In other words, you don't have to go far or wait long to get from one bloody thing to another. Different folks have conflicting ideas about cruelty and the meaning of freedom. "Did you know there are three things a fighting chicken thinks about?"

"No."

"Fighting. Covering hens. Feeding. In that order," says Ron Isaac, on whose land Edward Boone sleeps in everlasting horror of the scalper's knife. "They come out of the egg fighting," says Ron, speaking of his game fowl. "You can't teach a chicken to fight, you can only strengthen them, feed them right, keep them in top physical and mental condition, trained like an athlete."

"Cruelty to animals."

"They're not animals," Ron argues. "Any more than fish are animals. What is more cruel than hooking a fish, using pliers to pull out the hook, and throwing the fish back into the water to be caught again? Catch 'em again, reach for the pliers, twist out the hook, throw 'em back again?"

"Well..."

"What is more cruel than crowding baby chicks into broiler houses, blowing their fuzzy little yellow bodies up with high protein feed, then squeezing them into crates, and taking them to the processing plant to be hung up by their toes to have their throats cut?"

"Well, no."

"Or what about confining a hen to life imprisonment in a wired space hardly bigger than she is, feeding her a ration calculated to produce an uncontaminated egg a day, and when she misses a twenty-four-hour cycle, hanging her up and slitting her throat?" Her bland, pale, yellow-yolked days are over and done with, and if Grandmother Lala had been still living she'd have squeezed the hen's neck and thrown the rest of her in the general direction of the pot on the back of the cast-iron stove.

"It's the steel spur attached to the chicken that upsets opponents of cockfighting."

"It's more cruel *not* to use the steel spur. If I were to turn these one hundred cocks loose right now, there would be an awful, bloody fight and that would not end until there was one chicken still alive. Without gaffs they would bludgeon each other to death."

Each morning, in the new millennium, one hundred fighting cocks on the hillside send up a battle cry. Three families of game chickens, Albany, Kelso, and Claret—flaming red, brilliant yellow, and deep black—tense and tethered by tie strings, envision with wildly flashing eyes a simply delicious, deadly combat. Oh, the glory of it! The power of it! The desperately driven necessity of it!

Ron calmly cradles —one of his favorites, a pure Albany with lemon hackle feathers flared, in the crook of his right arm and takes him inside the barn stall where there's a conditioning table. Ron makes half-moon swoops and turns the cock loose so it can fly to the edge. Wings are flapping like foremast sails, the chicken's stern wheels taut and turning, winding with energy. Ron whirls the creature back in repetitive half-circle swings, and each time the cock closes the gap in anticipation that there just might be another cock on the table to engage in combat, a struggle that would continue until one chicken was dead, the other alive, ready to fight again.

"They're insensitive to pain. They just keep fighting to their last breath," says Ron. "The general public doesn't know anything about chicken fighting. There's nothing more beautiful than a fighting cock. I love to breed them. People are going to fight their fowl."

"That's illegal in Kentucky."

"There's a small group of people, who don't want you to do anything," says Ron, wearily, believing if it's all right to push to the bone-threatening limit a Thoroughbred (Bluegrass Downs, Churchill Downs, Ellis Park, Keeneland, Latonia, Turfway Park) or a horse in harness (The Red Mile and Thunder Ridge) or a Standardbred (county and state fairs) or a steeplechase horse (Dueling Grounds, Kentucky Horse Park), then it ought to be legal to allow fighting cocks to do one of the only three things they know how to do and want to do, especially the first thing on the short list. Do or die.

Assuming it is unacceptable to hold cock fights because it is cruel to animals, then it stands to reason (would it not be honestly argued?) that the breeders of the fowls ought to be shut down too? Ought not inspectors, representatives of the United States government, the Agency to Defend Society from Cockfighting, proceed forthwith to move in and confiscate the enemy, arrest the uncivilized perpetrators? Well, and if that is so, should not a species be sentenced to die? Should there not be a list of Most Rightly Endangered Species, so that America would be remembered as the Most Benevolent and Peaceful Civilization?

"You can't conquer a game cock," says Ron Isaac. "You have to be kind and gentle," a specious argument, opponents would say, for what could possibly be unkinder than to put razor sharp gaffs on chickens' legs and allow them to slice up each other until one falls dead? All the while, human beings placing bets as to which cock is more likely to conquer another cock?

A better way would be to breed a much larger chicken that could be saddled and bridled and ridden in Cock Racing. It might be the answer after the lottery has run its course. The annual Chicken Yearling Sales could take its proper place in the Commonwealth of Tracks for Every Taste. Young men and women could grow up to become chicken jockeys, and there could be a Kentucky Fowl Derby Breakfast at the Governor's Mansion. But it would be illegal to serve scrambled eggs, unless they had been inspected and cleared of any possible contamination by the damnable yoke that demands its day in combat, its moment of sordid truth.

On a wet afternoon in April, with Boone Creek gathering the waters of Plum Lick Creek, the spirits of Edward Boone and Shawnee warriors rest easier in the knowledge that justice has at long last been done. The fighting gene has been destroyed. From this day forth, there's no need for courage. When the invader comes, as he or she most likely will—the Vikings, the Huns, the Holy Crusaders—there'll be no need or reason to fight. There'll be peace throughout the land, and in the merry, merry month of May ladies will be bedecked in Derby hats for the Running of the Cockhorses.

Rings on her fingers and bells on her toes,
And she shall have music wherever she goes.

Plum Lick sits amid the headwaters of the South Fork of the Licking River.

It's reassuring to *be* at one of the countless fountainheads of such a huge hydrologic system, but it can be a curse for those living downstream. The flood of March 1997 is a painful reminder of the power of water. It ought to be a challenge to individuals to understand a natural and inevitable phenomenon. To ignore or underestimate the power of such a vast system is to invite tragedy and, at the same time, to lose rich opportunity. It's too late when national television crews come cherry picking in the name of recording the suffering. Lives are forever changed. Property will be restored, but at huge expense.

The people on Plum Lick bear witness to flash floods in their infancies. The water level rises and falls in approximately equal periods of time. They recognize it for what it is, and they watch it move downstream, out of sight, out of mind. The people and the cattle, the sheep and the dogs stay away from it. They know not to be trapped in it, and they don't need television to tell them what to do. They remain on high ground, yet dare not be smug. In March of '97, the flash flood was greater than anyone could remember. Plum Lick Creek, in drought time a trickle to bone-dry, looked as wide as a river. Falmouth, downstream, was devastated. It received the flash floods of hundreds of licks: Grassy Lick, Mud Lick, Salt Lick, Indian, Little Indian, Flat, Little Flat, Bald Eagle, Smoky Hollow, Happy Hollow, Aarons Run, Pretty Run, Strodes, Houston, Harper's, Big Cave Run, Little Cave Run, Peter Cave Run, Slate, Sycamore, and Graveyard Branch—only a few of the tributaries in Bourbon, Montgomery, and Bath Counties. On the banks of each of these tiny veins in the long arterial system called Licking stand the homes of proud and gifted Kentuckians, and the nation is richer because of them.

Kentucky and Little Kentucky

It is a part of eternity,
for its end and beginning
Belong to the end and beginning of all things,
The beginning lost in the end,
the end in the beginning.

Wendell Berry
A Timbered Choir

It is befitting that the Kentucky River, flowing with a theme of now, ends near the home of Wendell Berry. The beginning, arising in the east, descends from Beattyville in Lee County to Carrollton in Carroll County. In summer, whether in season of moistured plenty or parched despair, when he looks out from his hillside writing place on the Henry County bank of the 259-mile main stream, Wendell Berry witnesses for those who cherish pure water, clean air, and conserved soil. In like manner, he stands steadfast among those who compose for the soul of Kentucky, the essence of humanity, mirrored in the great cycle of water.

In the Inner Bluegrass center of Kentucky's deepening length, a weathered, abidingly thoughtful man quietly works amid his books in a companionable, close-fitted townhouse on Kentucky Avenue in Lexington. Historian laureate Thomas Dionysius Clark remembers life

81

intimately along the Commonwealth's namesake river as it exits from the Daniel Boone National Forest near Shade, then coils northwestward across Estill County. On foot, he has traveled the banks and the fertile bottomlands of all three forks of the Mother River, he has paddled his canoe from St. Helens to Valley View to bear witness to the Palisades, and he has equally contemplated histories of the smallest tributaries. His classic, *The Kentucky*, is essential.

Thomas D. Clark has gone in search of "the first drop of water." He has traversed North Fork toward Jenkins, following the forks of Right Beaver and Left Beaver, cataloging the respective watersheds of Kentucky and Big Sandy. The idea of the "beginning" and the "ending," a complexity worthy of clarification if not solution, includes perhaps the greatest truth: "ultimate truths" are as elusive as they are futile, and potentially fatal.

The search is eternal, the beginning in the end, the end in the beginning.

With his faith in sturdy trees, Dr. Clark, at age ninety-seven, strolls through his beloved timberlands less often but no less impassioned in his latter time. After nearly a century of studying his adopted Commonwealth of Kentucky, writing about it for generations to follow, he is an inspiration for students to continue the work that he and other historians have begun.

James Still, another of Kentucky's beginning and ending spirits, master of local language and expression, has created his words at the headwaters of one of the Kentucky's Appalachian forks. His thoughts, like his voice, are clear and mellow, his mind is resolute, his good nature lively despite a fall that resulted in broken toes, now mending. In early summer of the new century, recovering from pneumonia, James Still was approaching his ninety-fourth birthday.

In his log house beside Dead Mare Branch, one hundred yards from Wolf Pen Creek facing Little Carr Fork in Knott County, the former poet laureate of Kentucky sits quietly in the center of the 1836 fireplaced, mantled room filled with books, the ancestral home of Jethro Amburgey. Thunder lumbers across the mountaintops, and rain softens the moss-covered ground between the gate and the steps to the front door. And now the conversation turns to creativity and the living of a long life.

"When I come here I'm at home. No other place on the earth gives me the feeling of absolute contentment," says the quiet and gentle man who wrote *River of Earth*. Other works include *Hounds on the Mountain, On Troublesome Creek, The Wolfpen Poems,* and *Jack and the Wonder Beans.*

"I never wrote anything until it overcame me, and then I was ready for it, and I didn't know what was coming next, either....I've known many of the famous writers of my time—they didn't seem to enjoy writing," he says, recalling Robert Frost, Ernest Hemingway, Elizabeth Madox Roberts, and Carl Sandburg.

"Would you like to look upstairs?" Mr. Still asks, as if wishing he too could still climb the steep wooden steps. (As autumn came he had fallen again.)

"Yes, I would."

An overhead panel must be carefully pushed back, making footing tricky. But it's worth the extra effort. Along the second-floor wall there are broad shelves containing neatly stacked vintage copies of *Harper's, Virginia Quarterly Review,* and *Esquire.* Marilyn Monroe smiles seductively from the cover of *Life,* as was her want. A small cot and a kerosene stove await the return of the writer. There is silence. The writer waits at the table in the center of the first-floor room where he worked for two years to create *River of Earth.* "I wrote without light. I wrote chapters and published them," he explains, opening the May 10, 1941, issue of the *Saturday Evening Post,* which includes his story of "The Proud Walker." On the opposite page is an advertisement for a new Cadillac. The price is $1,345.

Outside the log house the fragrance of the Sweet William textures the air and the rain continues falling to replenish Carr Creek Lake, well to the north. Troublesome Creek winds its way past Carrie, Emmalena, Fisty, and Dwarf, then north to Ary and Hardshell before emptying into North Fork of the Kentucky. Amid these headwaters James Still's "Heritage" is a sustaining bequest of the hydrologic cycle—water, like creativity, arising from the earth, where it has permeated interfacing layers of rock. The moisture that suffuses mankind appears in springs up hollers along distant watersheds, forming countless branches, licks, creeks, then rivers. The late Jim Wayne Miller proclaimed: "James Still's early poems are a headwaters where the river of earth rises."

Heritage
I shall not leave these prisoning hills
Though they topple their barren heads to level earth
And the forests slide uprooted out of the sky.
Though the waters of Troublesome, of Trace Fork,
Of Sand Lick rise in a single body to glean the valleys,
To drown lush pennyroyal, to unravel rail fences;
Though the sun-ball breaks the ridges into dust
I cannot leave. I cannot go away.

Being of these hills, being one with the fox
Stealing into the shadows, one with the new-born foal,
The lumbering ox drawing green beech logs to mill,
One with the destined feet of man climbing and descending,
And one with death rising to bloom again, I cannot go.
Being of these hills I cannot pass beyond.

James Still
With his permission

The main stream of the Kentucky begins in the Beattyville section of Lee County with the convergence of three rambunctious currents: North, Middle, and South Forks. By all rights, these streams deserve to be counted as four rivers because the notion obliges cultural differences among people who for generations have chosen to carve out hallowed, protected places for their individual selves. From Beattyville to the confluence with the Ohio at Carrollton, the Kentucky River completes the drainage of an area of seven thousand square miles, larger than Northern Ireland.

Troublesome Creek lives up to its name when "furiners" try to travel or trace it. To simplify the difficulty, Troublesome begins in the area of

Hindman with the confluence of the querulous creek's Middle, Right, and
Left Forks. The Middle Fork more or less originates at Malley southeast
of Hindman. It gathers Cave, Parks, Perkins, and Combs Branches. The
Left Fork more or less begins east of the Garner community, collecting
Alum Cave, Mill Creek, Possumtrot, and Owens Branches.

Standing in dry, late summer in the center of Hindman at the meeting
of Left and Right Forks of Troublesome—the water but a trace, barely
moving—is like viewing innocence before the onrush of passion. The
nearby Hindman Settlement School was founded in 1902 by Katherine
Pettit (1868-1936) of Fayette County, Kentucky, and May Stone (1876-
1946) of Owingsville, Kentucky. The school, one hundred years old in
2002, has each year for the past twenty-three years hosted a Writers'
Workshop—a week of exchanging ideas about creativity and the *word*.
On KY 496 from U.S. 80 to KY 15, tramping the Troublesome through
Ary and Rowdy, there's a collection of thirty-four swinging footbridges
(some decayed and dangling, but all reminders that the little creek below
rises in floodtime and cuts off homes from the highway). Troublesome
twists westward from Hindman toward the Carrie community, thence to
Emmalena and Fisty, all in Knott County, then crosses into Perry
County, where it passes through the community of Dwarf. Picking up
Engle Fork and Combs Branch, Troublesome turns north to Ary, then
northwest to Stacy.

At Ary, Troublesome is joined by Balls Fork, whose headwaters roll
down from Soft Shell in Knott County, the community that produced
new Kentucky author Chris Holbrook. In 1995, he wrote *Hell and Ohio*
in which a definite preference is stated for Hell. The quip may offend the
state that has produced so many presidents of the United States and so
many jobs for Appalachians down on their luck, but deeply rooted
feelings of inferiority have not been helped by equally deeply rooted, ill-
gotten notions of superiority. Indiana and Illinois also have acquired a
bad habit of treating Kentuckians as if they were doormats on the long
haul to Florida. Chris Holbrook has spoken for many Appalachians worn
down to nubs by these cultures on the northern side of the Ohio. He
might have said, "If I owned both Heaven and Kentucky, I'd give
Heaven to them and live out my days in Kentucky."

Troublesome crosses into Breathitt County, gathering Fugate Fork before reaching the Hardshell community, rolls on to the Flintville and Lost Creek communities, and empties into North Fork of Kentucky. The waters of Troublesome are in timeless fellowship on the journey to the Ohio, the Mississippi, and the Gulf of Mexico.

North Fork of the Kentucky meets Middle Fork about one mile upstream from Beattyville, around the bend near Maloney. South Fork glides into Middle Fork in Beattyville proper (once popularly called "Three Forks"), established in 1872 as the county seat of Lee. It's estimated that there are approximately sixty creeks in Lee County, and the main waterway out is the Kentucky.

Middle Fork collects Wilder Branch, Grassy Branch, and Hell-fer-Sartin (sometimes spelled Hell-fer-Sartain, and sometimes, regrettably, Hell for Certain) in the area of the Confluence community in Leslie County. Leonard W. Roberts has written *South from Hell-fer-Sartin and Up Cutshin and Down Greasy*. Recent reprints by the University Press of Kentucky are helpful in understanding the folk culture of the people who live beside these waters. Roberts' books are fine examples of the essential role of oral history, an art form often ignored. Almost everybody has a story to tell, but typically the tales are lost for lack of listening.

One of Middle Fork's origins is in the western pinch of Leslie County on the slopes of Kentucky Gap, Rainbow Gap, and Phillips Gap. Middle Fork turns north at the Saylor community, gathering Spruce Pine Creek, which drains the western slopes of Deep Gap, Chestnut Gap, and the half-mile-high Chestnut Knob. From the Spruce Pine community it continues northward alongside state road 1760. The stream passes the Warbranch community and winds on toward Hyden, birthplace of the Frontier Nursing Service in 1925. By now, the river has collected White Oak Creek, Sam's Branch, Upper Bad Creek, Lower Bad Creek, Trace Branch, Saltwell Branch, Greasy Creek, another Lower Bad Creek, Johns Creek, Camp Creek, Hurricane Creek, and Muncy Creek.

Judge Muncy is a mountain woman who hasn't needed a Hollywood cosmetician or a central casting headhunter. She'd be unintimidated by a

New York network television news crew digging up old War on Poverty bones. She'd patiently endure an Ivy League linguist's reproving insistence that "it" should not be pronounced "hit." Far and away above nonsense and pretense, she's a twenty-first century eastern Kentucky judge who chooses not to wear a robe.

"I don't need that robe for people to know I'm a judge," says Forty-first Judicial District Judge Renee Muncy as we lunch on tasty hamburgers and French fries in her chambers in the Leslie County courthouse in Hyden, a mountain town close by the junctures of Rockhouse Creek, Hunt's Creek, and the Middle Fork of the Kentucky River.

In her tenth year on the bench, Judge Muncy helps one other district judge, Oscar House, to serve the people of Clay, Jackson, and Leslie Counties—total population less than 50,000 (1990 census)—three counties with about as many people as in one small town—say, a Circleville, Ohio, or a Wheeling, West Virginia. Leslie County is predominantly Republicans and trees. One of its communities is named Thousand Sticks ("sticks," a mountain word for logs).

Something tells us not to get caught doing something illegal in Leslie County and be brought up before her, we were thinking when we first laid eyes on Judge Muncy, flanked by her three female court assistants. The walls of the courtroom are blue green, the rug is grey, and the presiding dark-headed woman has eyes that don't blink. You can tell right away that her mind is sharp. She commands respect without saying a word. But when she does speak, it's with a voice that's low, steady, and measured in the way of her mountain upbringing.

"I try to set an example, be patient, tell it like it is, and not take myself too seriously. I've devoted my whole life to this job," says Judge Muncy as she makes us feel at home in her office. Her careful smile communicates strong conviction. She doesn't seem ruffled or restless. But she has a presence, she fills space well, without pretense. She doesn't have to prove a thing. The ceiling of her chambers isn't made of glass. She tells us she hates it whenever men go to talking about "that woman judge" being hard on men brought before her. "I try to treat people the same." We appreciate the truth of her statement when a lame, crestfallen man in orange jail clothes hobbles before Her Honor. She reduces his sentence, and he won't be spending any more of the Christmas season behind bars. She tells us later that it doesn't make sense to impose maximum fines and jail time for somebody who can't afford to pay the minimum. In court, as the grateful man turns to leave, Judge Muncy says with a reassuring smile, "Hope to see you again under more favorable circumstances."

We're beginning to think that facing Judge Renee Muncy might not be as frightful as we'd first imagined. We'd be less certain in Circleville, Ohio, or Wheeling, West Virginia. Here's a woman who didn't get a high school diploma. At age sixteen she entered Hazard Community College, then went on to the University of Kentucky, where she earned a degree in education. She tells us that she'd wanted to be a veterinarian but "realized I had very poor math ability." After a stint of teaching at Henry Clay High School in Lexington (she also wanted to be a writer), Renee had a call from her mother, who worked for an attorney, and she said, "I want you to think about going to law school."

"It sure sounded pretty good. My mother worked two jobs to get me through college. But when I took the LSAT [Law School Admissions Test] l came home and cried because I did so poorly."

Once again proving that test scores don't always tell the whole story, Renee was accepted at the Salmon P. Chase College of Law at Northern Kentucky University. "I was tied for second in my class at the end of the first semester, ninth in the graduating class of 1985."

With her husband she returned to the mountains to begin life as a lawyer, her mother working in the office with her (she's presently Leslie County Treasurer). Renee passed the bar exam and, in 1987, became a mother herself. Twelve-year-old Robin has a rich heritage for making good things happen. Her judge-mom cares about what befalls less fortunate children.

"I want people to wake up and see that their child is a person and their rights need to be protected. I want to see children's rights protected in court. If I lost my job I can say I stood up for a child," says Judge Muncy, who likes to meet privately with children in her chambers: "I tell them to let the judge know where they want to be. Things they say to me will be kept confidential." On call twenty-four hours a day for cases of domestic violence, Judge Muncy, born October 5, 1959, is the first eastern Kentucky woman elected to the bench of District Court. She figures she considers up to fifteen thousand cases each year: civil, criminal, juvenile, small claims, traffic, probates and wills.

Renee and her husband, "Mack" (he's the finance officer for Leslie Fiscal Court) live with their daughter Robin in a modest home high and dry above the twisting Middle Fork of the Kentucky River, a serpentine stream that bears watching. It has the capacity to make swinging footbridges look purposeful.

Favorite sight on the river?

"Moonrise. It's beautiful."

Secret to success?

"I have every confidence that my faith in God has given me whatever I have or may have in the future."

Advice to young women?

"Take advantage of every educational opportunity that you can."

Judge Muncy takes us for a ride in her mini-van north along Middle Fork of the Kentucky. State Road 257 follows the river, the river doesn't follow the highway, so we talk about the "tides," when Middle Fork floods and the churning, brown water laps at doorsteps. We acknowledge rusting abandoned cars along the shoreline, and we observe the swinging bridges. Rickety they may appear, but probably reliable for years to come. We resist do-goodery as easily as judges and reporters do on a typical day in New York City, but if we see somebody in obvious trouble, we'll stop and do what we can.

We visit "Owl's Nest," Judge Muncy's mother's home, where once lived great-uncle Will Sandlin, Kentucky's answer to Alvin York. Sergeant York single-handedly assaulted a German post and captured one hundred and thirty-two soldiers. One version has it that Will Sandlin captured three German machine gun nests; another is that he knocked out seventeen pillboxes. There's no disagreement that Sandlin was awarded the Congressional Medal of Honor. A movie was made about Sergeant York, but Will Sandlin's legacy is a historical plaque at the Hyden County Courthouse, two sentences in the *Kentucky Encyclopedia*, and a swimming pool named for him alongside Middle Fork of the

Kentucky River.

We drive on to Confluence, where the backwaters of Buckhorn Lake begin and then sprawl west and north to the dam site near Buckhorn in Perry County. The stillness is deep. There's light moisture in the air. There's a feeling of *being*. There's no rumble of elevated trains as on State Streets, no vibration of subways plummeting toward Brooklyns. There's a feeling of *oneness* with the water cycle. There's continuity.

South Fork of Kentucky begins at Oneida at the confluence of Red Bird, Goose Creek, and Bullskin Creek (also spelled Bull Skin). During winter thaws, especially then, each of these three muddy streams has many tributaries. There are countless stories to be told about this area: the people who've made it home, their isolation and the disunion deepened by the American Civil War. It would be easy to focus only on the legendary feuds ("wars" and "troubles"). The Baker-Howard feud, for example (also called Baker-White and Garrard-White), has been described as "probably the largest and longest of the feuds" in Kentucky. It outdid the Hatfields and the McCoys by a long shot.

James Anderson Burns was a man caught up in Kentucky's longest and largest vendetta. There's an account of him in Darrell C. Richardson's book *Mountain Rising*, the story of an individual who saw through the futility of feuding and did what he could to educate people. He showed them that accord was better than discord, no matter how much mountaineer pride might be involved. James Anderson Burns was the founder of the Oneida Baptist Institute where South Fork of Kentucky begins. Born in the West Virginia Mountains on August 2, 1865, James was the son of a Primitive Baptist preacher in Clay County, Kentucky. The family had moved to West Virginia to escape the feuds, which were expected to erupt worse after the end of the Civil War. In his autobiography, *The Crucible*, Burns recalls the words of his father: "Jim, I can never give you an education. I have no money. But I do want to teach you this: Never accept anything you do not earn."

After his father died, Burns returned to Clay County, irresistibly drawn there by tales of blood feuding. He became a legend in private, church-sponsored education. He was one of a kind, tall and rugged with a jaw that looked as if it were carved from a rock castle. "He was an individual of few words who rarely smiled. He usually did the unexpected," Richardson has written. Once Burns was hit over the head and left for dead. It was a turning point that led away from feuds to education. He is remembered as having said: "I have been as dead. I have been brought back to life again. It is for a purpose. That purpose is God's. Now I shall try to find out that purpose and follow it....I wanted to make peace among my kinsmen and fellowmen. But how? I was up against a feud spirit generations old. It seemed to me insurmountable."

Burns briefly attended Dennison University in Ohio. He returned to Kentucky and taught school at Rader's Creek (also spelled Rader Creek) in Clay County. This stream's headwaters are at the foot of Pilot Mountain, just east of Grace. The water joins Little Goose Creek, which loops the north side of Manchester, then winds north to Oneida. Burns first preached at Pleasant Grove Baptist Church near Benge in northwestern Clay County, at the juncture of Alderson Branch and Mill Creek, a tributary of South Fork of Rockcastle. He preached at numerous churches, including Pleasant Run Baptist Church near Sidell and Rader Creek. He taught school at Crane Creek, a tributary of South Fork of Kentucky, in the heart of feud country.

"It had been quite some time since a teacher had taught at Crane Creek. The last one had not lasted but a few weeks. The conduct of the students was frightful. Women teachers were beaten up and thrown out of the school almost as soon as they arrived. Men teachers lasted a little longer because they could usually whip at least some of the pupils." The account appears in Richardson's *Mountain Rising*. Burns was a disciplinarian who began to gain the support of even the leading feudists. Richardson describes one scene in which Burns picked up a student troublemaker by his neck and the seat of his pants and threw him out through the school door.

Burns married Martha E. Sizemore in 1875 on Red Bird, and she birthed six children. James and Martha divorced after World War I, but they are buried near each other at Oneida. James Anderson Burns taught for a brief time at Berea College. It was there that he and a Baptist preacher, H.L. McMurray, planned the beginning of Oneida Baptist

Institute, patterned after the Berea College concept that work is a good four-letter word. Burns called a summit meeting of the feudists at the mouth of Red Bird, a tense moment in the history of Clay County. "As I looked into their faces—faces I knew so well—I realized that the opportunity of my life had come at last—the one thing for which I had been born and for which my life had been spared," wrote Burns in *The Crucible*. "Men, let's all join in together and build us a school of our own. Let us put our children into it at the earliest possible age, and teach them the story of our Saviour's love every hour in the day. When they learn the story of that love and contrast it with the cruel, murderous hate of the feudists they will never seek each other's lives again. Let us bring our boys of the warring clans into our school, side by side, so closely together that their elbows will touch. And when our children learn to love each other in place of hating each other the feuds will stop."

James Anderson Burns's words are the foundation upon which has risen an internationally respected school upon the hill at the confluence of three streams of water. For the past one hundred years, Oneida Baptist Institute has opened its doors *free* to any student in Clay County, grades six through twelve. In recent years, students have paid to come here from Atlanta, Detroit, Lexington, Los Angeles, Louisville, Miami, and New York City. International students have come from Brazil, China, Eritrea, Ethiopia, Iran, Japan, and Thailand. A student doesn't have to be a Baptist to attend school on the campus on the hill overlooking South Fork of the Kentucky. Atheists are not turned away. Nonbelievers are shown respect, and they in turn are expected to be considerate of those whose faith is wedded to evangelical Protestantism. "We welcome atheists to share daily chapel, share our faith, and at the same time we'll not be too pushy," says Denise Spencer, Oneida Baptist Institute's publications director. She's the wife of the school's chaplain. They make no apologies for their belief, rooted in individual freedom.

Attendance at daily chapel is not an option for the more than four hundred students and one hundred and fifty full-time faculty and staff members. On a day in February, the huge chapel is filled with voices singing favorite hymns upon request. Those in attendance call out the page numbers from the Baptist Hymnal—"The Old Rugged Cross,"

"The Lily of the Valley," "Great Is Thy Faithfulness," "Amazing Grace," and "When the Roll Is Called Up Yonder." Neither is work an option. Some students clean floors. Others work on the school's twenty-cow, eighty-sow farm. Ken Martin is the farm manager. His wife, Nancy, supervises students' work and learning in the greenhouses. It has been said that the main crop on the OBI farm is the young people.

Words on a bulletin board tell the story, which might have brought a smile from the tall, dour James Anderson Burns: "If you ever need a helping hand you'll find one at the end of your arm." "Act as though it were impossible to fail." "This is the day the Lord has made. Let us rejoice and be glad in it." Even a person such as Bonnie Consolo, a friend of ours, born without arms in Menifee County, would probably smile too. She has said, "God has given me everything I need." Bonnie writes with her foot. Amazing outcomes fill the Oneida Baptist Institute Craft House and the adjoining James A. Burns Museum. Mrs. Donna Atto began it sixteen years ago, and she continues as the manager. It takes her longer now to climb the stairs from the large basement work area. She does it because she believes in her Faith and her commitment to work. "Because of the many materials that are donated to us and the wonderful host of volunteers who help us, our expenses are kept very low. This enables us to donate up to 80 percent of our profit to the Student Aid Fund." The fund is for students who need financial help.

Mrs. Atto reaches inside a display case and takes out a peach-pit angel. "Here," she says to the visitor, who has just bought a copy of Burns's *The Crucible*, "Take this home to your wife." The students at Oneida Baptist Institute are living the vision of an angel who survived the feuds, who said in his opening address one hundred years ago: "Some day this infant institution's influence will have had much to do with people far beyond the borders of these rugged hills. These hill dwellers will expand to all parts of this great country. You children must be obedient. You must respect authority and do the tasks assigned you. You boarding children will be looked after as if you were at home. You are admonished to live according to the Golden Rule."

Today at OBI, when a student is disciplined for misbehavior, the suspension from classes is spent working. The faculty and staff would be the first to acknowledge that there is no perfection this side of Heaven. Working in that direction is a common calling handed down, the inheritance of James Anderson Burns.

Fort Boonesborough is located on the south bank of the Kentucky between the mouths of Otter and West Fork. Whenever we cross over the new bridge on our way from Winchester to Richmond, we feel the presence and the fellowship of Daniel Boone, who canoed the river and walked the surrounding woods. At the annual Christmas festival at the replica of the fort, we sign and inscribe our books at the giant fireplace beneath the portrait of Boone. We can't imagine Kentucky without him, about whom so much has been written. Would we have had a fraction of the courage of Daniel and Rebecca Boone and the other pioneers who came into this land, looking for places to establish homesteads? Most likely not. And why? Because we're spoiled.

One of the last ferries regularly operating on rivers in Kentucky is located near Valley View at the juncture of the Fayette-Madison-Jessamine County lines. "Kentucky's oldest recorded commercial business," according to the *Kentucky Encyclopedia*, Valley View Ferry has been in operation since 1785. It takes about two and a half minutes to cross the river on the ferry, three cars at a time— hardly a match for the towering upstream Clay's Ferry Bridge with its constant north- and southbound I-75 traffic. The Valley View Ferry is right for those who yearn to experience a slower time on the road from Spears to Stringtown.

Lexington, the fabled "Heart of the Bluegrass," is the only major Kentucky city not located on a river. Town Branch flowed through the heart of Lexington and was responsible, in 1833, for the spread of the cholera epidemic that killed ten percent of the population. Today, Town Branch is covered over with concrete (Vine Street), but the stream is visible after it emerges near Rupp Arena and flows on to the south fork of Elkhorn Creek near the meeting of the Fayette, Woodford, and Scott County lines. McConnell Spring, located near Town Branch on the eastern side of Lexington, was once the precious water that attracted pioneers in the summer of 1775 and led to the development of the city that became known as the "Athens of the West."

Where it forms the Jessamine-Madison county line, the Kentucky's tributaries include: Marble Creek, Stony Fork, Silver Creek, and Paint Lick Creek. From the mouth of Paint Lick Creek, it's a winding way to Brushy Fork, a stream flowing in from Berea, site of Berea College. Founded in 1859, the college was established to educate former slaves and the children of poor families living in Appalachia. The Berea concept—work and scholarship—has spread and has taken hold in surprising ways.

"It came from outside of me, I'm not sure why," says Frances Figart, as she sits with a cup of coffee at Café Collage on Main Street in Winchester near the Clark County Courthouse. "I felt a calling to bring together a group of women—professionals, artisans, musicians—I called it a 'women's web,'" By November, the café has gone out of business, but the group that was meeting there is still going strong. In its first year, Greater Opportunities for Women, GO Women, Inc., has been a life jacket for sixteen women. Half of the graduates have gotten jobs and are still employed. All have returned to school or picked a new direction.

Let's say you've been freestyling along in your job, but lately you've been treading water. A reverse current is slowing you down, threatening to pull you under. You're seeing the shoreline slipping away. You're by yourself and you feel lost. Maybe you had your kids when you were young and now want to move into the workforce, but you lack confidence. Perhaps you didn't complete high school, but now you have a desire to get a better education. How do you go about getting the know-how of where to start to get a GED or go on to college? What if you have a talent for music or you've written a song but don't know how to connect with the industry? Or what if you'd like to reach out to someone else and give her the benefit of what you've learned?

GO Women, Inc., could be just the life jacket you need to aid in the pursuit of your dreams for a better life. The life jacket is the brainchild of Frances Figart of Winchester, and she, along with a group of volunteer mentors from various professions, are tossing out enough skills and self-esteem to save many a woman fallen overboard. What began as a "mostly social" occasion has evolved into a Kentucky nonprofit organization whose mission is "helping low-income women gain the skills and self-esteem to procure greater employment opportunities."

According to Frances, a former employee of the *Lexington Herald-Leader*, this will be accomplished in two ways: exposing women to a series of workshops to improve their skills and confidence, and pairing these women with professional female mentors. Workshops consist of a series of free, two-month-long sessions with professional leaders who assist women to achieve computer literacy, acquire resumé-writing skills, learn money management, and develop increased self-esteem. Health and nutrition are taught. Some optional sessions include hair styling and makeovers and women's issues.

Some of the eligibility rules: You must be a woman over age eighteen in central or eastern Kentucky; you don't have to be unemployed, you may simply want a better job; you probably have a financial need, but you must not be expecting a handout; above all, you must be motivated to make changes. Need transportation to the workshops? Someone will pick you up. Need child care? They've thought of that too, and it will be provided if necessary—both services at no cost. The first sessions for GO Women were held in April through May 1999 and were completely booked to the limit of ten participants. The next session was from September through October for fifteen participants. In 2000, there were three sessions with a limit of fifteen women per session.

"I have a dream of being able to award a yearly $7,000 to $10,000 arts scholarship to a woman who shows special promise in art, music, or writing," says Frances. GO Women has received corporate sponsorships from Winchester Farms Dairy and Hart's Dry-Cleaning, whose workplaces were toured by workshop participants; but more corporate financial support and mentors are needed. "After all," says Frances, "we're training their future workforce."

The Kentucky Palisades were not cut, opened, and exposed by highway construction dynamite. The majestic cliffs towering higher than a Commonwealth Stadium standing on its head evolved from millions of years of cycling water crumbling the porous limestone, pushing downward the dolomitic, sedimentary rock. *The Palisades of the Kentucky River*, published in 1997 by the Kentucky Chapter of the Nature Conservancy, is stunning. With photography by Adam Jones, a foreword by Barry Bingham Jr., and text by Richard Taylor, it's alternative food for acculturated, video-driven generations.

Boone Creek forms the southern portion of the Clark-Fayette County line, and it empties into the Kentucky River just upstream from Clay's Ferry. Where Boone Creek tumbles down steep, rock-strewn ravines near the Boone Station State Historic Site, John Jacob Niles (1892-1980) lived with his Russian-born wife, Rena Lipetz, on Boot Hill Farm. Niles died there on the first day of March 1980 and is buried nearby in St. Hubert's church yard on Grimes Mill Road. Rena Lipetz (1913-1996) is buried next to him. They rest near the grave of Bishop and Mrs. William P. Moody, where the words on a centerpiece monument are good news:

Peaceful is the day within this garden
Where they rest who have the need of rest.
Here they know our Father's gift of pardon
Here they lie by holy Angel's blest.
Here the sun shines sweetly in its season
Here the waiting fields receive the rain.
All things here look up to God's own reason.
The dead here bless us in their quiet way
And point us to our God's triumphant day,
He who made the world now wills them peace.

A small dogwood tree's blossoms are about to burst at the end of the corridor of eight cedar trees leading into St. Hubert's church yard. The day is overcast. There is moisture in the air, and the sweet remembrance of music, "I Wonder as I Wander," and "Black Is the Color of My True Love's Hair." A new age beginning, a new century of Kentuckians may wonder as they wander through the entranceway of tiny St. Hubert's Church. The double doors were carved with mallet

and wood chisel by the folksinger John Jacob Niles, who loved
woodworking and who did not come there to worship in the usual way.
The doors contain words, a translation of Psalm 84, carved laboriously
and lovingly in longhand by Niles:

O how amiable
Are thy dwellings
Thou Lord of hosts!
My soul hath desire and longing
To enter into the courts of the Lord,
My heart and my flesh rejoice
In the living god.
Yea the sparrow
Has found her an house,
And the swallow a nest,
Where she may lay her young...
Blessed is the man
Whose strength is in thee,
In whose heart are thy ways,
Who go through the vale of misery
Use it for a well,
And the pools are filled with water...
I had rather be a door-keeper
In the house of my god
Than to dwell in the tents of ungodliness.

In the foyer, there's a large framed picture of the craftsman at his
work. John Jacob Niles and the hand-carved doors of St. Hubert's above
Boot Hill, Boone Creek, and Kentucky River are an inspiration. They
tell us that deep down there's something both lovely and fundamental
that is missing in this life. That "something" may not be found at St.
Hubert's or the Oneida Baptist Institute. It may be discovered in the
most unlikely of places—corridors and conditions of the heart and mind.
It may come when least expected. It may have nothing whatsoever to do
with a specific river. It may have something to do with watersheds of

life, evolving in patterns as interrelated and connected as springhouses, runoffs, rivers, and the sea.

Bonnie Quantrell Jones was four years old when an undertow took her "out with the freighters" off the Florida coast. Her father rescued her and that became "an early God experience." Bonnie has lived much of her life on water, including a houseboat in Georgia and the upper Mississippi at Minneapolis-St. Paul. She was twenty-two years old with a degree in philosophy from the University of Minnesota when she went to work as an office girl at the Pillsbury Company.

This Bonnie "has done a lot of living." When she was twenty-five years old she was vice-president and creative director of a new video production company. In the 1970s she was a freelance writer. In the late '70s, "...it occurred to my father that he might not be immortal....He began to talk to me about taking over his automobile business." In 1979 she moved from Minnesota (land of lakes) to Kentucky (land of rivers) and rejoined her father's business. She worked in sales, service, parts, the body shop, and the office. In 1984 she became president of Quantrell Cadillac. The same year she married Billy Gatton Jones, a food broker. A year later, her father died. Her mother passed away in 1991.

Arthur E. Quantrell had moved his business from Minnesota to Kentucky. When Bonnie became president and chief executive officer of Quantrell Cadillac, Volvo, Saturn in Lexington, something called the "energy crisis" came down hard on big cars. When Bonnie was twenty-nine years old, the bottom also fell out of budgets for sales meetings and multimedia shows. "Too many people got in when times were good. It taught me the cyclical nature of business. Taught me to salt some away and to prune."

Early in her life, she went to live in Europe for two years. Home was a Volkswagen panel truck named Eleanor (after her mother). "In the late '80s I had a conversion experience," Bonnie explains. "I'd gone to a prayer breakfast and heard a senator from Colorado talk about his life and family and how everything he had done had worked. But there was something still missing in his life, and he didn't know what."

For the senator and for Bonnie, that "something" was a spiritual calling. "When I wrote a spiritual biography it was a path that God had been calling me to—the burning bush—but I was always there with the fire extinguisher. It was like going down a chute getting narrower. I struggled for five years. I spent two years at Lexington Theological Seminary to learn more about the Bible."

She gave up her Porsche-Audi franchise in Lexington and sold Quantrell Chevrolet-Buick in Harrodsburg. She acquired a Saturn franchise to go with her Cadillac and Volvo business in Lexington and found time to enter the seminary, where she moved from the Master of Arts to the Master of Divinity program. On May 31, 1997, Bonnie Quantrell Jones was ordained to the priesthood in the Episcopal Church. On June 17, 1998, she became Associate Rector of St. Peter's in Paris, Kentucky, the county seat for Plum Lick in Bourbon County.

Bonnie describes her journey as a balancing of the business world and the spiritual life, the car dealer and the person who takes communion to the sick as well as those who come to hear her preach. Short of stature, she rises to the occasion of consecration, bridging the worlds of commerce and heavenly considerations. "I believe that one of the things I was supposed to do is to take the language of both—infuse your business, carry into your business not a prayer service but how you operate it, how your treat your customers and your employees, reinvesting money in the community for the betterment of the community. The more I do for the community the more the community responds."

On a quiet afternoon at St. Peter's on the hill above Houston Creek just before it empties into Stoner, she laughs and talks about life being fun, not having limitations. "I never hit the glass ceiling. I went around it or ignored it."

"Crashed through it?"

"Yes, crashed through it."

"Are you a feminist?"

"I don't know. Perhaps I am growing especially for the feminine side. It took so long to get to this point."

"What do you do now?"

"I know I'm where I'm supposed to be. I cannot give specific goals. I want to be faithful to what God wants me to be."

"Your advice to younger women?"

"Find something you love to do and do it well—any number of things. Pay a lot of attention to your family. Your business and career will change as you change and grow. The thing that will keep you sane is your family. Too often women in a career mode are doing the same things as men do, putting business ahead of family. Stay on a successful path, whatever that means. Have fun, don't take yourself so seriously, you're going to make mistakes."

This is not a commercial for selling cars, I tell myself as I return to my own life as vice president of my own company, Plum Lick Publishing, chief cook and bottle washer, chalice bearer at St. Peter's, mother of a daughter soon to be eighteen years old in a house by the side of Plum Lick Creek, where there are no glass ceilings. I believe she, my husband, David, and I are growing older with "enjoyment based on wisdom" that we've learned from individuals like Bonnie Quantrell Jones.

Cedar Branch flows into the Kentucky River near High Bridge. The Kentucky next forms the Mercer-Woodford County line, and the tributaries include Shaker Creek (which flows through the Shaker Village at Pleasant Hill), Shawnee Run, Brushy Run, and Landing Run. The Shakers realized the importance of the waterways as an outlet for their talents. Dr. Thomas D. Clark and F. Gerald Ham have described the early days in their book *Pleasant Hill and Its Shakers*:

> *Farming in Kentucky in the first half of the nineteenth century tied the state's economy to the developing Lower South. The Kentucky River by way of the Ohio and Mississippi formed an artery of transportation all the way to New Orleans. By the end of 1816, a new gristmill was constructed on Shawnee Run and, in January 1817, began grinding the Society's corn for market. All up and down the river and along the side branches there were mills grinding meal and flour, but perhaps none of*

them was so ingeniously equipped as the Shaker mill.
A cardinal tenet of Shaker communal living was industry
and ingenuity.

When we are invited to come to Pleasant Hill in the Christmas season of 2000, snow falls softly and settles on burdened tree limbs. People arrive from many states, drawn to the Shaker shrine out of a sense of caring about the past and what it meant to be committed. Looking out through the windows of the craft shop, where we set up our table and display our books, we wonder how much we are intruding. Even though we know we could not abide the celibate life, we realize the importance of sincere, beneficial outcomes, and we rededicate our own lives to writing as well as we are able.

The Kentucky River passes beneath the Vic Hellard Jr. Memorial Bridge and separates Anderson and Woodford Counties. Tributaries include Craig Creek, Bear Branch, Griers Creek, Bailey Run, Sharps Branch, and Buck Run. Shortly after entering Franklin County, Glenns Creek flows in. Vaughn Branch empties into the Kentucky on the southern edge of the state capital, Frankfort, where the Capitol dome, refurbished and polished, serves as a beacon for the Kentucky Book Fair and the Kentucky History Center.

On the northern side of Frankfort, Benson Creek flows in from the west to join the main stream. U.S. 421 knifes through deep cuts of limestone, and from this point the Kentucky travels on a curving course to the north. Tributaries include Tucker Creek, Duval and Steeles Branches and Elkhorn Creek, comprised of two main forks, the North and the South.

Forks of Elkhorn, on the eastern edge of Frankfort, is the location of the Switzer covered bridge, built by George Hockensmith in 1855. The flood of March 1,1997, swept it off its abutments as if nothing were sacred, as if the water itself were directed by the hand of Great God Almighty. Many came to witness what *Water Bearer* had poured from vengeance (human beings might ask, what else could have been the reason?), and they tried to remember the youthful days of their lives when death had been so inconceivable. Surely some things are not meant for destruction, they thought in vain.

Restoration occurred, and the bridge is standing again, but it would not be, could not be the same, not exactly the same. Kentucky author Vernon White, friend of covered bridges, has described the reconstruction: "Not much of the old timber had been used although much of it was probably good. They had set the braces too far apart, which left a space between them and the counterbrace. They should have been set against one another. Some of the spaces were blocked before they were bolted but most were not. I had seen the bridge while they were rebuilding and had pointed out the mistake and suggested they correct it but they left it like it was. If we are not going to restore something to its original condition maybe we should not do anything to it and let it die an honorable death."

Dobree Adams and Jonathan Greene live and work downstream from Frankfort where she weaves tapestries, and he writes fine poetry, gracefully designs books, and manages Gnomon Press.

Jonathan opens the door of a tall house, where the guarding animals—a goose and a large white dog—seem to have an acute sense of danger or the absence of it. Their presence is attention-getting. The goose does not crave a pat on the head.

Dobree, who graduated from the classrooms of mathematics at Wellesley, stepped out of the arena of state government computers in Frankfort to become a full-time "spinner, dyer, weaver, and shepherd" at Riverbend Farm. Her tapestries, with titles like *Swan Pond*, *Blue Licks*, *The Knobs*, *Big Black Mountain*, and *Blanton Forest*, can be seen in the main dining room of the Hilary J. Boone Faculty Center at the University of Kentucky and in Capital Gallery in Frankfort. Emerging from the land along the Kentucky, her work is in public and private collections in England, France, Guatemala, Japan, Puerto Rico, and the United States.

Dobree juggles her time: another lambing season, another garden to be started, a rare horse to tame, another tangled aftermath of floodwater.

As we struggle to restore our Kentucky River farm after the third major flood (over five feet in the barn!) in twenty years I

*am reminded all day long why I love this farm and my Lincoln
Longwool sheep. As we struggle with deposits of sand and mud
in our pastures and repairing broken fences, I think of how
close we are to the earth. As I work on fine-tuning the size of
my flock to the carrying capacity of the farm I am mindful of
the possibilities of summer drought and extreme cold as well as
the ever-present threat of flood.*

*It's difficult to describe the sense of the rightness of work,
that morning chores are daily pleasures: feeding and watering
my critters, being there for my ewes when they lamb, cleaning
sheep pens and mulching the garden, scratching in the dirt. I
am fascinated by the landscape and by how the light changes
the contours from dawn to dusk and from season to season. I
never tire of watching and recording how the light falls on the
hills behind our river bottom, of how the light creates layers of
trees and mist and fog. My greatest hope is that my rugs speak
of my passion for my animals, of my love of the land, of my
fascination with the colors and contours of the landscape, of
the joy of being able to weave the wool of my sheep.*

Jonathan Greene's work—founder, "CEO, and shipping clerk" of
Gnomon Press—has been to publish a wealth of writings by Kentucky
authors, including Wendell Berry, Chris Holbrook, Harlan Hubbard, Ed
McClanahan, Jim Wayne Miller, Gurney Norman, Martha Bennett Stiles,
James Still, and Richard Taylor.

Gnomon Press has also published authors from North Carolina, West
Virginia, Tennessee, New York, Vermont, California; as well as translations
from Provençal, Spanish, Latin, Japanese, Egyptian, and Russian.

Guy Davenport, a native North Carolinian, Rhodes Scholar, author of
more than twenty books, distinguished professor at the University of
Kentucky, has said of Jonathan Greene and his work: "Gnomon Press
will figure in the history of American letters as one of the brave and
distinguished oases of excellence, taste, and adventuresomeness
whereby good writing survived in this age of popcorn for the mind."

University of Kentucky archivist James D. Birchfield says: "Jonathan

Greene is truly a cultured poet and designer, an artist intimately aware both of his literary contemporaries from coast to coast and of graphic tradition from Gutenberg to Bill Gates. Whether designing a Kentucky chapbook, a poster about Shakertown, or a sumptuous volume of Italian photographs, his superb taste is always in evidence."

As we sit with Jonathan and Dobree in chairs covered with Lincoln Longwool pelts, sipping hot tea, the conversation turns from publishing books and weaving rugs and tapestries to the art of survival on the farm in Kentucky in the new century. We take a long walk and sit on a log that has fallen across a steep, rocky, dry, no-name creek bed, and we talk about being "a steward of the land" and "shepherd of the sheep." It's one thing to weave works of exceptional quality. It's another thing to raise the sheep that provide the rare wool to weave these creations. The Lincoln Longwool is a rare, endangered old British breed, no longer commercially popular. It's not unusual for the wool to be twelve inches in length. The fleece is very strong, very curly, and so lustrous and shiny it looks synthetic. Dobree Adams's prize-winning flock ranges in color from white to silver, gray to brown, charcoal to black.

It's the sheep that undergird the art so rooted in the land. Each strand of Dobree Adams's Lincoln Longwood lies at the heart of her work. "This piece of land is really important to me. I want to take care of it, leave it better than it was." The springtime light filters through the windows of Dobree's studio, and it falls on thick bundles of spun yarn hanging from tall racks and wooden pegs that line the walls of the fourteen- by twenty-foot workspace built in 1977. It's home for her handmade walnut loom and sliding bench, where the artist sits with her tools at her fingertips. "The bench is made from a Kentucky coffee tree that came from this farm." Peacock feathers that spray from a nearby vase sitting on the windowsill pale in comparison to the jewel-like hues of Lincoln Longwool. "I spin the wool, then I paint it with a brush rather than submerge it in dye. I can do so much more with the color," she says, holding a thick, coiled skein of shiny gold-to-sienna-colored strands of fiber.

To sit with Dobree Adams in her studio or on a fallen tree trunk in the cool of an April morning is to respect her wisdom. "Your terrain is so important to your operation. What I can do might be entirely different from what it is that you do. Having the stamina to accomplish something of worth is difficult."

Suddenly, the first butterfly of spring flits across the opening, touches down lightly on the fallen tree, then rises in its dancing, weaving motion to fly off out over the Blue-Eyed Mary carpet beneath the trees.

The Kentucky crosses into Owen County close to where Flat Creek empties in. At this juncture, the Kentucky forms the Owen-Henry County line. Tributaries of the lower Kentucky River include Stevens Creek and Sawdridge Creek, which flows past Monterey, where "Kentucky's Gutenberg," Gray Zeitz, meticulously hand-sets type for his Larkspur Press. "I don't have deadlines," says the smiling man with the long, straight, white beard. Alabama-born, he came to Kentucky as a child and found abundant reason to stay. He's fifty years old now, contented for his work to be as fine as the best of the fine print presses in the United States.

Since mass production schedules are not prescribed, Larkspur has a reputation built upon extraordinary quality. "It takes four years to produce a book once it's in my hands, and I'm one- to one-and-a-half years behind. I teach authors patience: 'Make haste slowly,'" says Gray, who has produced the works of Kentucky's foremost writers. There are collectors who buy everything Larkspur produces no matter who the author is. "It all starts here in the type case. All books are set a letter at a time, a line at a time, a page at a time. Everything is inverted, so you must watch your "P's" and "Q's!" Gray laughs. "After it's proofed, it's locked into the chase. The lines have to be set to exact width. The chase fits onto the press."

The antique equipment (the 1880 paper cutter was rescued from a county courthouse), does the work as deliberately as water rolling down Sawdridge Creek to the Kentucky River. "How did I get started? I published a magazine, *handsel* (e.e. cummings, you know), and I worked at the King Library print shop [at the University of Kentucky]. In 1974, I started Larkspur."

"Do you have a philosophy?"

"I have no philosophy. When I decided that Larkspur would be the name of the press, I didn't want to have a philosophy, because I might be held to it."

Gray's wife, Jean, has been a teacher in the public schools of Owen County, but she's also "a big part" of Larkspur. There are two apprentices who come in one day a week. There's a golden Labrador retriever, and there is peace. Larkspur Press stands on the slope of a hill, purposefully lost in time near stone-bedded Sawdridge Creek, where water murmurs and in troubled times roars over myriad rocks, bordered by palisades in microcosm. "We don't have flash floods, we have slow rises," Zeitz has been quoted as saying in *Kentucky Living* magazine. "When we went through the 1978 flood, I had water navel-deep in my shop, and I still have type I haven't cleaned."

In the first week in May, the vegetable garden is plowed, the richness of the soil awaiting the seeding of corn and beans, the planting of tomatoes. On the other side of the shop—where Gray Zeitz works on a new book by Dianne Aprile, *The Eye Is Not Enough: on Seeing and Remembering*—the flower garden is blooming with columbine, clematis, iris, peonies, tulips, daisies, dahlias, day lilies, lambs ears, and—larkspur. Two chairs. A place to talk, quietly. A place to remain silent, too, to watch a red-bellied woodpecker, rose-breasted grosbeak, cardinal, gold finch, and bluejay.

The lines of Beatrice Warde grace the corner inside the door of Larkspur Press, the first and last words upon the coming in and the going out.

This is a printing office.
Crossroads of Civilization
Refuge of all the arts
Against the ravages of time.
Armory of fearless truth
Against Whispering rumor.
Incessant trumpet of Trade.
From this place words may fly
Abroad, not to perish on the

Waves of sound, not to vary
With the writer's hand but
Fixed in time, having been
Verified by proof.
Friend,
You stand on sacred ground.

As the Kentucky turns more to the northwest, the tributaries include Severn Creek, Pot Ripple Creek, Sixmile Creek, Clay Lick Creek, Sulphur Creek, Drennon Creek, Mill Creek, Big Twin Creek, and Little Twin Creek. By the time Cane Run flows in, you're near the home of Wendell Berry.

"When you come we'll drive around. I'll show you my home watersheds of Emily's Run, Cane Run, and Drennon Creek." The voice of Kentucky's preeminent living writer is kind and thoughtful to a degree seldom matched. Giving "sense of place" a valid, valuable meaning, he has authenticated the agrarian experience. Along the final miles, through Wendell Berry's "Port William Membership," there's a feeling of caring about *places* and *sense of places*. The water and the earth and the people are entitled to be in accord. Human intelligence has the opportunity to furnish meaning. Yet some do, some don't.

After Gullion's Branch empties into the Kentucky, the main stream flows into Carroll County where the final tributaries include Eagle Creek, Goose Creek, Mill Creek, Whites Run, finally Majors Run and the long journey has ended—or has it really begun? Wendell Berry's mythical Port William is closer to Port Royal, a tiny village, a lasting place preserved and perpetuated. So "ended" is not the correct word. No, now. Not at all. To sit with Wendell, his wife, Tanya, their children, and their children's children at their dinner table on Sunday in December, in the "last" month of the "last" century, is to know the pleasure of living purposefully. The tall glasses of water on the table symbolize the connection with the cycle that "began" with "the bench on Pine Mountain." The lamb on the oval platter came from the flock grazing on the hillside overlooking the Kentucky near Port Royal. The conversation ranges from Cheviot sheep to weather, to fence building and mending, to the hydrologic cycle.

"Would you like to go and look at the river?"

"Yes."

In a cold rain, we walk to the river's "edge," where the view upstream evokes images of a misty Chinese landscape painting. The harmony of "beginnings" and "endings" is natural and satisfying. The fog, fragile and refreshing, for a moment lightens the breathing of earth's atmosphere. But how long will mankind endure? Are we in danger, even here? Dare we suppose there'll always be a hidey-hole for the favored few? The sweetness of the air at Port Royal bears a hint that presumptive thinking can be beguilingly deceptive.

The following month brings news that Kentucky is on the "Ten Worst" list for bad air. The cause is said to be automobile and lawnmower exhaust, ozone-related. The progress piper must be paid. But it will be difficult to convince the consumer-driven public. Then a distillery fire and the spillage of bourbon into the Kentucky River cause the worst fish kill in the state's history.

Wendell Berry's is a plaintive, rueful voice in the age of high-speed boats and other recreational watercraft whose wakes damage the banks of rivers not only at Lanes Landing Farm but throughout the Commonwealth. Civilization is spilling over despite the warnings. Prime agricultural farmland has been converted to cul-de-sacs. Broken barn skeletons have appeared on the wings of $300,000 to $500,000 houses, each one equipped with can openers, snow blowers, and electronics of every sort. The news is full of technological growth stocks, mutual funds, and internet shopping malls to replace the ones that have supplanted pastures and cropland. Super Bowl commercials include new advertising campaigns, the latest laugh-o-mercials, from "herding cats" to "money coming out the wazoo." The *Atlas of Kentucky* estimates the population of the Commonwealth will be "rising about 23 percent from its 1990 level of almost 3.7 million to approximately 4.5 million by the year 2020." Lots of cats, lots of wazoos, little quiet thinking.

Wendell Berry points to the wooden shelter where he writes. Out of personal respect, the impulse to invite oneself in is set aside. Retracing squishy steps up the slope is task enough. The cold water wants to penetrate thin Sunday shoes. It dampens the socks and sends a message of reality by the riverside. The warm ride in the pickup truck is enough to hope for, a friendly place to ponder years not yet begun, water still to be recycled. There are beginnings and endings on Emily's Run, Cane Run, and Drennon Creek. In a cedar-stumped field, a gazebo drips in wet disrepair. A place for a stolen kiss in a long ago summer, the scene nurtures thoughts of Drennon Springs, the nineteenth-century spa where the wealthy came to "take the waters," and Union and Confederate forces came to kill and maim. The spa and the war are history. The water returns each year, pledged to take no prisoners.

Wendell Berry's team of Percherons, descendants of horses that once pulled artillery, have been bred for peaceful purposes. The agrarian advantage is no threat to the ozone, yet such an idea is not popular in a mechanical, technologically gee-whiz culture. Like other zoo animals, draft horses are on display at Busch Gardens in Florida, in Christmas parades, and in occasional, nostalgic television commercials for a beer company, but rarely seen working on farms in the new millennium. The tradition of the family farm is an affirmation of what could be but is not likely to become in a culture consuming too much with too little.

Wendell and his brother, John, understand this. They work to convince others to consider what has been lost and what might be returned. Lessons seem clear. Native intelligence is a basic tool, but greed will undo likelihoods.

Along narrow, twisting roads the view from the window of the pickup truck is too often marked with doublewides and strewn litter. It seems as destructive as the dreaded zebra mussels, the imported species with deadly consequences for native mussels and other aquatic life in the ecosystem of the rivers of the Commonwealth.

The literature of Kentucky helps to point the way. Creativity and rivers share a concept of perpetuity, beginning internally in the minds of individual human beings and the smallest of waterways, ending in accordance with the laws of nature. One without the other is an unfinished journey of the soul.

As there are four Kentucky Rivers—North Fork, Middle Fork, South

Fork, and main stream—there is also a Little Kentucky River. Lake Jericho is the largest of five flood-control impoundments on the Little Kentucky, the work of men like Nick Coleman's father, chairman of the Little Kentucky River Watershed Conservancy Group, a community-supported project. Nick remembers how it was, forty years ago.

"Flooding was a big problem. The little town called Sulphur—every time the creek came up it cleaned Sulphur out," says Nick. "I mean it flooded it. The Christian Church there—I've seen water up to here on me [he touches his midsection] in the church—and my mother was a member of that church, and every time the creek came up we'd have to pull the carpet out of the church and dry it out."

The Sulphur community is located on the Henry County line where three streams—Fallen Timber Creek, Bartlett's Fork, and White Sulphur Fork—all converge with "Little Kaintuck Creek," which is the way local residents usually say it. They generally refer to the Little Kentucky River here as Little Kaintuck Creek because, they say, to call it a river upstream from Sulphur is to take on airs. Eighty-year-old Coleman Sibley lives in a two-hundred-year-old house on the Little Kentucky, downstream from the Sulphur community. He and his wife have many times watched the water rise and cover their hallowed bottomland farm. Mr. Sibley is one of the founders of the Little Kentucky River Watershed Conservancy District.

"Come in here! How you doin', Larry?" says Coleman Sibley to our guide, Larry Jeffries, who knows the people of the Little Kentucky watershed like the back of his hand.

"How do you do, sir?" he says to us, and "Where did you pick that up?" nodding in the direction of Nick Coleman, who has come along on the one-day tour. We all go to the front room built with hand-hewn logs. "Just sit around here anywhere," says Mr. Sibley. His wife, Caby Jean, joins us.

"Did the Little Kentucky River ever have any other names?"

"As far as I know, it never did," says Coleman.

"You're about to get your tobacco housed, I see."

"They're cutting on it this morning."

"Tell me a little bit about the nature of the Little Kentucky River.

Where do you say it begins? At Sulphur?"

"No sir, begins right outside of Eminence."

"Does it flood every year?"

"About three years ago we had a terrible rain, and it got out of its banks then, but since we've had the Conservancy District, it hasn't flooded to amount to anything but two times."

"What's your favorite Little Kentucky River story?"

"I got caught on the footbridge across the creek here and it might not have been my favorite, but it made more newspapers than anything else. We owned a farm across the creek at that time and lived over there."

Caby Jean says, "We had to leave the car on this side."

"Well, I came down, right on the footbridge," says Coleman, "and got across on this side and couldn't get off. So I stood there about five minutes, and then went back toward the house, but couldn't get off on the other end, so I stood there and watched our car float down the river a couple of hundred yards. It lodged on a stump down there."

"You were there from about 6:30 in the morning until, say, 1:30 in the afternoon," says Caby Jean.

"Were you scared?"

"No, sir. I went back to the other side of the creek and there was a big sycamore tree there and the limbs were about this high from the water, and so I figured if the bridge went I'd catch one of those limbs and climb up the tree. A neighbor came in on a horse from that side and got me off." Coleman Sibley doesn't look like a man who's just turned eighty. He looks and acts more like sixty.

We say our goodbyes and head over in the direction of Steve and Karen Bess Smith's place farther downstream, in Trimble County on a horseshoe bend of the Little Kentucky River. They're a young couple with bushels of young ideas about modern farming advertised in their brochure: "Michihili Chinese cabbage, Burpless Muncher cucumbers, Japanese Hulless popcorn, Trevisio Radicchio, Spring Song Daikon, Sunburst Yellow Scallop squash, Yellow pear, Roma, Golden Jubilee and Branywine tomatoes. Plus, all the tried and true favorites, Garden Goblins & Fairies, Kindred Spirits, Mystery, Romance and Adventure you've come to expect."

The Smiths are involved in CSA, which is not Confederate States of America but Community Supported Agriculture. Their newsletter defines it: CSA "...puts the community back in farming, in a fresh, new way. Through this arrangement, you can join with farmers to create a local food economy by purchasing annual shares in their crops, doing away with middlemen, bureaucracy and waste. CSA brings the freshest possible food to city folks, while sharing with them a rural way of life. This support of community allows small independent farmers to not only stay in farming, but find a better way to farm."

We sit in Steve and Karen's tool shed at their Ewingsford Farm and talk about their main concern about the Little Kentucky River today: expansion of the Trimble County landfill and potential leeching into the stream, "Seventeen million tons, over seventeen million *tons* of additional garbage, ninety-eight percent of that is out-of-state garbage dumped on the banks of the Little Kentucky River. Now, that in itself just boggles the mind. It's incomprehensible that a human being would do something like that," Steve laments.

We don't have an answer for it. We know that garbage has to go somewhere. The population is growing and so is the garbage. The real reason why we don't complain on Plum Lick is because it's once again the old "NIMBY" thing—Not In *My* Backyard. So maybe the question is, why is there so much garbage in the first place? Well, we've trapped ourselves in this big, fat garbage can because we live in an increasingly disposable society, getting and spending and laying our waste wherever we may. Were we all to live as the Amish and Mennonites do, then where would we be as leaders in our hell-bent global consumerism? The talk turns to Wendell Berry, a major influence in the life of Steve Smith. "He has a spirit that's in tune with reality. He's not deceived by the counterfeit," says Steve. "He can see what's real in this age where reality doesn't really matter—see it and then verbalize it. Yeah."

It's confession time for the authors of *Rivers of Kentucky*: "We've got a lot to learn about farming. We now have 214 acres, but we used to be land poor with 495 acres. We were trying to put together our family farm that dates back to 1799, and that wasn't working. So we think we can hold on to what we now have, although if we were not writing books and selling them—that's one of our crops, that's our major crop—then we'd die on the vine. We raise tobacco and cattle, but we don't have vegetables the way you do, and we don't have a market such as the one you have developed."

Steve and Karen deliver their produce every Thursday from April through November to St. Matthews Episcopal Church on North Hubbards Lane in Louisville. Customers pay $425 in advance for a half-bushel of in-season vegetables for thirty-one weeks, or about $13.70 per week. Confession time too for Steve, as he recalls his farming methods before he discovered Community Supported Agriculture: "Rip and tear agriculture. It was a destructive way to farm, and I had bought this place, trying to pay for it, and renting tobacco all over the county, handling a lot of money, but keeping none of it. None of it. My net was zero. Just being honest. I was handling a lot of money though. My main crop was red ink, so I did that as long as I could and finally I had to change." Presently, by their calculations, Steve and Karen make $10,000 an acre and keep $6,000.

In 1990, Steve discovered organic farming, sustainable agriculture, and Wendell Berry. "I met Wendell the second year of my co-op. Somebody gave me a copy of *The Unsettling of America*, and I read that and it was my story, the story of my people. This is what happened to my family. We're in a pickle, a real bad situation. If we would look to the Amish and study them, there is a solution there—self-sufficiency, self-reliance."

As we drive back to Sulphur and on to Eminence, there's time to reflect on what Steve and Karen could mean to all communities. Before Steve was born, back when horse-drawn plows were a common sight along the Little Kentucky River and throughout the Commonwealth, when farm life was so much simpler, there was far less need for landfills. The family farm had not yet surrendered to the new age of huge equipment and a mountain of debt. World War II was over. "Progress" was the new watchword. Students poured into the University of Kentucky and other institutions of higher learning. Too many were looking for quick answers. The unsettling of America was about to begin. Thank God, there were other voices.

This year's trip to Henry County to help his neighbors pay tribute to Wendell Berry was also a quiet road curling back to the memory of that other mostly forgotten writer born in the little county named for Patrick Henry. His name was Hollis Summers, born June 23, 1916, in the Baptist parsonnage in Eminence. Paying tribute to Wendell while ignoring Hollis would be a most serious, yes, maybe, unforgiveable omission.

The headwaters of Little Kentucky are entirely in Henry County on the western outskirts of Eminence, birthplace of Kentucky novelist, short story writer, poet, and educator Hollis Summers. His birth in this quiet land—slow, free-flowing light through arching trees and winding pastures along Little Kentucky—was as unheralded as fern growing greener with textured, timeless moisture. The leafy hillsides brush the horizon to hail the boundaries of childhood's domain. In the season of prepubesence, thoughts as pure as spring water feed Little Kentucky, sending it on its short journey toward the Ohio River, then on to the sea. The river of toys and dreams and improvisations has not the capacity for real steamboats, towboats, and barges. Little Kentucky is a kindly lacework, sensitive to the touch of a mother's fingertips. Yet this river, like all rivers of Kentucky, has its moments of flooded pain, despair, convulsive flashes tumbling down like the walls of Jericho.

Hollis Summers was hired at the University of Kentucky for the 1949-50 school term. There in his thirty-third year he patiently suffered nineteen-year-old neophyte writers, according them a sensitivity they craved but hardly deserved. He was especially kind to the one who insisted, under his breath and sometimes out loud, that Robert W. Service was a poet. With a gentle, hushed nature born of Little Kentucky, Hollis Summers taught creative writing and short story courses. He instituted the strange novelty of requiring students to bring to class in McVey Hall (now mainly occupied with computer technology) original ideas on smudgy, dog-eared, three-by-five cards. One submission was a list of the names of the trains passing through Lexington—Hummingbird, South Wind, City of New Orleans. Dr. Summers patiently listened to the nervous calling out of the names, and he smiled his soft smile. Didn't preach. Didn't suggest. Made room for youthful fantasies, gave them a chance to grow of their own strength. His presence was enough. A student could meet with Dr. Summers in his office, could sit and smoke a cigarette with him, could talk about words and how to give them structure and form.

There were no student evaluations of teachers then. No submarine torpedoes fired, on moonless midnights, at innocent unarmed merchant vessels. Little desire to arm wrestle for an "A," especially if it meant "artificial." It was sufficient to be in the class, to see Professor Summers walk in, take his seat, and make way for new ideas. There was no Microsoft Word. Dr. Summers (no undergraduate student called him "Hollis") and his class experienced the joys of writing out by hand, reading out loud, savoring words. There was lively, forgiving discussion, playful yet serious purpose. Some found it to be a new, challenging assignment, for they did not know where to begin. Not knowing where to begin, they did not know where to end. They had come face to face with a truth spoken later by a dean of the College of Communications: "You can't write if you can't think, and if you can't *think* you can't *write*, damn it." Hollis Summers might have thought that, but he wouldn't have said it.

Even before the television epidemic, students in the late 1940s and early 1950s did not conceptualize, they memorized, and only when it was required. In high school had they been expected to stand in clodhopper shoes before a class, to repeat from embarrassed memory lines of Longfellow and Tennyson without ever once knowing what anything *meant*, or how it felt, or possibly what joy might have come to one who wrote her or his *own* poetry. After all, poetry was something written by poets a long time ago. Poets, who were studied were mostly old men who wore long beards. Hardly any were women—Elizabeth Barrett Browning and Emily Dickinson were rare exceptions.

"Trees" had been an especially sturdy oak in high school. "Poems are made by fools like me" was, we were told, Joyce Kilmer's popular explanation of the relationship of God, nature, and the sorry human condition. "Trees" was piously assigned and prayerfully recited. Any smirks about "hungry mouths" and "sweet flowing breasts" brought stifled murmuring and willful looks from distant corners of the room. "Trees" was assumed to be and widely accepted as a ringing truth for the wrong reasons. Professor Summers helped his students to improve their understanding of poetic design, to resist the temptation to mix their images.

After he was buried in Millersburg, near Hinkston Creek in Bourbon County, Hollis's widow, Laura, attended a writer's workshop at the University of Kentucky. To her teacher, who had been Hollis Summers's awkward, callow student (suddenly self-conscious about a definite lack of literary credentials), she presented a first-edition copy of her husband's 1988 volume, *Other Concerns & Brother Clark*. The "student" who had become "teacher" was still not able to understand many of the lines of "difficult" poetry, but he gratefully added it to his personal library, along with the other "S" authors, hoping that one day he might graduate from his Robert W. Service mentality long enough to discover new values from Hollis Summers.

The student of fifty years ago could not have imagined the writing of *Rivers of Kentucky*, or the discovery of an epigraph about a stream, Little Kentucky, that had run through the childhood of that patient, long-suffering teacher who left the University of Kentucky to live and teach to the end of his career at Ohio University, where he was again the recipient of the highest faculty honor.

At this late hour, the year of a seventieth birthday, on a—well, on a kind of three-by-five card—here's an original thought, a posthumous gift for Dr. Summers, who mainly taught by listening:

please

why must you go
and leave me here
why not stay
with me here

you are a part
and I am two
parts of a part

but both apart

There was a bright and beautiful student in that class. She was from Harlan on the Cumberland River, and she wore a buckskin jacket. She wrote stories about Big Black Mountain before the time of controversy about stripmining. She said she liked "please," and she wrote lines on a coffee shop napkin, and then she handed it over as a gift to the one who so desperately wanted to become a writer.

because

to leave
is
not to go

but

to stay
is to go

what does it matter

it has been
and once having been

is

Jane Ellen Tye Matthis
Abingdon, Virginia

"Hollis Summers is gone, and the world is a little colder since his passing," Jane wrote in a letter in 1992.

Little Kentucky makes its rendezvous with the Ohio at Carrollton, hurrying toward the city of New Orleans.

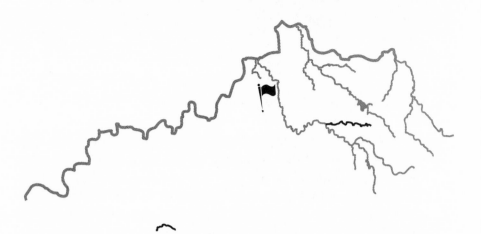

Red

*We have carved something beautiful out of the wilderness,
haven't we, Jibbo?*

Governor Bert T. Combs
December 2, 1991

*We are in for a terrible siege, Judge. Let's go in and stay up as long
as we can and keep vigil over the house.*

Sara Walters Combs
December 2, 1991

Two days later, on December 4, 1991, when Sara Combs was in Louisville, the Red River was in flash flood stage, and its waters swept away former governor Bert T. Combs. He had turned left at Rosslyn onto KY 615 near the foot of Mill Knob, his car stalling at the bottom of the slope where, during frequent floods, the Red spills over from its narrow, tangled channel. With the increased water volume from Right Fork, Hall Branch, and Cat Creek, the force of the water's tide swept his body beneath the Bert T. Combs Mountain Parkway, which he had been responsible for building and which he had proudly dedicated on February 26, 1961. A little more than three decades after that dedication, searchers found the former governor's body in the next bend of the river. He was buried in Beech Creek cemetery in Clay County on December 6,

1991. Beech Creek flows from Combs Lake and empties into Goose Creek, headwaters of Red Bird River.

It was on that day, nine years ago that our friendship with Sara began. We never fail to feel the presence of the governor when we visit Fern Hill, the mountainside farm where "Jibbo," his widow, Sara Walter Combs, lives and loves to welcome friends. She will not allow the memory of Governor Combs to fade away. When Lalie and David were assembling stories for the book *Peace At The Center*, in 1984, we sat at Sara's breakfast table and she shared her thoughts about the wholeness of life.

> *Last night when you used the word integrity—I thought that was a very good beginning for* Peace at the Center. *When I think of integrity, I think of it as more that just the sense of honor to which we all value and aspire, a sort of Cyrano de Bergerac sense of honor. But, it's more than that. It goes back to the Latin root "integer," which meant wholeness We even use that in mathematics—a whole number is an integer, not a fraction but a complete number in and of itself.*
>
> *I believe that one doesn't arrive at that philosophical and mathematical purity until having undergone many life experiences. Now, I think it arrives in a person in different stages, maybe based on one's training and experience and background. My concept of it is simply this: whatever values, training philosophy, even religion one has learned in the course of a life, the childhood values from the cradle, through adolescence, through college, are all there.*
>
> *They are part of the person, but not until one undergoes the crucible, perhaps, puts all those values to the test in the crucible of life experience—you know—a great love, a great passion, and, I think, a great sorrow. I think one has to suffer before all these values can be tested. No doubt, we can select what's necessary for our survival and then go on and arrive at a kind of ability to deal with one's self as a whole person. Then, turn outward after you grab all this in from the outer*

*universe into yourself and come to terms with what it will take
for one to cope and survive with a sense of one's own honor
and integrity. Then one starts to deal differently with the
world, and that's your peace at the center.*

Sara Walters Combs was elected in 1994 to the Kentucky Court of
Appeals. She hoped it would be her new beginning. She still lives in the
cabin at Fern Hill on Lower Cane Creek Road. In the past nine years,
there have been pressures for her to move back to "civilization," but she
has so far resisted the idea. James Still's words from "Heritage," framed
on her dining room wall, capture the spirit of Sara's better understanding
of what constitutes "civilization."

Being of these hills I cannot pass beyond.

There are three Red Rivers in Kentucky: the one widely known for its
Red River Gorge in Wolfe, Menifee, and Powell Counties, a second in
Simpson and Logan counties in south-central Kentucky, and a seldom
mentioned third in Shelby County, a very short stream arising on Cat
Ridge and emptying into Little Beech Creek at KY 636 between the
communities of Junte and Mt. Eden. Creeks usually empty into rivers or
forks of rivers. This is one of at least three rivers in Kentucky that empty
into a creek. (The Chaplin River empties into Beech Fork, a tributary of
Rolling Fork River.)

None of Kentucky's three Red Rivers is one hundred miles long,
again defying conventional wisdom. In fact, most of Kentucky's
approximately fifty rivers are less than a hundred miles long. The
longest of the three Red Rivers is ninety-six miles from start to finish. It
rises near Burkhart in Wolfe County. The main stream flows generally
westward past the communities of Lee City, Helechawa, Daysboro,
Hazel Green, and Tolliver in Wolfe County. It cuts deeply across Daniel
Boone National Forest, through Clifty Wilderness, Red River Gorge,
Red River Gorge Geological Area, Gladie Historic Site, Red River
Gorge National Recreation Trail, near Natural Bridge, Natural Bridge
State Resort Park, and Natural Bridge State Park Nature Preserve.

121

Geographic place names in the Red River section of the 660,000-acre Daniel Boone National Forest are a testament to local creativity—Angel Windows, Castle Arch, Cloud Splitter, Courthouse Rock, Double Arch, Grays Arch, Half Moon Arch, McKinney Cliff, Nada Arches, Princess Arch, Raven Rock, Ravens Window, Red Byrd Arch, Rock Bridge Arch, See Rocks, Short Creek Arch, Silvermine Arch, Slade Twin Arches, Star Gap Arch, Tower Rock, Turtle Back Arch, and White's Branch Arch— enough visual pleasure here for a lifetime of annual visits. One time is not enough. One season is insufficient. So many arches and natural bridges have time on their side. To become familiar with these geologic wonders, witnessing them in relationship with mankind, is to be fulfilled.

We—Michael, Willie, Rocky, and David—put our two canoes in on the southern edge of Clifty Wilderness in Menifee County, and we look as ragtag as anybody, but there's nobody in sight with whom to compare, so it doesn't make any difference whether we are formal, figleafed, or in the buff. All-weather running shoes are a help in sliding down the mudbank where we ease our two canoes into the water.

We're on the last canoe trip of the year, through Red River Gorge, until next spring when the water level rises and it'll be a smoother ride down the nine miles of the lower gorge from Sky Bridge Arch to Raven's Rock. Michael and David are in one canoe, Willie and Rocky in the other. Lalie and Miranda stay home because they've better sense about mud wrestling and dogwalking canoes over so many bottom-scraping ripples.

The only capsizing of the day occurs between Sky Bridge and Tower Rock when Michael, who has gotten out to push-pull through the first riffle, loses his footing and over we go. The water is cool, bordering on cold, but refreshing. It's a funny thing how at such times everything seems in slow motion. You think first about not drinking any more of the river than necessary, although it looks relatively clean at this point. You see yourself in relation to the overturned canoe and calculate whether it's a boomerang threat that's going to spin around and knock you down again. You try out your legs to be sure they're not broken, feel the breast pocket to be reassured that the notebook is still there, pat the left hip pocket to make sure of the lump that is the billfold with the $100 in it, fish out the DeLorme and Red River Gorge Geological maps before they float farther downstream and add a colorful touch to the community of debris, retrieve the black Nikon cap, look at your Wal-Mart watch but not care if it's still running, congratulate yourself on the decision not to bring a tape recorder or camera.

You are wet.

"That wasn't supposed to happen," says Michael, who prides himself on years of canoeing experience. He rescues the lunch and his sunglasses, disgustedly throws the cushions back into the canoe, and mutters apologies.

"That's all right," David jabbers, tasting Red running down from his hair to the corners of his mouth. "No goddamned problem at all."

With cheerful, knowing looks on Willie's and Rocky's faces, we're on our way again. They understand that every canoe cuts along the sharp, leading edge of awareness, making smugness an immodest burden. This is no race to the finish line. Gliding past straight, tall tulip poplars, fuchsia-colored trumpet vines, silver birch, and sycamores with roots exposed, we pick our way through boulders as big as trucks, some as large as houses. The river's rate of descent is gradual, unlike the upper Red River Gorge, where the river falls much more steeply and rapidly, breaking and gobbling canoes for Sunday supper.

"I'm going up there next spring," says Michael.

"I'm going with you," I say, "to stand on the side and send for help when you need it."

"I'm not going," says Willie with conviction.

The Upper Gorge begins at Spradlin Bridge, where KY 746 crosses Red River, and ends where we more cautiously put in at Sky Bridge. Willie respects the Upper Gorge's "Canoe Eating Rock," where you say a prayer and close your eyes if you're fearless or crazy or both. The passage there is narrow and the water flies by and the chances are great that mortal human beings will taste a lot of Red and be reminded that the ancient rock is simply passionate about canoes. Maybe Canoe Eating Rock figures that if man survives it could mean another day of boldness, another feast of canoe, man embracing the great lust for retribution.

The challenge is enough in the Lower Gorge, where the rocks are formidable—some as big as pickup trucks, others as big as doublewides—but the chutes are wider, and the water is clear and quieter. It's nice for meditation.

"What in hell is that?"

Automobile tires begin to appear in the riverbed. They're easy to spot in the clear water no more than a foot deep. At first there are one, two, or three, then they multiply into the tens and hundreds, almost too many to count. Should have counted them, damn it. Now, in addition, there are truck tires. Red River is gray and blackening, and there's a feeling of canoeing over a rubber graveyard. It's saddening that human beings, Kentuckians, would abuse the Red River in such a way. Perhaps they dump the tires in by the truckload from one of the bridges.

"The state should consider paying to recycle the tires before they're thrown into the river," says Michael. "Or people could be paid one dollar for every tire pulled out of the river, then recycle them. People are just not going to pay several dollars a tire to process them."

I sit in the canoe and think what would happen if everybody considered Red River to be a handy, practical junkyard for wornout tires. Probably whole cars and trucks, abandoned refrigerators and stoves, aren't thrown in with the same impunity because they're so much more noticeable and traceable and apt to invite out the National Guard. Old tires fit snugly in the riverbed, and if you're not canoeing in low water you're not likely to notice them—out of sight, out of mind—until there are so many there's a tirejam.

"Isn't it the same thing as littering on the highways?"

"Of course it is," says Michael, feathering the canoe with his paddle as we glide in silence past Tower Rock, the mouth of Gladie Creek, and then, downstream—reaching heavenward—Cloud Splitter. At least for the moment, the soaring peak lifts meditations up from the despair of old automobile and truck tires. Clouds, parted by the slender, solitary rock formation, are a way of seeing a relationship with creation and the hydrologic cycle. We are water, we have descended from fissured clouds, we are returning forever downstream to the sea to be buried in vastness, we will be taken up into the atmosphere to be brought home again, and the earth, needing us, will welcome us as prodigal children, reborn from preceding generations, ready to forgive us for sins of pollution. Who knows, maybe we are the pollution.

When we stop for lunch we select a rock on the Wolfe County side, a huge rock that descended eons ago from the higher elevations. Stepping from the canoe at the base of the rock, we find that the only way to the top is up a muddy slope where each footprint sinks into muck past the ankles. Michael extends a hand and slowly we make it to the moss-covered summit. Willie and Rocky follow and the four of us sit down as if we've found the finest of tilted picnic tables. When sandwiches and cookies are unwrapped, the paper finds a temporary home in our pockets. To have thrown anything into the river would have earned serious reprimands.

We slide down the muddy bank on the downstream side of the rock, step carefully into our canoes and head back in the direction of "civilization."

There's another, lesser-known Red River that flows north from Tennessee into Simpson County, Kentucky, just south of the community of Providence. (There are three other Providences in Kentucky: in Knox County, Trimble County, and Webster County.) This Red River flows through Price's Mill and westward into Logan County. It passes the edge of Mortimer Station, Schley, and Dot. After picking up Whippermill Creek, Red moves south into Tennessee. Then, as if by rueful afterthought, it curls back into Kentucky before reentering Tennessee. The mouth of this Red River is on the Cumberland at Clarksville, Tennessee.

On May 30, 1806, at Harrison's Mills on the Red River in Logan County, a fatal duel was fought involving a future president of the United States. Andrew Jackson shot Charles Dickinson, who died the same night at the home of William Harrison. Jackson, who was seriously wounded, had lodged at Miller's Tavern. The duel was fought across the line in Kentucky to avoid legal complications in Tennessee, the home state of the adversaries. Although Jackson went on to become president, he eventually died of the wound he'd received in the duel.

This south-central Kentucky Red River has a West Fork that begins at Tabernacle in Todd County. The South Fork originates in Tennessee, enters Kentucky south of Adairville, and joins the main stream just west of Dot.

The Black Patch War, a dark era in Kentucky's history, evolved from a declining economy in the Reconstruction period following the Civil War and was waged along these waterways. The Planters Protective Association, organized in 1904 in Guthrie, was a strategy to combat the low prices paid by companies to tobacco farmers. Violence—murders, whippings, and property burnings—was visited on growers who resisted joining the organization. The hostilities were heightened when the tobacco companies refused to buy the commodity from members of the Association.

Jefferson Davis, another future president (of the Confederacy), was born in the Fairview community near the West Fork of this Red River. His monument shoots skyward along U.S. 68/80, a reminder that the waters of Kentucky produced the presidents of the two opposing sides in the American Civil War.

Kentucky's most celebrated writer, Robert Penn Warren (1905-1989), was born in Guthrie near the headwaters of Spring Creek. In 1980, nine years before his death, "Red" Warren published *Jefferson Davis Gets His Citizenship Back*: "Davis died without rancor, and wishing us all well. But if he were not now defenseless in death, he would no doubt reject the citizenship we so charitably thrust upon him. In life, in his old-fashioned way, he would accept no pardon, for pardon could be construed to imply wrongdoing, and wrongdoing was what, in honor and principle, he denied."

The third Red River has the curious distinction of being about one mile long. It drains the Cat Ridge watershed near the meeting of the county lines of Shelby, Spencer, and Anderson, flows northwest, and empties into Little Beech Creek at the juncture with Back Creek. Little Beech flows west along KY 636 toward Mt. Eden on the Shelby-Spencer County line, turns northwest, and picks up Rattlesnake Branch before emptying into Beech Creek near KY 53. Beech joins Salt River headwaters to form the northern neck of Taylorsville Lake.

The littlest Red River illustrates discovery in unlikely places. Ask almost anybody where it is and a puzzled look is usually the response. The few who know are unaware of how the tiny stream acquired its "river" status. After spotting it first on the Delorme map (*Kentucky Atlas and Gazetteer*) and using a lighted magnifying glass, we decided there was nothing to do but go and take a look.

The Shelby County judge/executive said he didn't know he had a Red River, but he recommended octogenarian Marvin Perry of the Mt. Eden community, just south of Little Beech Creek. Mr. Perry led the way and for him it was the final time. He passed away last year.

The rocky road off KY 636 crosses the meeting place of Little Beech, Back Creek, and "Red River." The woman who steps out on the front porch of what used to be "Grandma Mattie's old family place," where Mr. Perry once lived, is neither bonneted nor barefooted nor pregnant. She's urban in appearance and urbane in speech. Catherine Tuggle lives on eighty-six acres with her husband, Kenneth, two German shepherds—Topher and Nellie—a canary named Raphael, and a cat that looks like Mr. Mestophines. At last count there were ten peacocks.

Catherine and Kenneth moved from Louisville to this remote area in 1996. He commutes to his law office in Louisville. Catherine says she's happy to be out of the city because now she can do whatever she wants to do. She can go out to her studio and oil paint God's little Red River, or she can garden, or she can drag rocks up from the stream and build walkways.

"I really love to be connected with the earth—this quiet, the total quiet, the isolation—and I can see the Milky Way. I love wandering in the woods—Venus coming above that pink stretch. Smelling the earth. You don't smell it in the city the way you do out here."

"What do you hope to find here and have you really found it?" she's asked, as we sip tea at the kitchen table beneath Raphael, who throws down a chirpful greeting, then remains respectfully quiet, as if listening.

"I guess I really wanted a more comfortable way to live, as I want to live and not up to others' expectations." Catherine recalls her two acres in an "upscale" section of Louisville and how she wanted to let part of it "just grow" and not mow it at all, and how this led to murmurs about,

"Oh, it's those Tuggles." On Red River, Catherine can turn off "all the electrical stuff" and *listen* to the fire burning and *feel* the heat. She can cut the wood herself. And, she adds with a nice double meaning, "It's so easy to become *disconnected*."

Catherine Tuggle is a Kentucky woman busy connecting with herself. But she has anything but shut herself away. She's reaching out to the rest of the world. "By profession I was originally an artist, and I wish I could continue, yet another thing keeps evolving...this thing that comes from here [she touches her heart] needs to happen. I have to get it out in a way that some people will hear."

Catherine gives *ecumenical* a deeper, richer meaning. She goes beyond connecting just one church with another church, this congregation having supper once or twice a year with that congregation, here and there, once in awhile, talking the talk but not really walking the walk in a way that brings more people even a little bit closer.

"It's this human ecumenical movement to separate it from what most people mean. People within religions create the problems. The church gets problems from its humans." One definition of "ecumenical" relates to "the worldwide Christian church." Another broadens the idea: "Concerned with establishing or promoting *unity* among churches or religions." Catherine wants to be sure she's understood: "The last thing I want to do is to create another dogma. What I want to do is to give them [all churches] a good reason to put their dogma aside. The spirit functions the way the spirit wants to do it." This is one Kentucky woman's idea. Her passion, really. She aspires to win the endorsement of the National Conference for Community and Justice, and she welcomes the opportunity to travel away from the little Red River to spread her message.

What does her husband think about such a daunting adventure? "He agrees, and he's very supportive."

"What's ahead?"

"True security comes in that one minute when you separate yourself from fear. I'm talking about fear and security on the unconscious level, securing living patterns, stop treating myself as a doormat...there is no absolute security...it's what resonates with you...not to be afraid to question...the importance of thinking."

She's a Kentucky woman after our own Kentucky hearts. Who would have thought that you wouldn't have to hike through Red River #1, or go stand on some idiotic duelling site on Red River #2. You can discover your own Red River #3 or whatever number you want to give it. And there you, like Catherine Tuggle, will find *yourself*.

Dix, Redbird, and Horns

*He told 'em that was his river...hit was Dick's River, an' they
ortent to be huntin' on it.*

Janice Holt Giles
Hannah Fowler

Dix River (formerly Dick's River) rises in the Brodhead area of
Rockcastle County, where it gathers the waters of Long Branch,
Bowman Branch, Boone Fork, Negro Creek, and Little Negro Creek.
Originally named for the Cherokee chief "Captain Dick," the river is
about forty-five miles long. Short but determined, and proud as the man
for whom it lives in memory, Dix feeds and forms Herrington Lake, a
long, deep impoundment of water, then empties into the Kentucky
River upstream from High Bridge. Rocky Fork joins the lake near the
dam, which is 275 feet high. Cane Run, Tanyard Branch, McKecknie
Creek, Mocks Branch, Spears Creek, Clarks Run, and Boone Creek are
also tributaries.

South of the mouth of Hanging Fork is Logan Creek, which
originates at Buffalo Spring on the western side of Stanford, county seat
of Lincoln. Buffalo Spring was the site of Logan's Station, or St. Asaph,

131

established by Benjamin Logan in 1775. Janice Holt Giles provided her own description of the fort in her historical novel *Hannah Fowler*. "The fort was oblong in shape, being a third again as long as it was wide, and the strong, sharpened poles of the stockade fence looked invincible to Hannah." North of the mouth of Hanging Fork, in Mercer County, is Cane Run, site of Bowman's Station, established by Colonel John Bowman in 1779. He was the military commander of Kentucky.

Dix River converges with the Kentucky River between Bowman's Bend and Lock No. 7. The mouth of Dix is just upstream from High Bridge, a community and a bridge. In 1877, when the original railroad span was constructed, it was the highest bridge in North America. In the new millennium, with mournful cry, CSX diesel engines roll on phantom-like train trails against the Bluegrass sky pulling long freights north- and southbound across the cantilevered bridge connecting Lexington and New Orleans.

Steam has vanished, but the rails still pulse with energy, while deep inside the Palisades, on the Jessamine County side, groundwater grinds its own tracks, as it has for hundreds of millions of years. Since the Middle Ordovician age, water has highballed through the limestone strata, cutting holes, setting its own deliberate estimated times of arrival and departure, waiting for human passengers to discover plenitude. As is often the case, fortuitous unearthing happens in curiously connected circumstances.

At High Bridge, at the beginning of the twentieth century, rock was mined in an ancient quarry. Engineers excavated the rugged riches to build modern highways. In 1923, after the exterior parts were exhausted, the Kentucky Stone Company burrowed inside the rock formations. The quarry beneath the rail lines was the source of megatons of building material. When the operations ceased in 1971, there was nothing left but the fifty-foot by fifty-foot stone pillars supporting the quarry ceiling. Seemed a likely spot to grow mushrooms, the ideal place to establish a commercial source for edible morsels to garnish dishes and gratify palates. The enterprise benefited from the natural, constant underground temperature of sixty degrees, but another agricultural "alternative crop" bit the dust. The venture lasted several years until the property was eventually sold on the courthouse steps in Nicholasville. One of the investors, William Griffin of Laurel County, was the high bidder.

His vision for the one hundred surface acres and the abandoned limestone quarry beneath was as a storage facility: boats, recreational vehicles, and maybe a vault for banks, legal firms, universities, hospitals, and corporations. From this beginning, Kentucky Underground Storage, Inc., evolved and today stretches for thirty-two acres comprising millions of cubic feet of space, the only facility of its kind in Kentucky. Do you live in Canada in the summer and Florida in the winter and don't want to pull a recreational vehicle the entire distance? Park it in between seasons at Kentucky Underground Storage for about two dollars a foot per month. Live in Kentucky and don't want to undergo the expense of winterizing a boat? Same solution. At present there are about two hundred boats and RVs lining the pillars of a cave aching for better days.

This New World fortress near the mouth of his river would have flabbergasted Captain Dick. Neither he nor William Griffin could have anticipated all the hidey-hole possibilities. Pioneers came before the hi-tech era of backup tapes and discs for corporate computers, archival materials of institutions of higher learning, microfilms and -fiche. The bottomless pit of paper generated by technology cries out for a safe place to be stored. The cave has mushroomed light years beyond simple sporophore. The president of the company now is one of William and Jo Ann Griffin's five daughters, Gale Reece.

Then, there was this little problem.

Water was constantly flowing through a hole in the ceiling. It came from a spring beyond the rear of the cave. Mineral water, Adam's ale, percolated through miles of clay and limestone, never mind rock removal, mushroom farming, or high-tech storage. The water was actually an unnamed river that discovered its course and took it. More than two hundred years have flowed by since Captain Dick cupped his hands in pure spring water and lifted them to his lips. He could not envision the coming of a civilization that would have to bottle the water and load it onto trucks for distribution, then figure out a way to recycle all the plastic. The same simple drink that sustained Captain Dick and his warriors was cycling into another civilization.

Highbridge Spring Water, founded in 1981 by the William Griffin family, is today located in the vast quarry off KY 29 and River Road on the Jessamine County side, four miles south of Wilmore. Production of bottled drinking water is now about 20,000 gallons a day. The president of the company is another of William and Jo Ann Griffin's daughters, Linda Slagel. "Our Reverse Osmosis System takes out all but a little of the mineral content, leaving a trace of sodium," says the president, sitting by the side of her father, Chief Bill, deep in the High Springs cave.

"But the hydrologic cycle insures purity, doesn't it?"

"No. There is more unnatural contamination."

"Oh?"

"There is groundwater contamination, and a lot more things to test for," says Linda.

"I suppose I thought that when the water evaporated, returned from the Gulf of Mexico, back here to the springs, it was O.K. I mean, unpolluted."

"Rain is not 'good' water anymore," says Linda, who, with the help of a quality control chemist works to improve what is bottled and sold to the public.

The source of the elixir of the Palisades becomes problematic as more chemicals infiltrate the soil. Groundwater contamination necessitates a filtration process. Almost one hundred years ago, when Booker T. Washington said, "Put your bucket down where you are," the metaphor for self-reliance might have included an admonition: Look to the bottom of the bucket and make sure of what's there before you drink it.

The mouth of Red Bird River is at Oneida in Clay County. Goose Creek and Buckskin Creek join it there, and the three streams form the South Fork of the Kentucky River. Red Bird begins as Red Bird Creek in northern Bell County. By the time the "creek" winds its way through the southeastern corner of Clay County it has attained "river" status. Legend has it that Red Bird River was named for a Cherokee, Chief Red Bird, who, after his furs were stolen, was killed and thrown into the river. His companion, "Jack," was killed on what would come to be named Jack's Creek. The facts of the murders are lost in time, but there is speculation that Chief Red Bird's amorous nature and possibly a troubled past in North Carolina may have gotten him into more trouble with early pioneers streaming through Cumberland Gap. There may have been interbreeding, which led to jealousies and overheated rivalries. So be the fruits of passion.

We drive down I-75 to London and take the Daniel Boone Parkway over to Manchester. The road follows a portion of Red Bird River. We take Exit 34, where we pick up KY 66, then we continue southeast, deeper and deeper into Daniel Boone National Forest. The state road follows Red Bird, and we pass through what the map says are Peabody, Marcum, Creekville, and Spring Creek. Names of creeks, rivers, roads, and settlements on a map don't always correspond with current usage. Terminology varies with time and circumstance. Even "Red Bird" sometimes becomes "Redbird," but the surrounding nature is nameless, without beginning or end.

It reminds us of the rain forest in Puerto Rico as we drive down the winding road where trees—poplar and sycamore—shade the rock formations and cover the slopes dropping down steeply to the narrow Red Bird. Trees look like feathers in layers of green. Memories return— the flat tire we had in the rain forest in Puerto Rico, back when we were much younger and thinner, better able to scrounge on our bellies in roadside gravel and muscle up the rear end of the car with a tricky jack. We didn't worry for a New York second about trucks rumbling by in the dark. Our older concerns today are oncoming coal trucks and dropoffs that might lead to a flat car.

At the junction of Upper Jack's Creek and Red Bird, we bear to the right and pass Red Bird Mission School, graded K-12. Then, less than a mile further, we reach our destination—Red Bird Mission, the Queendale Center at Beverly. We cross over the small concrete bridge and enter the enclosure that includes the hospital, medical and dental clinics, pharmacy, early childhood development center, bookmobile, dormitories, cafeteria, food pantry, community store, and craft shop.

"Are crafts a major part of Red Bird Mission?" We assume as much because we harbor the simplistic habit of thinking mainly in terms of crafts when acknowledging achievement among Appalachians.

"A minor part," says Craig Dial, director of retail operations, with abundant modesty. Actually many people initially do learn about Red Bird Mission through its extensive crafts program. We walk past floor-to-ceiling shelves of wooden objects—birdhouses made of tree sections, handcarved toy trains, expertly woven baskets, laboriously carved dough bowls—into another room with several small mountains of bagged used clothing for distribution to those in need. At lunch in the mission restaurant, we sit and talk with Craig and his wife, Karen, an ordained minister. Afterwards, we go to look at the main focal point of the United Methodist Church's outreach to Appalachia—the place in the valley where Cow Fork branch joins Mud Lick to form Red Bird River. (Some maps show Mud Lick coming in a little to the south—there'll always be friendly disagreement about exact beginnings.)

We stand together at the meeting of these two small mountain streams, which care not a tinker's damn about names, and we quietly celebrate creation—no fireworks, no festival, no cotton candy or flavored popcorn. The confluence of the two rock-strewn rivulets becomes a water hole for baptizings—spiritual new beginnings for the believers. The water is about three or four feet deep where Cow Fork and Mud Lick surrender their man-given identities. We choose to walk up Cow Fork past the old Beverly United Methodist Church, where "Uncle Willis" Sizemore long ago worshiped.

According to his friend Sam Lawson, Uncle Willis had never experienced a bath anywhere except in his old galvanized tub. One day, while "taking the night" at the home of Red Bird Mission Superintendant. John Bischoff, Uncle Willis was asked if he wanted to bathe. He declined. Heck, for one thing, he saw no water or anything to put it in. Superintendant Bischoff showed him the faucet, something the elderly man had never seen before. Had no idea what it might be. Uncle Willis was amazed, and for the rest of his life he would tell the tale of how he once knew a man who had water coming out of the wall of his house.

Uncle Willis didn't get his wish to be buried in the casket he had personally selected and had lain in to try on for size. His body is moldering somewhere out there in California, but his friends believe his soul is still residing on Red Bird River in Kentucky. Family feuding drove Uncle Willis out West, and he just never got back. The casket he had purchased in advance became the final resting-place of an old woman who had no other accommodations. Uncle Willis said she was welcome to take it.

Sam Lawson and his wife, Esther, are fountains of Appalachian Mountain wisdom. She was the Red Bird bookmobile lady from 1954 to 1990. Esther emigrated from North Dakota to eastern Kentucky in 1946 and found her home of homes at the headwaters of Red Bird. She married Sam Lawson and never saw reason to be anyplace or anybody else. Esther taught English, and whenever she could she saved books for the mission library.

As for Sam, he never cottoned to "higher education." "I didn't want to go to college," says Sam. "I wanted to be with the building trades, and I never regretted that decision." Sam Lawson, whose specialty is wielding a paintbrush, figures he's been at Red Bird Mission longer than anybody. When we talked to him, sitting inside the shade of his pickup truck, he was planning to retire this year. He speaks of the '47 flood: "Found the post office safe four or five miles downstream."

Problem with snakes: "Esther and I are hikers and never in our lives have we seen a poisonous snake—rattlesnake, copperhead, or water mocassin."

Isolation: "Before roads we never knew what was going on from one side of the mountain to the other."

"If you get your feet wet in the Red Bird River you'll always come back," says Sam with his soft smile and the voice that is as mellow as a day in the new millennium. Praise God, there's nothing to do but to sit on the bank of Cow Fork, remove shoes, ease down the ferny slope, and step into the sharp coolness of clear water churning down from Bear Wallow and Rainbow Gaps. A youth approaches. He's holding out two plastic bottles. One is store-bought distilled water, the other is filled with water straight from Cow Fork. "Can you tell the difference?" he asks. They do look the same. And in time of thirst, a feller might be grateful for a swaller or two of water from Cow Fork. It would seem a safe bet. But it would be a mistake to become too sculptured. After all, there could be hidden surprises in out-of-the-way places. Darting tongues and itty biddy eyes.

"Any snakes around here?" is about the same as yelling, "Any fire in this theater?" But the words are sometimes tolerably good for opening conversations.

A young girl yells back: "Don't even use that word!" She and other religious folk from Methodist churches in Southern Illinois are here to build a new picnic shelter on the original Red Bird Mission grounds. The wary don't ever forget the possibility of poisonous snakes in their mountain homes. Nor should human beings, believers and nonbelievers, discount the likelihood of small streams turning furious in flood time, like that dark day in the summer of 1947.

"About 2:00 a.m., on June 28, rain came down in sheets, and I knew we were having a cloudburst similar to the one experienced at the Jack's Creek Community Center six years ago." This description is in the preserved account of Red Bird Mission Superintendant John W. Bischoff.

> *Then we stood there helplessly and watched the Schaeffer home go by. The sidewall broke off and we could see the furniture in the house as it swept across the tennis court and the ball diamond and crashed into the porch of the boys' dormitory. It struck so hard that the house seemed to bounce, then whirled around the corner of the dormitory, and we have never seen it since. A few scattered articles like the bathtub and sink were found down the river a way, but the doctor's household goods were completely swept away.*
>
> *Shortly after the Schaeffer house floated away, Uncle Millard's store and post office started down the Red Bird. Crashing into a huge tree it began breaking up. Pieces of homes, big trees and logs went floating by. We could hear the roar of rocks tumbling in the water, many of them weighing as much as five hundred pounds. Afterward we found that a large boulder estimated to weigh about two tons had been moved near the bridge by the water.*
>
> *It was with great relief that we saw the flood beginning*

*to fall. Stopping to think about it, we realized that we were
practically blue with cold; so we changed into borrowed
clothing.*

*Our Jack's Creek Community center was the least affected,
although people living a half-mile or more away on the river
lost homes, other buildings, fences and gardens. At Beech
Fork the Helton Post Office, the bridge just below the school,
and several homes between our Beech Fork and Lower Beech
Fork churches were taken. The Mill Creek community
experienced even higher water than Red Bird; good homes
being washed away, and all three stores were severely
damaged. The church was washed off its foundation and
lodged between the mountain and the stone parsonage
constructed last year [1946].*

*Almost every chicken on Mill Creek was lost, and fine
apple orchards were uprooted and washed away. Just across
from the parsonage two men were trapped in a home which
appeared doomed, so they climbed into an apple tree.*

*Throughout the area as far as we know only one life was
lost, that of a girl on Straight Creek.*

Red Bird Mission moved from its original northeastern Bell County
location to what is now called the Queendale Center at the new Beverly,
just over the line in southeastern Clay County. The center is named for
Chris G. Queen, instrumental in persuading the Henry Ford Foundation, in
1951, to donate sixty acres of land upon which to build the future. Today,
Red Bird Mission serves churches in eight counties in southeastern
Kentucky and has extended its outreach to six other countries. It claims to
be "the largest home mission project in the United States."

The beginning was the murder of Chief Red Bird. The ending lives in
a simple idea—service to people. Beside the pulpit in the old Beverly
Church on Cow Fork, the bibilical "Fruits of the Spirit" are proclaimed:

Love

Joy

Patience
Kindness
Goodwell
Faithfulness
Gentleness
Self-Control

My heart is here.

Eugene French
at the head of the holler
Horns River

Along Red Lick Road to Horns River in southwestern Estill County, the mountains are called "Kneeling Elephants." They pleasure men, women, and children for free. They'll always be there for everybody, because they don't go anywhere, don't wrap their trunks around the next feller's tail, get on and off trains, lumber into town, eat a lot of peanuts, and take pleasure in watching human beings cleaning up with big shovels. The circus crowd might not understand or appreciate the fact that there are some elephants that can't be bought, borrowed, or trained to rear up and bellow when tapped on the snout.

What matters is knowing that there are lots of visions for the taking, just by being there. The mountains stretching from the Kentucky River at Irvine—Curtis Mountain, Peter Mountain, Preacher Estes Mountain, and Wilson Mountain—resemble peaceful, resting creatures. In early March, with the pickup truck's window rolled down, the sound of birds has returned. Jonquils are in their glory. Forsythias are bursting with yellow. Dogwood buds are straining to be born again. Hound dogs "Ba-roooing," crows "Caw-cawing," squirrels looking lean and stringy after winter. Farmers plowing the rich bottomlands. Long, swinging footbridges rocking in the breeze.

Horns River takes its good old time emptying into Red Lick Creek, just south of Jenks. What's the hurry? Red Lick Creek is a tributary of Station Camp Creek, which connects with Crooked Creek and Clear Creek, then joins the Kentucky River at Irvine. Always has. Always will. 'Less somebody tries to dam up all creation. Horns River comes down— twisting and turning, sometimes rippling, sometimes pooling for a spell—from Zion Mountain and Brooks Mountain.

KY 499 leads from Irvine to Wisemantown. A left turn at KY 594, known locally as Red Lick Road, begins a journey that Francine and Tom Bonny of Wisemantown call "one of the most beautiful drives anywhere." They use it to go over to Berea. It's not necessary to throw good money after bad going to the Pigeon Forges and the Gatlinburgs unless there's a contest and the main object is to spend money or ogle Dolly. At Jenks, there are a little store and a few houses. On the other side of Jenks, Horns River Road is on the right. It's gravel. It follows, more or less, the little two-mile stream, possibly named for a tree, then again, might've been named for a person. Some Horn surnames trace back to the stream and its holler, where there's been a wealth of trees. The American Hornbeam tree "is frequently found along streams or about springs well up in the hills." Take your choice. According to Grimm's *Book of Trees*, the American Hornbeam "is often used for levers, homemade tool handles, and for fuel," the basic stuff that has given Kentucky its strong beginnings.

Early pioneers cut the logs, dragged them with mules, built their cabins, and settled in the holler along Horns River. The settlers were known by traits still found today in the Kentucky highlands: identity with earth, streams, and trees; family connections with Aunt Della, Aunt Nannie, and Uncle Oakley; resourcefulness, integrity despite a perpetuated picture of poverty and ignorance. Ingenuity has included the right to call a tiny stream a river, if somebody has a mind to.

"Imagine a river emptying into a creek," says Tom Bonny.

"Has happened before."

"Where?"

"Shelby County. And there's another one in Allen County."

"Well, now," says Tom, not wishing to burden the difference into a dispute.

He says, "Follow me in my truck, if you want to, and I'll lead you up Horns River. That way, you can stay as long as you like."

We ride past the "Kneeling Elephants" on the left hand, Station Camp church and cemetery on the right. There are no gridlocks, no traffic signals, but every once in a while there might be a bearded man on a horse, a young woman following on hers, their energy sweating pleasantly, eight horseshoes jingling like wind chimes.

A man in bib overalls stands at the head of the holler, the base of the triangle formed by Zion Mountain, Chrisman Mountain (1,499 feet), and Lily Mountain. The meeting place is beyond Turkey Pin Branch, about as far as a pickup truck wants to go. Eugene French's outstretched hand is large with the forbearance of years of work, the grip as strong as an elephant handler's, yet sensitive too in its enthusiastic grasp. He is a Horns River man, born and bred, as was his father, Lloyd, and *his* father, Richard, and *his* father, Preston.

"Where does Horns begin?"

"Well, now, in a spring inside a cave back up there on Mount Zion," says Eugene, speaking in a direct way, without beating around the bush. He likes to talk, doesn't mind questions but, while getting right to the point, does it politely. Doesn't lash out, or growl, or bark except when he absolutely has to. When that time comes it's more than likely best to watch out. Not to say that he's anything like a pit bull or a rattlesnake. Mostly, he'll be all right if the other feller's all right. There's a quality in Eugene's voice. Mellow. Knows where it's going.

"Uncle Oakley—wish you could have known him," says Eugene with pride. "No formal education. There was the Garrett School House, sat in double seats, 'In' and 'Out' card tacked up on the wall. If it said 'Out' it meant somebody was using the outhouse. It was a one-holer. One time Uncle Oakley felt the call of nature, but the card said 'Out.' He had to sit there, and he had an accident. Came home with his pants soiled. We were poor, but we didn't know it."

"Much misbehaving around here? At the present time, I mean to say?"

"Awful good people here."

"How do you account for those who don't do right?"

"Devil's still with us."

"Is?"

"Some don't correct. Some don't work. Resent you having something. Won't pick up a blackberry. Or a black walnut."

"What kind of horses are those?"

"Rocky Mountain and Kentucky Mountain Saddle," says Eugene, handing over a card with a picture of his stallion, "French's Slick Willie."

"Not named for the president," says Eugene. "Man said he wouldn't breed to him if he was a Democrat," he adds.

"What did you say then?"

"I did tell him I was a Republican."

The conversation in the middle of the graveled Horns River Road moves to the edge of political philosophy: self-sufficiency, closing the door after passing in or out, turning off the lights, "how to take care of stuff and how to be conservative." Eugene recalls: "My grandfather and me, we'd go to the barn. He'd set me down on a bucket to shell corn. You know how that's done, don't you? Well, if one grain jumped out, I got up then and got it and brought it back."

Eugene's mother and father believed in work. "They'd go up there on that hill, cut trees with a double handsaw, snake them down with mules, dig the post holes by hand. Didn't have chain saws or tractors." There was entertainment: "We'd take a straight dogwood stick, use Mama's thread to clear a passage through the center, use it for a gun to burn a blister on somebody."

Eugene French spends part of his time with family in Ohio, part of his time on Horns River Road. He and his wife, Janet, have a passel of children: Eugene Jr., Tim, Steve, Dale, James, and John. Sharon Jane came along between James and John. When told about Chris Holbrook's *Hell and Ohio*, Eugene laughs deep down inside his ability to turn a witticism upon himself. A Kentuckian, especially one uprooted from Appalachia and transplanted north of the Ohio River, is usually bedeviled by multiple personality.

The native bears the brunt of "hillbilly" while working in the Promised Land of Mechanical Labor in Ohio. Yet, on visits back home to Kentucky, sometimes on weekends, sometimes for the balance of a lifetime, the trick is not to appear too blue-collar improved. "Up there," for example, speech is damned when the "g" is dropped from words ending in "ing," or when the long "I" is not properly pronounced, and when the "h" is intruded to make "it" become "hit." At the same time, the long "I" of "I've got a job in Ohio" is the sure mark of "taking on airs" up the holler of Horns River. It's much easier and more friendly for a Kentuckian to pronounce the name of the state as "Kintucky" using the short 'i" instead of the short "e." It's enough to make a reasonable feller want to "rent out Ohio and live in Hell"—assuming there's half a chance of a job at Toyota. At least that would be in the Bluegrass and a hundred miles closer to home. At the same time, Ohioans can go right on with their superior pronunciations and lifestyles, and they can go to their graves believing that all Kentuckians are brainless and to be barely tolerated. Kintuckians can go to their graves remembering the time when they had to go to Ohio for a job, suffered the ridicule, and then returned home to agree with Chris Holbrook that if "I had to live in Hell or Ohio, I'd rent out Ohio and live in Hell."

Salt, Rolling Fork, Nolin, and Chaplin

At this moment I am at a special place, a little park on the river in West Point, Kentucky, where I come as often as possible to meditate, savor the view or just to be. Today, a particularly cold day, I've seen more than the usual amount of waterfowl, heron, geese, duck, and sea gulls lifting and circling at the mouth of the Salt River and of course the tugs are colorful too.

Mary Hite
A letter in January
Bardstown

The mouth of the Salt River is normally narrow at the place where it pours neatly into the Ohio River. In March 1997, floodwaters shrouded the juncture one mile north of West Point, making it next to impossible to know what was Salt River and what was Ohio River. Upstream on the Salt, devastation visited Shepherdsville, the county seat of Bullitt. The *Courier-Journal* estimated the damage in the Kentucky-Indiana region to be $500 million. No price could be placed on the twenty-one lives that were lost.

The origination of the usually peaceful Salt is in Boyle County near the intersection of Persimmon Knob Road and Cream Ridge Road, due west of Junction City. West of Danville, the Salt picks up Quirks Run, then continues a twisting northward passage to the west of Harrodsburg and on to Vanarsdell in Mercer County. When Bill Irvine was a farm kid in Boyle County, he used to fish in the headwaters of Salt River, used to catch sunfish, used to wade in the little stream, more creek than river at the place where he was born and raised. "It begins about two miles up in the hills, the Knobs area, and there was a spring on my farm that empties into the Salt River about two miles from the place they call Pumpkin Run. Starts there as a little branch, then becomes twenty or thirty feet wide in places and comes on down through my farm." At eighty-seven years of age, Mr. Irvine remembers with pleasure his wading days, the old swimming hole where he learned to swim. "I lived there my whole life except for the war." But, five years ago, Mr. Irvine cashed in the farm, sold all six hundred acres, and moved to Danville. "Couldn't get any good help," he explains.

"I drive out and look at the old home place," he says with a touch of longing in the tone of his voice.

"Did it used to flood?"

"It would flood a hundred yards wide, flash floods at times, but didn't take it long to run down. It could be quite a bit of water."

"Tell us more about the farm. Was it your father's before you?"

"Yessir."

Asking questions about the sale of the old home place is a throwback to being CBS-nosy, but every once in a while old reporter dogs regress, and they're glad they did. "Who bought your farm?"

"Bunker Hunt. Do you know him?"

"Well no, yes, sir, I know of him. I walked up to him at a Phyllis George Brown fundraiser for her husband. He wanted to be governor again, but she seemed to be the one that was pushing it the hardest. I reminded Mr. Hunt that on a Sunday afternoon I'd knocked on his door in Dallas, which was as far as I got. Later, I covered his and his brother's wiretapping trial in Lubbuck. I guess, Mr. Irvine, you got to know him better than that."

"He bought five hundred and forty-three acres, but he doesn't own it any more. A bank took it over, a bank in New York paid me."

"Did you ever see Mr. Hunt?"

"He and his wife came to our home."

"What was he like?"

"He was just a plain old guy. Everybody spent money for him. You just can't throw money around." Mr. Irvine recalled the days of Nelson Bunker Hunt and his brother cornering the worldwide silver market. "I think he was playing with too big of an auger," says Bill Irvine, understanding and appreciating simplicity. He always carefully hung his Burley tobacco, spaced it so that air could cure it, minded his cows and calves as all good animal husbandry requires. He sold out of sheep when coyotes kept coming over the hill, and he sold the whole kit and caboodle when Bunker Hunt came down the road and the price was right. Mr. Irvine is a Salt River man, born and bred. He was not, as they say, born yesterday.

Salt River and its tributaries form Taylorsville Lake, 3,050 acres stretching from east of Driscoll Hill to the dam on KY 2239 in Spencer County. The Salt flows through Taylorsville, gathering Brashears Creek and Elk Creek. Near the community of Elk Creek, on July 19, 1829, James Morrison Heady was born. He was blind and deaf through much of his long life as "a musician, writer, composer, inventor, poet, architectural designer and philosopher." Heady's mostly forgotten life has been preserved by Ken D. Thompson in *Beyond the Double Night*. The old man with the long white hair and beard died December 20, 1915. There have been many who have lived unnoticed and unheralded along the rivers of Kentucky—their lives becoming springs from which to draw good water.

At Smithville, the Salt crosses into Bullitt County, passing beneath Interstate 65 at Shepherdsville. Just to the north, at Gap in Knob (or Gap-in-the-Knobs) on U.S. 61, is the birthplace of Kentucky novelist Frances Barton Fox (1887-1967). While she grew up to write agrarian-based books—*The Heart of Aresthusa* and *Ridgeways*—her brother, Fontaine Talbott Fox Jr. (1884-1964), conceived the popular comic strip *Toonerville Trolley that Meets All the Trains*. The contrast illustrates reality in early twentieth-century Kentucky and throughout America:

caricature, parody, lampoon, satire, and burlesque have built-in audiences, while literary accomplishments demand lifetimes of education and delayed gratification.

A community that marches to its own drummer, the Sisters of Charity of Nazareth, Kentucky, is located in Nelson County at the headwaters of Froman Creek, which flows into Cox Creek, a tributary of the Salt River. One of the sisters, Patricia Kelley, has written *Fifty Monsoons: Ministry of Change Through Women of India* (1999). The flow of water in India, she found, as in every part of Earth, has its own idiosyncrasies, its own patterns and pathways.

The Salt River bears southwesterly, forming the county line of Bullitt and Hardin northward from Pitts Point near the mouth of Rolling Fork River. The Salt then snakes past Arnold Rocks and Buzzard Roost, through the center of Fort Knox Military Reservation, and finally empties the waters of almost 3,000 square miles into the Ohio River. Usually it accomplishes this task in an orderly way. When provoked by a foot of rainfall, as in March 1997, it's time to consider certain hydrological truths: unwise to build on floodplains; smart to accept the fact that water has a mind, a power, a will of its own.

The one hundred and forty-mile long Salt River was named for Henry Crist's 1779 salt operations. The expression "up Salt River" refers to an incident in 1832, when presidential candidate Henry Clay was supposed to be transported *down* the Salt, then to Louisville for a speaking engagement. Instead, Clay's opponents bribed the boat's captain to go in the other direction, causing the candidate to miss his speaking engagement. Clay lost the election to Andrew Jackson, but the margin (219 to 49 electoral votes) would not seem to hang on one campaign speech in Clay's home state or going the wrong way on Salt River.

Today, defeated candidates for public office are on special occasions offered the balm of honorary membership in the Salt River Navy, where everybody's an admiral. Nobody has to chip paint, and keelhauling is against the law. Membership includes the advantage of not having to worry about patronage or getting reelected. No re-votes or recounts.

Rolling Fork River empties into Salt near Pitt's Point in southern

Bullitt County, the river formed by North Rolling Fork and Big South Fork at their juncture at Bradfordsville in Marion County. North Rolling Fork's headwaters are in southwestern Boyle County, including Shelby Branch, Johnson Branch, and Carpenter Fork. KY 37 follows North Rolling Fork past Forkland, site of an annual festival of local artisans.

To the west, where Little South Fork empties into North Rolling Fork, is the location of Penn's Store, believed to be the oldest continuously operated family store in America. The tiny store sits in the shadow of Connie's Knob. On a crisp afternoon in late November of 1999, on the edge of a new millennium, three men and a boy in a pickup truck drive up to Penn's Store. All pile out. "Does anybody know where this creek runs to?" asks the driver, speaking directly, just short of insistence, referring to North Rolling Fork.

"Lady inside might," says a man sitting on the weatherworn front porch, where a black dog named Mollie scratches fleas as necessary and challenges all wandering, out of place, four-legged creatures. Jeanne Penn Lane opens the screen door and steps forward. She's a damn good-looking woman, but when she walks out onto the front porch to speak to a stranger who has dropped in from out of the blue, her voice is as authoritative as a colonel hearing a knock on the door at midnight at central headquarters.

"Can I help you?"

"This feller's lost," says the driver, nodding toward the third man, short of stature and two fingers missing.

"Got separated from my dogs," says the third man, quietly, earnestly, humbly too. He is, as they say, hat-in-hand, slowly stroking the brim of it. A man on the front porch wonders about the two missing fingers but has enough good sense and common decency not to ask, at least not at this crucial moment. But he wonders about it. Losing two fingers is not all that much of a tragedy, but usually there's a good story behind it, wanting to be told, hungering for audience. The ghost of Charles Kuralt sends up a message that if paths were to cross again, if two men were seated somewhere on the bank of Rolling Fork, one might just might quietly inquire: "How did you lose those fingers?"

"Don't know where my truck is, either," says the man, who looks for all the world like "E.T." just landed near the corner of Casey, Boyle, and Marion Counties. Not that the man looks grotesque—he just looks pitifully and profoundly lost. He's down on his luck with two fingers missing. It's no time to complain or raise a ruckus. If he did, it wouldn't make a bit of difference. If he were Frank Sinatra, Jeanne's manner would be the same. It's like the Great Equalizer's Nude Beach at Guadaloupe: young and old, male and female, large and small breasts, hair where God planted and intended hair to be, the sun shining equally, rain falling fairly when clouds become overburdened, gravity needing no passport, Rolling Fork rolling as Rolling Fork must roll.

Jeanne calmly makes her recommendation. "Go out here to the road, turn right, go about two miles, turn left over a creek, and that's where you'll find the man you say you know."

E.T. and his rescuers, along with an earth-boy who's not spoken a word, load themselves back into the pickup truck and down the road they go. There might be a whimsy to follow them, even to take up with them, but prudence and patience pay, as they say. Besides, there's too much going on right here, right now.

Inside Penn's Store, a hunter named Steve resumes his guitar picking, accompanying Dawn, who plays her guitar, holding it in close to herself, mothering it, making most any warm-blooded mammal wish to be strung out on such an instrument. She and her twin sister, Dava, the beautiful daughters of Jeanne, go on singing around the wood-burning stove as if nothing has happened. It could've been E.T. or Sinatra, it wouldn't have made a particle of difference. They would have smiled and kept on playing "If You Love Me, Really Love Me" and "Coming Home to You."

The waters flow. The days roll on. There's no turning back. No, not ever. We were on the road and hadn't heard the news from Penn's Store—not until we received word from Jeanne. "Our hearts are broken," she wrote.

The last E-mail from Dava had been dated March 7, 2000, 9:13 a.m.: "We are all fine. Busy with the store, of course. There's some big things going on there right now. We have made some history. The store's porch has been shored up and the rotten wood has been replaced. It looks so nice and feels so much better under your feet!!! I'd best get to the store.

Hope you all are doing fine and are enjoying this great weather that we have been having!!! Hope to see you soon!! Love, Dava."

Dava died in the summer of 2000.

How can a beautiful woman in the prime of her life be gone forever? There is so little time, so precious little time. We had not known about the seriousness of Dava's heart condition. "The challenge is to live and love as best we can while we have the time," says Lalie, breaking the numbing silence after receiving the news.

Now there'll always be something missing at Penn's Store on North Rolling Fork. But the water won't stop, will it? We are caught in it and by it and for it. And the questions become: Where are we going? When will we arrive? Will it all have been worth the effort? We like to think of it as a voyage we never asked for in the first place. But having been set upon it, we have come to an understanding. There's a life force at work in us, designed to keep us on a reasonably even keel sometimes but not always—if we cooperate with the flow.

Scrubgrass Branch, Mill Creek, and Wards Branch empty into North Rolling Fork south of Gravel Switch, home of nineteen-year-old Michael Lanham, the nation's youngest Rhodes Scholar. Gravel Switch, Kentucky? "I've become a kind of poster boy in the state for the acceleration of gifted and talented students," says Michael, six-foot-eight, who instead of playing basketball and dreaming of joining the NBA, sings and plays the piano and French horn. His destination: Oxford University and a doctorate in mathematics.

Lovers Leap, named for a distraught man and woman who jumped to their deaths, is located on "Devil's Backbone," above a bend in North Rolling Fork. Tradition has it that the eighteenth-century lovers had wanted to be married, but their parents didn't approve. The height of the jump was about a quarter of a mile. Their spirits ride the night air as the river gathers the waters of Followell Creek.

Abe Lincoln was born near the South Fork of Nolin River, but his boyhood home was on the edge of Knob Creek, a tributary of Rolling

Fork, both places in LaRue County. Rolling Fork gathers Pottinger Creek on the eastern side, Knob Creek on the western side. Lincoln's family moved to Knob Creek in the spring of 1811. The site is described by Carl Sandburg in *Abraham Lincoln*: "That Knob Creek farm in their valley set round by high hills and deep gorges was the first home Abe Lincoln remembered....He scrawled words with charcoal, he shaped them in the dust, in sand, in snow. Writing had a fascination for him."

Teachers today pound writing portfolios into the consciousness of sleeping young Abes and Abigales. Reasons for it: television, especially on snow days when there's no school. The new age resists formal education as much as Abe longed for it. Character has undergone woeful change, so that cheating is an amusing game. Flawed thinking would have many believe that an educated person is exactly what an uneducated person says he or she is.

There's a story told about Abe when he was president of the United States. He was holding a cabinet meeting, and the discussion became unnecessarily catawampous. Lincoln finally just up and asked, "How many legs would a dog have if you called the tail a leg?" There was a pause. Then, somebody said, "Well, Mr. President, it would be five."

"No," said the man who wrote in the dust, the sand, and the snow on the edge of Knob Creek in Kentucky. "It would still be four. Calling a tail a leg doesn't make it a leg." Calling a school an education does not detract from the truth of water. The cycle that produced the Great Emancipator at the same time created opportunity all along the rivers of Kentucky. There, good people can reach for the stars, for spirituality, daring to *want* to be saints, reaching from within their selves, trusting in the lordship of intuition, believing in values derived naturally, needing no external confirmations.

Nolin River converges with Green River opposite Indian Hill. The mouth of Nolin is upstream from Brownsville in Edmonson County, downstream from Houchins Ferry. The North and South Forks of Nolin join near Mathers Mill in Larue County. The North Fork flows through Hodgenville, site of the Lincoln Museum. Its headwaters drain the western slope of Cecil Ridge near the sixteenth president's boyhood home. The South Fork of the Nolin gathers the headwaters of southern Larue County. It flows past the Sinking Springs farm, where Lincoln was born on February 12, 1809.

Nolin River gathers Barren Run, then crosses into Hardin County. The community of Nolin sits at the juncture of Nolin River and Cox Run, just south of Glendale. The Nolin flows northwesterly to gather Valley Creek, then turns southwesterly at Boiling Spring toward Harcourt and White Mills, thence southward to Spurrier and Millerstown. Berry Run and Sinking Fork have joined the Nolin, which forms the Hardin-Grayson County line. Nolin River Lake, sprawling across 5,795 acres in Grayson, Edmonson, and Hart Counties, was built in the 1960s. The dam is located near Dismal Rock. Tributaries to the lake and its backwaters include Hunting Fork, Barton Run, Laurel Run, Bacon Creek, Round Stone Creek, Cane Run, Little Dog Creek, Dog Creek, Wolf Creek, Long Fall Creek, and Brier Creek.

Nolin Lake State Park can be reached by KY 1827 just north of Mammoth Cave National Park. The Nolin River loops south past Whistle Mountain inside the park. The main forks of Nolin River should be as recognizable to Kentucky school children as the name of the sixteenth president of the United States. In these waters is the essence of generations that have followed almost two hundred years since his birth.

He it is also that is born each instant in our hearts: for this unending birth, this everlasting beginning, without end...this is the life that is in us.

Thomas Merton
The Seven Storey Mountain

The Abbey of Gethsemani is located on Monk's Creek, a tributary of Pottinger Creek, whose Nelson County headwaters descend from Holy Cross, Loretta, and St. Francis. Pottinger flows past New Hope, then converges with Rolling Fork. The Trappist monastery's spire soars above the countryside, as stunning today as it was the first time Thomas Merton viewed it.

"But, oh! How far have I to go to find you in whom I have already arrived!" Merton's words, clear as water trickling from an eternal spring, have the power to sustain us in the now of our lives. As we stand beside his simple grave in the monk's cemetery at Gethsemani, we acknowledge to each other that we are ready to die at this instant, in this place. But we do not know the time of our ending, do we? In that burning moment, standing hand-in-hand by the side of that small cross, we dare to imagine a new beginning. Often we think of death, of that day when one will precede the other, or die together in each other's arms. We may be in the same canoe on a wild river in Kentucky. We may see the white water ahead, as if with one eye, knowing for a certainty that our end has come. Or we could hope that lightning might strike us as we lightly place our hands upon Merton's cross. Or no such theater will occur, and we will simply look longingly at each other from separate beds pulled close together in ancient, anxious time. Whatever our demise, may it happen by riverside. And may that New Orleans jazz band return from the gravesites, may they be playing "When the Saints Go Marching In." May everybody set their tears aside, and may they laugh and laugh and laugh.

In northwestern Washington County, Chaplin River empties into Beech Fork, which flows into Rolling Fork River in Nelson County. The terms "river" and "fork" are interchangeable in the minds of those who are loyal to Beech Fork, for if *it's* not a river, how can Chaplin be called a river? There is no rule, no rhyme, no reason. Kentucky streams acquire their names through long usage—once a name sticks, it usually stays.

The Chaplin originates between Parksville Knob and Chestnut Grove Ridge west of Parksville in Boyle County. The river moves northwest, picking up Buck Creek before passing directly through the community of Perryville. Doctors Fork and Bull Run empty into the Chaplin near the site of the Battle of Perryville, where, on October 8, 1862, Confederate General Braxton Bragg and his forces met the army of Union Major General Don Carlos Buell. The two generals were doomed to remember thereafter the slaughter of 1,355 men, each side suffering more than

2,000 wounded. The battle, the largest of the Civil War in Kentucky, is sometimes called the Battle of Chaplin Hills.

Who was the victor? Who the vanquished? It was said to have been a victory for Buell and the North, for it was the last major battle of the Civil War in Kentucky. Psychologically, it may have ended vaingloriously for the South, the survivors limping home to taste again the water from the springhouses that had nurtured them in the beginning. Many now knew that it would be only a matter of time until the Chaplin would again flow without the blood of such a horror as the Battle of Chaplin Hills.

Kentucky novelist and poet Elizabeth Madox Roberts was born in Perryville. *The Great Meadow* was her historical novel of the founding of Kentucky. "There's a river through the land, he told us, a deep river with banks that make a sharp cliff in the white limestone, trees and growth over the hills. He said it was one of the wonders of the world, a river you might travel halfway over the earth to see, a wonder. He said it was called Chenoa, or Cho-na-no-no. Or some called it Millewakane," the Indian names for the river that would later be called the "Louisa" by Dr. Thomas Walker and in time be named "The Kentucky." The University Press of Kentucky has now reissued Roberts' out-of-print novel *The Time of Man*. As Robert Penn Warren has written: "By the time of her death in 1941, Elizabeth Madox Roberts had lived past her reputation and her popularity. Now she is remembered only by those who read her in their youth when she was new, and news. The youth of today do not even know her name." The challenge and the saving grace is to reintroduce the name of the school teacher whose passion for writing flowed in midlife from Kentucky to the University of Chicago and back to Kentucky again. The cycle of water brought her home.

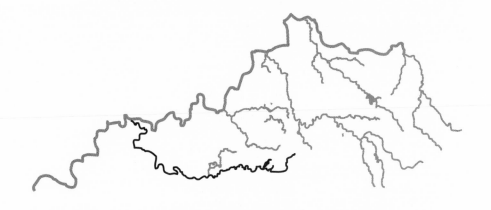

Green

...Right through the middle of this acreage,
right through the front yard in fact, a sparkling, clear, rushing little creek
known as Spout Springs Branch made its way.

Janice Holt Giles
A Little Better than Plumb

Spout Springs Branch murmurs into the Green River one mile south of
KY 76, about two miles on a direct line southeast from the Dulworth
community, a little more than two miles down the road from Knifley.
(Local residents say "Nifley," but they don't seem to mind when
outsiders intrude the "K" sound.) Janice Holt Giles, author of *The
Enduring Hills, The Kentuckians, Hannah Fowler, The Believers,* and
twenty other books is buried in Caldwell Chapel Cemetery near the
intersection of KY 1104 and the Ray Williams Road at the headwaters of
Spout Springs Branch. She was born March 28, 1905, in Altus,
Arkansas. One of Kentucky's most prolific writers, Janice Holt Giles
attended Transylvania College and worked for a time at the Louisville
Presbyterian Seminary. In 1943, she met her second husband, Henry
Giles, when he boarded a bus she was on in Bowling Green. They
corresponded during the war. Married two years later, they eventually

built a rambling cabin on the edge of Spout Springs Branch. "The only way I looked at the branch was with love," Giles wrote in her 1963 book *A Little Better than Plumb*.

Jim R. Dowing, born in 1837 in Ohio, was a Union soldier, survivor of Gettysburg and Andersonville. In his *Uncle Jim's Green River Diary*: September 1894, he wrote: "Green River is a beautiful stream of nice clear water winding in and out through the hills and bluffs of Kentucky. Sometimes it gets on a big tear and is not so clear and nice....The river is mostly fed by springs and little glens that run back into the hills a short distance. The water is generally soft and cool, good to drink any time."

There are flood times when love turns more to sobering respect, sometimes fear, sometimes loathing, but usually something short of hating. The Mennonite and Amish communities of Casey County understand this relationship. They practice pacifism, and they are rooted deeply in their adopted land.

On the South Fork of the Green River, east of Knifley between Teddy and Phil, Mennonite children walk and ride their bicycles home from school. The expressions on the faces, old before their time, seem on the edge of smiling. There is no pent-up laughter, no raucous behavior. No cigarettes dangling from their mouths or cupped secretly in the palms of their hands. Four small boys, ages nine to eleven, work on cleaning out a fencerow. There's a rhythm in the swinging of their manly scythes. Further on, three girls, ages eleven to thirteen, fork manure into a wagon. In the bottomland, a stalwart youth, tall and lithe with especially narrow hips and broad shoulders, balances on the small extension of a plow pulled by three horses. Outside a greenhouse, where a woman takes down drying garments from a circular clothesline, a child steps forward to receive an armload. He takes them into the house. No one is being punished for wrongdoing. Work is part of life at the headwaters of Green.

In a leather shop, a farmer has arrived by horse and buggy. He is looking for a piece of rubber pipe. "Will the plowed ground be used for tobacco crops?"

"No," he replies, gently. "We'd rather plant something to eat."

Green River rises south of Stanford in Lincoln County, then flows
westerly and northwesterly for 360-370 miles, cutting through the center
of Mammoth Cave National Park. In the northeast corner of the
sprawling park, the Green crosses from Hart into Edmunson County,
very near Crystal Cave.

Great Onyx Cave lies around the next bend. A myriad of underground
streams—Bretz, Candlelight, Crystal, Echo, Hanson's Lost, Hidden,
Logsdon, Houchin's Lost, Stevenson's Lost, River Styx—feed the Green
River and give it much of its unusual character and coloration.

Above the bend at Morgantown, memories of the old steamboat days
are alive in the Main Street home of a music teacher, "Miss" Ione Duke.
She's ninety-five years old. "Would you like to hear me play?" she asks,
reaching for her neatly organized sheet music.

"Yes, Ma'am, we would."

She walks on a straight line to the only upright Steinway in Butler
County. She slides onto the bench, straightens her back, and sits as tall as
her tiny frame will allow. "Miss" Ione elevates "Rock of Ages" and
"Blessed Assurance" through variations to make a body wonder that
such simple hymns could be so intricately beautiful. Miss Ione has spent
her life teaching music to the children of Butler, Ohio, and Webster
Counties. She has played them all—trombone, cello, violin, clarinet,
saxophone, and trumpet—but the piano is her passion. Chopin is her
favorite classical composer, but somebody else is her choice when
conversations turn to the days on the steamboats huffing and puffing
their twisting way from Evansville to Bowling Green. Scott Joplin!
"Maple Leaf Rag" fills the room on Main Street in Morgantown, and
there's a joyful rhythm in Miss Ione's shoulders, her slender fingers
finding the keys with the blessed assurance of a woman who loves many
kinds of music and holds dear the desire to share them all.

"Twelfth Street Rag," "Chicken Reel," "Peppermint Twist"—the
ragtime notes roll from the tip of her toes through her heart to the
keyboard of the stately piano. The floor, the walls of the house, and the
air inside the room vibrate. "I believe you just need something to keep
you going. You can sit down and fuss, but nobody wants to hear that.

Music will boost my morale," she smiles.

Each year, on the second Saturday in April, friends come for Miss Ione to take her to Onton, a little Green River town in Webster County. The lady who plays everything from "Rock of Ages" to "Maple Leaf Rag" had her first public teaching job in Onton. A reunion there wouldn't be a reunion without Miss Ione Duke to play the old songs. The larger community of Morgantown might be just another "go along to get along" Green River town if it hadn't been for the far-reaching life of Ione Duke and her upright piano. "It is fitting and proper to accord official recognition of Mrs. Duke, who has 'made a difference' in the cultural structure of the children she has taught," reads the proclamation signed in 1998 by Morgantown Mayor Charles Black and Butler County judge/executive David R. Martin. The difference can be seen, for example, in the lives of the graduates of the Children's Choir at the Morgantown United Methodist Church, although Miss Ione says, "I like to visit all churches."

She's been the chaplain and almost every other officer in the Butler County DAR. She received the "Rural Woman of the Year" award at the Louisville Conference of the United Methodist Women. Her long list of community involvement spans twenty-eight years as secretary and president of the Morgantown Women's Civic League, which oversees the care and direction of Riverview Cemetery, arising symbolically correct at the end of Main Street. "Do you remember seeing 'Sally's Rock?'"

"Yes. She'd be there to greet the boats," says Miss Ione of the legendary Sally Beck, who before Miss Ione was born, stood with her megaphone and shouted out the news from atop the promontory at the confluence of the Gasper and Barren Rivers. Ione Duke has played a variation of the theme of Sally Beck, both women reaching out to others, fulfilling their own distinctive callings.

"Do you play the piano every day?"

"I can tell the difference when I don't play."

The difference is communication beginning with a simple megaphone, coming of age on a keyboard, yearning to be a mighty chorus down by riverside.

The Green empties into the Ohio River just north of Henderson, the confluence about 197 miles from the meeting of the Ohio and Mississippi rivers. The Green River's main tributaries include Barren, Little Barren, Rough, Nolin, Mud, and Pond Rivers. Rangers Landing, Quinn Landing, Steamport Landing, and Roland Landing mark a long, graceful loop of the Green River along the western border of McLean County. The Green has been called the "deepest little river" in North America, its depth measured at two hundred feet between the mouth of Rough River and the Long Falls. Green River drains the Western Kentucky Coal Fields and the Pennyroyal region, named for the aromatic Eurasian mint.

On the Green, near the mouth of Rough, two small houses stand today on the site of the "Livermore Lynching," April 20, 1911. A black man named Will Porter or (Potter) shot a white man, Frank Mitchell. The sheriff arrested the black man and, according to a report in the *New York Times*, locked him up in the basement of "the opera house." A mob of fifty men took the prisoner to the upstairs stage, and there they lynched him. Other accounts appearing in Kentucky newspapers said the mob charged admission to view the lynching. Persons in the orchestra seats were allowed "to empty their guns." Those in the balcony were permitted only one shot (likely an embellishment, because the building was not an opera house in classic construction, and the enforcement of who was entitled to do what would probably have resulted in bedlam). No matter how much yellow journalism was involved, a lynching did occur, and after the N.A.A.C.P. protested to President Taft and Governor Willson, the mob leaders were arrested, but all were quickly acquitted.

Eighty-nine years later, the ladies working at the Livermore community library say they have not heard of the lynching, but they are helpful in locating the *McLean County Pictorial History, 1854-1992*. On page 75, beneath a picture of "the opera house," is the following account:

This Livermore building has served many purposes. It was
last known as the ACA (American Co-Op Association) building.

*It was located across the street from the Preston Hotel. The
hardwood floor upstairs was once a skating rink, filled nightly
with eager skaters. At other times it was a mill, grocery,
nickolodian, Whitaker's Operahouse, and a poolroom. The
nickolodian was a place to see movies for 5-cents. On April 20,
1911, Clarence Mitchell was killed. Wm Potter was arrested
and held in the operahouse. A mob of three hundred men
stormed the theater, killing Potter. Wilbur Calhoun razed the
building after 1940 and built three homes out of the material.*

No one is in sight at the houses occupying the spot where the hellish
thing happened eighty-nine years ago. The decision is not to knock on
the doors. Maybe we're cowardly. Maybe we wonder what will be
accomplished by asking old questions. We move on. Main Street in
Livermore is quiet and the Livermore Lynching is only a mention in
books on seldom-read shelves of history.

The nearby bridge, dedicated sixty years ago and remembered in
Ripley's Believe It or Not, begins in McLean County, crosses a point of
Ohio County, and ends back in McLean County. The bridge spans two
rivers, the Green and the Rough. The bridge is claimed to be unique in the
world. The steamboats are all gone, along with the happy times and the
bad times. The Livermore Bridge is remembered with a historical marker,
and the Livermore Lynching is a footnote in the annals of Green River.

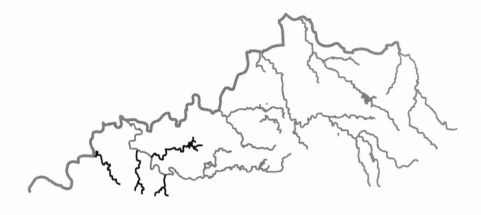

Pond, Rough, Mud, and Tradewater

You are a damned rough butcher, But cut on and be damned.

Micaja "Big" Harpe
His last words (maybe)
Harpe's Hill
August 1799

Harpe's Hill (also spelled Harp's) is the spot in western Muhlenberg County, less than half a mile from Pond River, where a posse caught up with the murderous, bloody Harpe brothers, Micaja "Big" Harpe and Wiley "Little" Harpe. It was in the last year of the eighteenth century, the year that Jacques Louis David painted the "Rape of the Sabines," but hardly anything could compare with the heinous crimes of the Harpe brothers in Kentucky. Accounts vary in details, but the legend has been repeated so often that much of it has become a part of the accepted background of the Commonwealth. The Harpes are believed to have been responsible for the deaths of at least thirty men, women, and children (including "Big" Harpe's own child). The total number of victims will never be known.

Micaja and Wiley were born in the frontier wilds of North Carolina,

163

"Big" Harpe about 1768, "Little" Harpe some two years later. According to Rothert's *The Outlaws of Cave-In-Rock*, the Harpe brothers began their trail of bloodletting in eastern Tennessee, and it stretched all the way to the infamous outlaw lair, Cave-In-Rock, on the Illinois side of the Ohio River across from present-day Crittenden County, Kentucky, about fifty miles upstream from Paducah. Seeming to find precious pleasure, perhaps perverted vindication by killing even the appearance of innocence, Micaja and Wiley moved northwestward through Kentucky, crisscrossing Pond River, a stream looping, snaking, letting go, and snapping like a sweating, hurried, hangman's noose. The mouth of Pond River is at Jewel City in Hopkins County, where the tortuous stream finally gives up its ghosts and empties into Green River.

On the night of August 20, 1799, about fives miles east of Dixon in present-day Webster County, the Harpe brothers used an ax to bash out the brains of a man sleeping in the loft of Moses Stegall's cabin. They slit the throat of the four-month-old Stegall baby boy, stabbed to death Mrs. Stegall, and set the house on fire. When Moses Stegall, who was absent at the time, learned what had happened, he gathered a posse and gave chase to "Big" and "Little" Harpe. Back and forth across Pond River—a tortuously, wearily narrow rope of a waterway forming the boundaries between Christian and Muhlenberg, Hopkins and Muhlenberg, and Hopkins and McLean Counties—the hunters and the hunted rode onward like the angels of Hell. No mercy. Not any.

The end of the chase is described in excruciating detail in Lyman C. Draper's *The Western Literary and Historical Magazine*, one of the sources used by Otto A. Rothert in *Outlaws of Cave-In-Rock*.

> *Harpe lay on the ground upon his right side, unable from weakness to raise himself, and rapidly ebbing his life away-Steigal* [there are various spellings] *stepped forward and pointed the muzzle of his gun at the head of the expiring outlaw* [Micaja 'Big' Harpe]*, who conscious of the intention, and desirous at least of procrastinating it dodged his head to and fro with an agility unexpected to the beholders, manifesting pretty plainly a strong disrelish 'to shuffle off this mortal coil.'*

*Perceiving this, Steigal observed, 'very well, I believe I will not
upon reflection shoot him in the head, but I want to preserve
that as a trophy;' and thereupon shot him in the left side—and
Harpe almost instantly expired without a struggle or a groan.
Steigal, with the knife he had so menacingly exhibited to Harpe,
now cut off the outlaw's head....Thus died Big Harpe, long the
terror of the west, and his decapitated body was left in the wilds
of Muhlenberg county, as unsepulchred as his merited death
was unwept and unmourned."*

After two hundred years, the bloodstains have been blotted out,
washed away by Pond River flash floods. The only traces remaining are
in the printed and oral histories passed down from generation to
generation. Moses Stegall placed "Big" Harpe's head in a saddlebag and
returned it to a place about three miles north of what would become the
Webster County seat, Dixon, where the object was put on public display,
and that location became known as Harpe's Head. Nowadays, this
precise place is next to impossible to pinpoint with irrefutable accuracy.
Legends are seldom improved with exactitude. According to the Draper
account, "...a superstitious old lady of the neighborhood, some member
of whose family was afflected with fits, having been told that the human
skull pulverized, would effect a certain cure, thus appropriated that of
the memorable outlaw of the west."

If there's something to be learned from this tale, it could be that life is
much like Pond River—defiled, doubled upon itself, dreadful in time of
frequent irrationality—in sharp contrast to Green River, for example,
with its deeper, more graceful nature. We have a saying here on Plum
Lick that something really awful "sucks pond water." Lilies stagnate.
Frogs strangle. Livestock muck up. In winter, cows and calves fall
through and drown. The nature of ponded thinking is that it doesn't
flow, doesn't cleanse itself except by stubborn, stupified evaporation. It
may be time to take a fresh look at the "Harpe Brothers" and what their
lives signify in an age when violence is standard fare on television and
in movies.

Rothert and other historians have called the motive of Moses Stegall into question: Why was he not at home the night of August 20, 1799? Did he know the Harpes? Was there a connection? An arrangement, real or implied? Was there twisted retribution? Did the Harpe brothers have reason to retaliate? Were Micaja and Wiley actually brothers? Who were the women claiming to be their wives—Susanna, Betsey, and Sally? What became of their children? Did Moses decapitate Big Harpe to keep him from talking after he was shot? (There have been conflicting accounts of whether he died of gunshot wounds.) And, after "Little" Wiley was captured, convicted, and hanged at "Gallows Field" in Mississippi "until he was dead, dead, dead" (as required by law), why was it necessary to decapitate *him*? A portion of frontier justice, to impale a head on a pole or lodge it in the fork of a tree as a warning to others? Such warnings hardly diminished the violence of Manifest Destiny. Was violence natural to the "Dark and Bloody Ground?" Was violence merely imported from North Carolina and Tennessee?

If capital punishment was barbaric in 1799, is it any more humane today? Lethal injection an improved method? Better than gas? Better than the electric chair, the firing squad, the gallows, the guillotine, for God's sake? We ask because we're as troubled as we are uncertain. A "Big" and "Little" Harpe, then and now, must be answered, must they not? Or should they be appeased, swept down a winding river of indifference? Reconciled as savage oddities feeding morbid curiosity? Eye for an eye? Life in prison or rehabilitation?

We have no answers.

The Ohio receives the Tradewater River at Caseyville and a short distance downstream is the ferry to Cave-In-Rock on the Illinois side. *The Outlaws of Cave-In-Rock*, is a winter-reading addition to our library shelves on Plum Lick. Written in 1924 by the then secretary of The Filson Club, Otto A. Rothert sets forth his purpose: "It [Cave-In-Rock] became a natural, safe hiding-place for the pirates who preyed on the flatboat traffic before the days of steamboats....The historian who passes them over [the murderous Harpe brothers] as mere blood-and-thunder tales misses entirely one of the high lights in the great adventure of the settling of the Mississippi basin."

Rough River "begins" at Head of Rough Spring just north of Saint John Road in Hardin County. The headwaters descend from the north-northeast in Nalls Valley, where the stream goes underground and emerges at the spring. Rough is quickly joined by Mays Run, which moves down from the eastern slope of Losenville Valley. The spring is not far from the home of Willis and Lottie Willyard at Blueball Hill, the highest point in Hardin County (1,017 feet).

Before the snowstorm in February 1998, Mr. Willyard agreed to be the guide for a visit to Head of Rough Spring. We sit with Lottie for a while on the closed-in side porch. We do not discuss Bill Clinton and Monica Lewinsky. We do, however, discuss a cow that refused to be loaded for the slaughterhouse. She went berserk, ripped through a double-gated holding pen, tore down a bunch of fences, and didn't finally settle down until she was back with the herd.

We touch on Punxsutawney Phil, a whistle pig if ever there was one. We equate "Ground Hog Day" with another pseudo-event, the Chincoteague ponies of Virginia, driven by volunteer firemen more than by "wild" stages of the moon. Willis and Lottie are not even a little bit interested in new ways of getting up crowds. As for what the weather may be on any given day, Mr. Willyard says, "Listen to the forecasters, then look up."

The talk turns to gates and latches. Willis knows how to weld, and he has made his gates to last a lifetime. The main thing about Willis's gates is that they don't sag like most of our Plum Lick farm gates. You don't have to muscle the Willyard gates in the opening or the closing. They swing like a gate ought to swing—free and easy. As for the latches, they're a miracle of ingenuity. It's hard to explain but here goes: There's a horizontal pin on the opposite end from the hinges, the fastening part. In the post, there's a device with a smaller pin, which holds a sturdy ring. When the gate closes, the horizontal pin strikes the ring, spins it around, and the gate is locked. It won't open until the ring is lifted manually. It belongs in the Smithsonian, but they've got other stuff and probably wouldn't take a second look at a farm gate that works every time in Hardin County, Kentucky.

We drive over the Vine Grove-Blueball Road and into Nalls Valley on the Salem School Road. We look at the large sinkholes where the fields resemble deflated balloons more than any pattern of simple holes in the ground. Water here finds it easier to travel under the ground than on top of it. It emerges beneath a rugged rock castle just off the St. John Road. With May's Run joining within a short distance, another river of Kentucky is off to New Orleans.

Rough continues south through the community of Vertrees, and shortly thereafter Vertrees Creek empties in. Rough River Dam is located on KY 79, southwest of the community of Axtel in Breckinridge County. Rough River Lake is an impoundment of 5,000 acres. Rough forms the entire southern border of Breckinridge County and the northern border of Grayson County.

Historian Hugh Ridenour has traced the lives of the Green family of Falls of Rough during the period 1795-1965, an era of vast land holdings, political connections, and young people astride their Shetland ponies. For the white establishment it was Camelot. Falls of Rough is located on KY 110 (or 80) in the southwestern corner of Breckinridge County. It can also be accessed by Tick Ridge Road. The river rounds Hog Knob and turns south to the community of Hites Falls before heading westerly to Davidson Station, which is located on the north side of the L.B. Davidson Wildlife Management Area. Rough passes along the edges of the communities of Narrows and Dundee, then heads south toward Dukehurst and Hartford, the county seat of Ohio County. Rough empties into Green River at Livermore.

Mud River is thirty-five miles long. It begins east of Russellville and west of Auburn in Logan County. Before the Civil War, the tightly winding stream was called "Muddy River" and "Big Muddy River." Near its beginning it once supplied the water for Hancock Lake, then twists its way to the north-northwest to the juncture of Logan, Muhlenberg, and Butler Counties.

The tributaries of Mud include Town Branch, flowing through Russellville. Not unlike the Town Branch cutting through the heart of

Lexington in the Bluegrass Region, this festering stream was once an open sewer playing a major role in spreading the Asiatic cholera epidemic of 1833.

The Russellville area is the birthplace of Alice Allison Dunnigan, born April 27, 1906, the first female African American White House correspondent. She wrote *The Fascinating Story of Black Kentuckians: Their Heritage and Traditions.* Her autobiography, *Alice A. Dunnigan: A Black Woman's Experience*, describes the night in 1963 in Frankfort, Kentucky, when she represented President John F. Kennedy's Committee on Equal Employment Opportunity. Refused public lodging, she sat up all night at the bus station. Alice Allison Dunnigan died May 6, 1983, and is buried in Maryland National Memorial Park.

Mud River is among the most twisting of streams. It forms the Muhlenberg-Butler County line to a point just west of Rochester, where it empties into the Green River. Other tributaries of the Mud include Larman Creek, Chick Creek, Motts Lick Creek, and McAdoo Creek. Near the juncture of these latter two streams is the site of Lost City (also known as the Page site) near Lewisburg in Logan County. In 1929, an archeological team from the University of Kentucky discovered here "one of the largest prehistoric Native American mound groups in Kentucky." *The Kentucky Encyclopedia* is a starting point for the trail leading to theories about Lost City, but the actual location is literally lost. W.S. Webb and W.D. Funkhouser's *The Page Site* is a valuable source of additional information. In the first and second centuries there were "three distinct cultures [who] inhabited the area during the Mississippian Period." On the Geologic Time Scale, the Mississippian Period predates human history. The Paleoindian Period covers 10,000-7,000 B.C. The Late Prehistoric Period begins about 900 A.D. Throughout each of these periods, the same hydrologic cycles worked as are working now. We recall Kentucky poet Langdon "Denver" Smith (1858-1908):

When you were a tadpole and I was a fish,

> *In the Paleozoic time,*
> *And side by side on the ebbing tide*
> *We sprawled through the ooze and slime.*

We check in with A.B. Willhite, local historian, at his home north of Russellville on the Cooperstown Road. Drought has withered the cornfields, and the sound of our footsteps on the burned up weeds crackles with the rush of granddaddy and grandmammy grasshoppers. "Mud River comes out of the ground and goes back into the ground, and when you're at Mud River Church you're actually standing on top of Mud River," says Mr. Willhite. His waxed and trimmed handlebar moustache tenses and twitches (almost as gracefully as Winslow Homer's, but not quite) as he talks about Logan County's early and more recent history of violence, problems of alcohol, family disputes, hearts of gold and hands of greed. Eighteenth- and nineteenth-century preacher men called it "Rogue's Harbor," famous for its tales of thievery and worse, a frontier haven for the lawless after the Revolutionary and Civil Wars. Some of it spilled over into the twentieth cenutry.

There are few private archives the likes of A.B. Willhite's, maybe none anywhere. Volumes and volumes of local histories fill two trailers behind his house, books alphabetized on steel shelves, newspaper clippings galore, a dependable copy machine, a computer, and an antique printing and binding operation in a barn. Mr. Willhite has a steel-trap memory—the stories he spiels are rich in saucy detail and tonality. "You know, when I was a kid, my Uncle Oscar taught me how to make whiskey, but he never taught me how to drink it. He would say a lot of times, 'They was two fellers in Lewisburg, one of them owned most ever'thing of any value at one time. The other, he lived there in a little old shack, looked worse than my trailer here, kinda leaning over sideways, hair usually down around his ears. He was kinda the feller that was the professional drunk. The preacher's son was the bootlegger, rode around in a new red Ford when ever'body else had a black one, and he wore a big Stetson hat.' And Uncle Oscar said, 'Now you can kinda look at the difference between a drunk and a bootlegger and make up your mind which one you want to be.'"

A.B. Willhite became a storyteller. He believes Jesse James got too much credit for every little incident. "Course, you know that Jesse James didn't have any way to get around except that old horse, and if he would have stopped and eat supper with ever'body's grandpa that would tell you that he come by and eat supper with his grandpa, that old horse would have looked like a basset hound—he'd had his legs pulled out so short."

Jesse James didn't get any credit for what happened in the twentieth century because he went to see his Lord in 1882. From that time until now, a long line of latter-day Robin Hoods and other redistributors of wealth have come and gone, each one caught in a complex web of thinking about what is right and what is wrong. "Two fellers with sacks over their heads—holes cut out for their eyes—had come into this grocery store over in Hopkinsville. 'Squeeky' was one of the two fellers. The other was his brother. Squeeky was the nickname given due to the high pitch of voice that he had. Squeeky had a voice that nobody heard anybody else that sounded like him."

A.B. Willhite warms to the telling. The handlebar moustache quivers.

"The first thing that they ever got caught robbing was the bank at Orlando, Tennessee. But Squeeky's brother said it was just not profitable to rob banks because they didn't have the money where you could get aholt of it. And if you hit a supermarket on a Friday night, they had money there to cash all them paychecks, had quite a bit of cash, so he liked supermarkets better. And I think that was what he did most of his time in the penitentiary for.

"At Hopkinsville, forgot the name of the store, but they robbed that store, and when they was robbing it, a woman was paying for her groceries and Squeeky walked up behind her and told everybody about the gun in his hand. Squeeky's brother was over at another cash register and they said it was a robbery and they wanted their money. When the woman ahead of Squeeky heard him, she didn't pay attention to what he said so much, just the voice. She spoke to him and asked him, 'How's your mama doin'? and how are you doin'? and he replied that things were not going too good for him. They got the money and went on out and the cashier asked, 'Do you know that man?'

"She said, 'Yeah, that's Squeeky. I went to school with 'im.'

"Said, 'Well, he just robbed the store.'"

"Said, 'Well, they done that before.' And so she went on and told about some other things they'd robbed.

"Squeeky and his brother left Christian County on Butler Road and they run off in a ditch out near Honey Grove, and they jumped out of that car and run over there to a widder woman's house and got her Plymouth, a '41 Plymouth, it was kinda rust-colored. And that's what they were driving when they come through Russellville out at the corner of 9th and Nashville Street, which is what we call around here the four-way stop, even though the four-way stop had been gone, there's been a light there since 1956 or seven. They come through there and they never meant to hurt anybody, but that's where they shot one of the dep'ty sheriffs here. One of the bullets hit old Clyde Darden—just took the top of his ear off. They dropped in behind Mud River Church out there, jumped out of the old car and started running. And that's when ever'body that had a gun went out there and shot all the ammunition they had shootin' that widder woman's car, just shot it all to pieces. I bet you that thing had two or three hundred holes in it. Course, they were well gone before they started shooting at it, made a lot of racket, and ever'body got a few shots at the old car, and ruined the woman's car.

"And they got some bloodhounds. It was getting on towards daylight the next morning and I hadn't been out of the army too long then and pretty good shape to walk. Helped 'em walk some of the bloodhounds, wound up over yonder on the railroad track and followed the railroad track back on down and across Stephenson Mill Road, got on out just before you get to highway 79 out here where the rock quarry crusher is now, wasn't there then. And I heard somebody down there, sounded like—'ugh-eek'—you know, cleared their throat a little, and them bloodhounds was wanting so bad to go down there, but George Shifflett had aholt of the reins of the bloodhounds then, and those bloodhounds couldn't drag old George off the railroad tracks. He made sure they wouldn't come on down the railroad track there toward Jackson's Crossing on into town. He didn't let 'em go down there."

"So they didn't catch them?"

"Naw, naw. They didn't catch 'em."

172

"How much money do you think they got?"

"Don't remember, but it was a sizable amount of money for that time, because I have the piece out of the paper that tells what it was that they got, pretty good bit of money for back then."

"Hundred dollars?"

"Naw, naw, it got on up to five thousand or something like that. I've got the paper that tells what it was. Seems to me they got less than a thousand dollars when they robbed the bank in Orlando, and that was the first thing they ever got kinda caught in."

"They both went to prison?"

"They both went to prison for robbing the bank in Orlando, and they went to prison over that deal in Hopkinsville, but they had just gotten out of prison when they robbed that store in Hopkinsville. I know they went as many as three times, and I think they went more times than that to prison through the years.

"Were they friendly sorts, or mean-spirited?"

"No, un-un, both of them was real good painters, real good. That whole family were extremely good painters and good paperhangers. They hung paper in some of the most prominent people's houses in Logan County. And they all liked 'em. They could go to the Citizens National Bank and borrow money anytime they wanted to. If they promised you something, they'd do it. I think they were just well-mannered and well-liked, I don't know. I quess it was just like people get a craving for things, they kinda wanted to rob banks or rob stores."

"They're both dead now?"

"Yessir. Squeeky was the one that was murdered in Warren County. Some bookie out of Louisville had hired him to collect. Well, Squeeky was doing a pretty good job of collecting and not doing too good of a job of turning the money over. Their grandmother was Thursday, just like the day of the week. Their grandfather was Wick. He lived in Adairville and he was pretty overbearing. He'd go down to the bar and usually on the way home he'd go by this old man where he was sittin' on the front porch and give him a cussin' and try to stir up trouble with him. So one night he went by the old man's house and badmouthed him a little. He just got down off of the porch with a baseball bat and beat him to death.

Wick's brother got mad about the situation and he come through Adairville shooting his pistol up in the air and the marshall chased him out of Adairville and they found the both of them out here on the west branch of Red River. The marshal was laying in the road, dead, and the other man was draped across the fence where he was—shot him off the horse, and he fell across the fence. And they killed each other.

"Would you say Logan County has been unusually violent?"

"In the early years, yes. In my lifetime, probably been a lot more murders in Muhlenberg County as there has in Logan. There was coal mines and union strikes and things like that. But in the early years most of your early people that came in here were running from something. They was either on the wrong side of the law or the wrong side of the Revolution. Course lot of these people that was on the wrong side of the Revolution worked their way into society. They just didn't one day say, 'This thing is over and we're all friends again,' you know that. Just like in the Civil War, lot of people wanted to change their name and all of that and not be kin to their brother and cousin that was on the other side. You can imagine it had to be the same way in the Revolution."

When we leave A.B. Willhite, a storm rolls across Cooperstown Road, and rain begins to fall, the first real rain in the drought of 2000. The grasshoppers are soggy, bulging eyes blinking, and we've a notion to take a closer look at Mud River. Looking down from the eastern side of Stephenson Mill Road, the stream is a foot to a foot and a half deep, perfectly clear to the stone bottom. In the flow of shallow water there were seventeen plastic gallon jugs and five empty wooden cable spools. Beer cans, pop cans, and styrofoam fast food containers littered the bridge, a sight repeated again and again across the Commonwealth. To litter a highway is one thing; to litter a stream of water is contaminating a God-given life support system.

You know, Billy T., there's lots of folks that don't have
any idea of where they belong.

James D. Ausenbaugh

Tradewater River is rich in nineteenth-century transportation lore, largely buried and forgotten in the modern webs of jet trails, rail lines, and interstate highways. Time was when coal, timber, tobacco, bourbon, and saltpeter were floated down Tradewater to the Ohio. Bootleggers devised a simple and ingenious strategy for staying ahead of revenuers. Stills were built on boats, which in turn were lashed to the bank. When the law moved in, ropes were cut and the moonshiners floated downstream.

It was a time when ladies with parasols and gentlemen in frock coats went for Sunday cruises on Tradewater. All of this is gone. But the stream, which had become unnavigable and so polluted that it no longer supported aquatic life, so drawn into itself that at times people could walk across it without getting their feet wet, has benefited from public concern. Today, at Dawson Springs, Betty Wagner Lafoon and her family have donated to the city a twelve-acre park with a wide, arching wooden pedestrian bridge and a mill dam in memory of Mrs. Lafoon's husband, Richard, "to be re-developed to equal and surpass its original greatness." It's a rare testimony to civic duty and pride on the Tradewater River, where there's a ballpark, "Home of the Tradewater Pirates," and a place for families to picnic on greenswards where trees reach across the stream, sharing leaves, shading the glen.

It was a Sunday in March, still too cold for picnics, but time enough for brave souls to fish in places quietly guarded by those who know where to go and what to do. Vending machines have appeared near the Tradewater, where an Isaac Walton (seventeenth century author of *The Compleat Angler*) could put in $1.75 and take out crappie minnows. Or $2.75 and what emerge are premium night crawlers. Leeches require $2.75, meal worms, $2.00. Should Isaac care to splurge, catfish dough bait costs $3.50.

The beginning of Tradewater River belongs to Buntin Lake south of

175

Kelly in Christian County. The stream flows to the northwest toward
Dawson Springs. Between Buntin Lake and Dawson Springs,
Tradewater gathers Dripping Spring Branch, Brushy Fork, Whitehorn
Creek, Sandlick Creek, Castleberry Creek, Morgan Creek, Sugar Creek,
McKnight Creek, and Buffalo Creek. The area between the Western
Kentucky Coal Field and the Pennyroyal is called the Dripping Springs
Escarpment, a subregion of sinkholes and disappearing waters in a web
of shallow cave systems.

The main stream forms the northern edge of the Tradewater Wildlife
Management Area and the Pennyrile State Forest. The overflow of Lake
Beshear freshens the river, which passes along the south side of Dawson
Springs, birthplace of retired Kentucky journalist, educator, and author
James D. Ausenbaugh. He graduated from high school in Nebo at the
headwaters of Rose Creek, which feeds into Weirs Creek, which joins
Clear Creek, which empties into the Tradewater close to Hickory Ridge
near the corners of four counties: Hopkins, Webster, Caldwell, and
Crittenden. The river, unmindful of courthouse conventions and structured
journalism curricula, continues northwesterly—twisting, turning, looping,
like a natural-born junkyard dog reporter baring her or his teeth for a
story. James D. Ausenbaugh, a member of the Kentucky Journalism Hall
of Fame, is seventy-three years old, and he's "getting burial expense
notices like I'd died, or something."
   "What do you remember about the Tradewater, Jim?"
   "The Tradewater was a favorite swimming hole for us boys in the
1930s. Our mothers would have fainted away if they had known about
our spot on a sweeping river curve and our rope swing tied high up in a
tree on the bank. We would fly far out and drop into the swirling water."
   The "good old days" on the Tradewater have passed by, and there are
relatively few in the state today who know there is, or ever was, such a
river. It earned only two paragraphs in *The Kentucky Encylopedia*.
"Tradewater" does not appear in the index to *A New History of
Kentucky*. A separate history could be written, with *Tradewater* as the
possible title. The most recent one was published thirteen years ago—
George B. Simpson's *Early Coal Mining on the Tradewater River*. "I

don't know the details of improvements to the river," writes Ausenbaugh. "But I do know that it was a wonderful stream in my boyhood, that it became a Dead Sea of coppery water (probably caused by underground mining, not strip-mining), and that in recent years it has been restored, at least to some degree."

Tradewater forms the Caldwell-Hopkins County line, where the tributaries include Montgomery Creek, North Fork, and East Fork. The region is dotted with springs—Beshear, Gibb, Cap, Chapel, Fork, Howton, and Lick Creek Spring.

Tradewater River forms the northern tip of the Caldwell-Webster County line, then the Crittenden-Webster County line, and the Crittenden-Union County line., The final tributaries include Cypress Creek, sometimes called "Cypress River."

Local journalist John Lucas lives on Tradewater Bottoms Road. "I've held on with determination to my little ninety-acre place here on the Tradewater River. Every day as I came down Rosebud Hill toward home, I could literally feel the pressures and stress of the job (*The Crittenden Press*) being stripped away and left behind. As one visitor said one day when he stopped as I was working in the yard and orchard, 'This is theraputic' (meaning the place). I thought, yes, and I've made it that way on purpose. Poor folks have got to work, though, and I guess now I've got to suck in my gut and get on with it. I've accepted a reporting job with *The Evansville* (Ind.) *Courier* covering western Kentucky for them. It will enable me to continue to live here on the farm. I look at it though with a little trepidation knowing that what is 'news' is tragedy. Nine thousand nine-hundred and ninety-nine people safely crossing the street is not news, it's the one who got run down mid-street by the semi which is."

Twisting and turning from Buntin Lake in Christian County, sixty-seven miles later Tradewater empties into the Ohio south of Caseyville between Poplar Ridge and Cedar Point, where the Ohio bends gracefully to shape the easternmost part of Shawnee National Forest in Illinois.

Barren, Little Barren, Gasper, and Finns

My daddy once owned almost two hundred acres, and he worked for it.

Dorothy Richards
Allen County, Kentucky

Marjorie Elizabeth Clagett was born one hundred years ago, on Chestnut Street in Bowling Green. She studied at the Sorbonne in Paris and, from 1928 to 1964, she taught French at Western Kentucky University. She left the campus just prior to the late Jim Wayne Miller's arrival (he was twenty-nine when he received his Ph.D. from Vanderbilt). When he described "people living a long time in one place" he might have had in mind—Miss Marjorie Elizabeth Clagett.

She knew as much about Barren, Little Barren, and Gasper Rivers as any living person, but her memory began to fade like one of the flowers she loved to photograph and study. She published a collection of her work in *The Waters of Gasper River*.

When we ring the old doorbell at the front door of the gray, two-story-and-attic frame house on a gray, Nathaniel Hawthorne kind of rainy afternoon in late summer, Miss Marjorie has her small feet pointed in the direction of a hot electric stove. A blanket is tucked around her legs. She's anticipating winter.

She smiles.

In that smile—memory darting like schools of minnows, concentrically around an abiding life on favorite streams of water—is the understanding that the teacher has passed the torch to the student. The hour is too late for depending upon others to do our thinking for us, and Miss Clagett's feet are past tramping the rivers. The books on her bedroom shelves—Dante, Melville, Longfellow, leatherbound classics that have endured, including her own *Waters of Gasper*—await a new generation of readers, thinkers, and writers. The pictures of her father, who taught English literature at Western Kentucky University, her mother, who possessed such grand poise, old Gasper River winding through the trees of winter—they are there on the edge of conscious recognition, blurring and dimming.

She smiles.

We see our own one-hundred-year times coming around the bend. In only thirty to forty-five years, if we're blessed, we'll be seeking warmth for the soles of our own feet far beyond the time of tramping, hopeful that our books will have made a difference in younger lives, students as yet unborn. But one day in late summer, eager to know, we come asking questions. One lesson seems clear in the school of rivers and people: don't delay, keep searching and sharing. If you wait, it may be too late.

Miss Clagett asks for help in standing. After our brief stay, she wants kindly to see us to the door. "Will you be walking outside today?" we ask.

"No, it's raining," she replies.

Later in the year, the afternoon of November 11, 2000, Miss Marjorie Claggett died in the same house where she was born.

The headwaters of Barren River begin in Monroe County, where the East Fork descends from Mt. Gilead. Barren River, once known as Big Barren, is the largest stream flowing into Green River. The mouth of Barren is in Butler County just southeast of Woodbury, where Lock 4 is barely a memory. The Barren forms the Butler-Warren County line from

Sprout Bend to the juncture with the Green River. "Barren" comes from "The Barrens," a word used to describe the area of south-central Kentucky where most streams move underground beneath grasslands where pioneers found relatively few trees; hence, an area unusually "barren" of trees—but not of fertility. In Allen County, the Barren begins the formation of Barren River Lake. Barren River Dam is located on KY 252 south of Finney. Barren River Lake State Resort Park is reachable by U.S. 31E between Scottsville and Glasgow.

Glasgow is the birthplace of prominent journalists, including Bill Goodman of KET, Julian Goodman of NBC, Arthur Krock of the New York Times, and Diane Sawyer of ABC and CBS. Bill Goodman hosts a weekly news and opinion program on the Kentucky Educational Television network; Julian Goodman was president of the National Broadcasting Company; Arthur Krock won three Pulitzer Prizes; and Diane Sawyer was staff assistant to President Richard Nixon prior to joining national television networks as correspondent.

Glasgow, Kentucky, is among the few small communities that can claim such journalistic preeminence. There are writers, poets, artists, teachers, politicians, craftsmen, and farmers who also call Barren County home. Former Kentucky poet laureate Joy Field Bale Boone, a local resident, says, "Glasgow is a creative place—and you can't say it's genes."

"Something in the water?"

"No, something in the soil." Joy Boone observes that Glasgow, Kentucky, is not a place of the rich-rich and the poor-poor. There's a big middle ground, where young people grow up thinking they're "as good as anyone. Other towns might be snobbish...there are class barriers in a lot of places...nobody laughs at you in Glasgow."

From Bowling Green to the Barren's mouth at the Green River, the tributaries are Rays Branch, Stall Creek, Reeves Creek, and Hightower Creek. Just before the Barren receives the Gasper River, there's The Narrows, where the Barren River Road is sandwiched between the Barren and the Gasper. At the confluence of the Gasper and the Barren between Sally's Rock and the mouth of Barren, Clifty Creek, Maxey Creek, and Little Muddy Creek are the last, or the first, of the Barren

River's tributaries, depending upon the direction you're going.

South fork of Little Barren, which is not navigable, arises at the foot of Lime Kiln Hill in Metcalfe County, where the total population remains below nine thousand. Edmonton is the county seat. Other villages and name places in Metcalfe County include Bald Hill, Beechville, Cave Ridge, Cedar Flats, Center, Clarks Corner, Cofer, Cork, Curtis, East Fork, Gascon, Goodluck, Knob Lick, New Liberty, Node, Randolph, Sulphur Well, Summer Shade, Savoyard, Sparksville, Willow Shade, and Wisdom. South fork of Little Barren gathers Scott Branch, Moccasin Creek, Oil Well Branch, Beard Branch, Skaggs Branch, Douglas Creek, Rogers Creek, Clay Lick Creek, Dry Fork Creek, and Sulphur Creek. It joins the east fork of Little Barren River northeast of the Sulphur Well community near the Edmonson-Green County line.

In 1845, Ezekiel Neal discovered artesian possibilities at Sulphur Well that attracted so many who came "to take the water" that the community grew up around the spot, and its popularity lasted until 1969.

East fork of Little Barren arises near the meeting of the Edmonson-Cumberland-Adair County lines. It gathers the waters of Delk Branch, Flat Rock Branch, Red Lick Creek, Reese Branch, Prices and Lawrence Creeks, Long Creek, Adams Creek, Dry Fork Branch, and Caney Fork Creek. With the two forks joined at the Metcalfe-Green County line, Little Barren loops northward past the community of Little Barren, gathers Greasy Creek, rounds Horseshoe Bend, accepts Trammell Creek, and flows on northward to South Bend, where it empties into the Green River.

Kentuckians always built handy to water. It was the first thing they thought about when picking a house site.

Janice Holt Giles
The Believers

The years 1799-1800 were the beginning of the Great Revival movement at the headwaters of the Gasper River in Logan County. The Reverend James McGready of North Carolina arrived on the scene with a fury not unlike the convulsiveness of Jim Jones at Jonestown almost two hundred years later. Reverend McGready lit the fire that threatened to consume the minds of Presbyterians, Methodists, and Baptists. Another prominent firebrand minister was John Rankin, who left the Gasper Presbyterian Church, taking many with him to join the "New Lights."

The Gasper is another of the rivers of Kentucky considerably short of the one-hundred-mile length. It's only about twenty-five miles long with headwaters that originate in Logan County northeast of Russellville and northwest of Auburn. One of the tributaries of Gasper River, Clear Fork Creek, flows near South Union, site of the present day Shaker Museum.

We park the car and walk in. The first impression is that the Shakers would feel right at home. We peek inside the rectangular cistern, which gathered the water for the faithful. The United Society Believers in Christ's Second Coming formed their community at 1807, and it lasted until 1922, when the property was sold. We take home with us a copy of a handbill dated September 26, 1922:

"The famous Shakertown estate of 4,113 acres divided into 60 farms 25 to 150 acres each, 15 five-acre tracts, 1 seventy-five acre tract having most of the large buildings, 1 beautiful hotel building, 1 store building. All live stock, implements and tools to be sold AT AUCTION, biggest opportunity ever offered farm seekers."

Shakers trusted in sure-handed craftsmanship and loose, wild spirituality. All that's left today of what once was six thousand acres of cropland and pasture, gardens and orchards, shops and homesteads is preserved by a nonprofit organization, Shakertown at South Union. Eldress Nancy Moore spent almost her entire life, eightly-two years, at South Union. During the Civil War, Eldress Moore kept a daily diary, rich in detail. She implored President Lincoln to declare South Union a pacifist community, but her efforts were only partially successful.

Today, the knives and forks are crossed on the empty plates in the dining room, chairs are hung on the pegs in the hallways, the voices of the dancing Shakers are gone. We drive away and head north to see what's left of the community called Gasper on our map. We discover what we'd expected. Gasper is no longer Gasper. The settlement is called Bucksville. There's a Bucksville Post Office and a Bucksville Store and scattered manufactured homes in a variety of conditions. Many are abandoned, pushed aside, and replaced with newer models.

Gasper River empties into the Barren River at "Sally's Rock" just to the southeast of Rockland. Sally Beck, a postmistress in the Rockland community, was a communications link with Barren River boat pilots, captains, and passengers. The year was 1886. Perched atop a jutting sandstone formation, Sally shouted the news down through a megaphone to those passing by. She raised eyebrows and caused jealous wives in town to harrumph their displeasure.

Today, there's a peaceful silence atop Sally's Rock. Her shouting voice is gone, remembered occasionally in chronicles of a noisy time on the water highways to the Kentucky interior. On a Friday afternoon in January of a new, technologically-driven century, there's a heavy stillness on the streams muddied by drought-breaking rains. It's whispery from Sally's Rock to Woodbury at abandoned Lock 4, where the Barren oozes slowly, almost remorsefully into the Green River in eastern Butler County.

It's not big enough to be a river.

Man in a gas station
Allen County, Kentucky

The little stream, Finns River, begins as much in scarce memory as it does in current thought. Its name is a part of a mostly forgotten puzzle waiting for solution. The water moving across generations and cultures—Cherokee to immigrant settler, possibly an Irishman named Finn—does not pay homage to a chieftain's cry or a word on a map or any piece of arbitrary paper. The natural watercourse, like the smallest vein of a little finger, trickles and seeps as it has for millions of years. Width, length, and depth don't matter. The water flows.

Finns River is 1.45 miles long. It's located in Allen County, south of Scottsville, about a mile from the Tennessee state line. It's one of the three rivers of Kentucky that empty into a creek. Finns River flows into Little Trammel Creek at the edge of U.S. 31E, along with Garrett Creek and Hinton Branch. These form the headwaters of "Big" Trammel Creek, which feed Trammel Fork, which empties into Drakes Creek, which flows northward, gathering the waters of Allen, Simpson, and Warren Counties, and empties into the Barren River on the eastern edge of Bowling Green.

Today, most residents in southern Allen County have never heard of "Finns River," or if they have they dismiss it quickly. "It's not big enough to be a river," says a man reaching for a soft drink at the cooler in the last gas station on the Kentucky side of the state line.

"You can't get there from here," a young woman chirps from behind the cash register. She has seen the stranger coming, map in hand, knowing right away that his arrival doesn't translate into a Lotto ticket, probably not even a twenty-five cent bag of salted peanuts. The native with the soft drink is patient, but he isn't about to be bamboozled by a citified idiot who doesn't know the difference between a creek and a river.

"See? Here, on this map, it's called a river."

"Doesn't make any difference. It's not big enough," says the man, opening the soft drink.

"All right."

"It's Little Trammel Creek."

"Yessir."

"Go back up there to the bridge. Turn right just the other side of it. There're some boys fishing over there. I just came by."

"I'll go see."

A pickup truck is parked by the side of Little Trammel. There's no sign of anybody fishing. It's a lonely-looking glen. The waterway is about twenty to thirty feet wide, shallow with room to flood on the western side. A rocky cliff protects the eastern bank. There may be minnows, there may be some little fishing holes for big old chub and horny heads, if you know where to look for them, if you know to stay away from sleeping copperheads.

The mysterious mouth of Finns River is not to be found, certainly not in a hurried moment. It is, at that instant, a phantom stream as lost in time as a darkened pool of eyeless fish in a forgotten cave. It doesn't seem prudent to go thrashing around in the woods, looking for something so godforsaken.

Another pickup truck approaches. A man, a woman, and a boy have come to stand on the bridge. They've come to look down into the flowing water, maybe to throw small stones into it to create new ripples, maybe to have a talk about something troubling them. They need answers, not interruptions from strangers rolling down their car window to ask questions.

"What's the name of that stream?"

"Little Trammel Creek," says the man, with a single-minded tone.

"On this map, it's called Finns River."

"It's Little Trammel Creek," says the man, as if reciting one of the Ten Commandments. He turns away to look again at the water, the round of his shoulders sending a message that the conversation is closed. The woman and the boy do not speak. It's time for an outsider to turn around and return to the main highway.

Three men are studying a riding mower by the side of U.S. 31E. An older man walks back and forth from a roadside stand, a place for displaying odds and ends, the makings of a valiant flea market. It's late afternoon. The men look up as the car stops. When they're approached, one of them, the one with a no nonsense beard—scraggly, lips unsmiling—wearily murmurs: "He's lost."

These are three men trying to make a living, bothering no one, not wanting to be bothered one minute more than necessary. The looks on their faces suggest that they can not be easily corrupted. They're willing to take the time to suffer a fool, kindly. "I'm looking for Finns River."

"You *what?*" asks the beard. The voice isn't unfriendly. It's as cordial as anybody has a right to expect in the Bowery, or the Bronx, or the south side of Chicago.

"On this map here, there's a Finns River. Right there. Finns River."

"Ain't no river 'round here."

"What do you call that stream over there?"

"Little Trammel. But it ain't no river. It's a creek," says the taller man, who says he's from Tennessee, and he knows Little Trammel because it begins in Tennessee.

"Thank you."

The third man, the eldest, is too focused on the work at hand to notice a stranger or to jaw about the names of creeks and rivers. He seems sensitive to the passing of time, the preciousness of it, knowing the irreplaceable value of it, not wanting to be wasteful. He is self-driven, respectful of his private need.

Down the road, farther south over the hill, a quarter of a mile from the state line, at Alderson Bridge, Carter Church Road connects 31E and Macedonia Road, an area populated by people living proudly, the best way they know how, in "manufactured" homes of every size, shape, and age. More substantial property owners in condominiums and rolling estates would look down upon rural survivors, might hear them mentioned as a statistic in a televised news report of a rash of tornadoes. Oherwise they'd go unnoticed by outsiders. Local concern, like water, sometimes emerges from a spring of charitable relief.

The Allen County Mission, a "second-hand thrift store," stands guard at the intersection of Carter Church and Macedonia. It's the outreach work of the Concord, Mt. Pleasant, and New Buck Creek United Methodist churches. "Come and shop. You not only save, but by shopping at the mission, you are giving a helping hand to others. The mission is a non-profit organization, supported entirely by donations and volunteering," reads the handbill made of heavy, economy-printed parchment.

Dorothy Richards sits behind the cash register. Her husband, Charles, stands nearby. They seem accustomed to unexpected visitors, more willing to entertain forlorn, quietly desperate pleas and questions. "I'm looking for Finns River."

"I was born on it," says Dorothy, straightening her back, sixty-three years old, possibly thinking she'd not be hearing the name again in an Allen County lifetime.

"You were?"

"Right over there. Can't see it from the road," she says with a soft and cheerful voice.

"Everybody I've met so far says there is no Finns River."

"Well, there is," she replies as she might to an inquiry about a distant relative.

"Or *was?*"

"That river ran back there behind the house. My daddy once owned almost two hundred acres, and he worked for it. He began selling it off. We became migrant workers, picked tomatoes in Indiana. Daddy had a heart attack over there in the back hayfield. He died and the one hundred and twenty-five acres that were left were sold. There were five of us kids. We should've bought it."

A man and a woman come to pick up a used mattress and bedsprings, which they've bought for thirty-five dollars, a real good price when you're trying to make ends meet. The mattress and bedsprings were donated to the mission. The thirty-five dollars go into the fund to help others. The man and woman load the treasures onto the back of their pickup truck and drive down the road. Another man comes in for groceries from the mission food pantry. He is unemployed. He helps some around the mission and comes upon three pairs of used shoes. He has a family to clothe and feed. His arms are full when he walks away.

"We give food to those who need it," says Charles. "We give clothes to families who've been burned out."

There are many racks of clothing in three rooms, used appliances, and a few shelves of books. Paperback copies of Dickens's *A Christmas Carol*, Defoe's *Robinson Crusoe*, and Michener's *Mexico* cost twenty-five cents each. A one-dollar bill goes into the cash register, and Dorothy returns a quarter with the books.

"How did Finns River get its name, do you suppose?"

Dorothy says she doesn't know for sure, but she says she'll call around and ask about it. She picks up the telephone and speaks with family and friends. Her mother, now in her nineties, is in a nursing home. She probably doesn't remember. Everybody's health is confirmed first, then and only then, the question about "Finns."

Dorothy hangs up the phone and speaks with authority. "It was about what I thought. It was named after a family. Somebody lived on that farm a long time ago," says Dorothy. "I could take you and show you."

"I'd like that. Can we go now?"

"What time is it?"

"Right at five o'clock."

"It's closing time. Lock her up, Charles."

The ride in the pickup truck down the lane and across the land that once was a farm is dotted with new, shiny trailers, used cars that need some tinkering, and riding mowers that probably were bought on time and asked to do too much on ground too rough. A woman looks straight ahead as she mows the rugged strip alongside the road. Men study problems under the hood of a car. Two young people seem contented where they sit on a small front porch. They're relaxing, their conversation likely cheered by such a new place to live. We wave. They wave back.

Finns River and the spring from which it begins are, Dorothy explains, out of sight beyond a wooded slope, "a flat bed stream with a little falls." Whatever it once was, it is no more. Dreams of stewardship of the land have turned to realities of another kind of marketplace. Cows not milked by hand. Hogs neither slopped nor slaughtered for meat house rafters. Bees not kept and tended to fill small jars against the winter. Horses not hitched to wagons. Dinner bells unrung. No old red roosters with necks well-wrung, feathers plucked, bound for glory in Sunday chicken and dumplings.

The decision is not to walk across so many private backyards. Dorothy's family doesn't own the land anymore, plain and simple. We're as close to Finns River—"swamp there, singing with frogs"—as close as we're going to be on this day in early spring.

The Finn family, possibly settlers in the late eighteenth century, have long since gone. Where did they come from? Where did they go? What caused their name to stick after two hundred years? There are no answers. Some researchers of census records may find some clues. It can't happen too soon. Mapmakers of the future may drop the name, and Finns will be completely forgotten.

Charles turns the pickup truck around, and drives back to Macedonia Road. A sign at the entrance reads: "One Acre Lots. E-Z Terms."

"My daddy would turn over in his grave," says Dorothy.

Echo, Logsdon, and Styx

The rivers of Mammoth Cave were never crossed till 1840.
Great efforts have been made to discover whence they come
and whither they go, yet they still remain as much a mystery as ever—
without beginning or end; like eternity.

Alexander Clark Bullitt
Rambles in the Mammoth Cave

"**Y**ou say, you want to see the place where Echo River empties into the Green River?" asks Tres Seymour, the patient Mammoth Cave guide.

"Yes, thank you."

"We can drive part of the way, but we'll have to walk down to it. We have a saying around here—whenever we walk down, we must walk back up!"

I had come reasonably prepared by reading Roger W. Brucker's *Trapped! The Story of Floyd Collins* (co-authored with Robert K. Murray) and *The Longest Cave* (co-authored with Richard A. Watson). These books had convinced me that I was not and never would be a true "caver"—too overweight and too cowardly. Claustrophobic since, as a reporter, sitting in the pilot's seat in the space shuttle mockup at the Johnson Space Center, I have cultivated a healthy respect for unusually tight squeezes. The idea of putting on a wetsuit and squirming through pitch dark crevices deep within a cave is not my idea of control.

The ride in the Mammoth Cave National Park minivan leads down an unlittered roadway bordered by tulip poplars and a profusion of other hardwood trees—pin oaks, sugar maples, and Kentucky coffee trees—in the midst of winter sleep. Deer are crossing the road where there are neither billboards nor "For Sale" signs, neither junked cars nor abandoned refrigerators. The forestry service has left a simple and direct message for the public on a vantage-point sign:

Rural Kentucky
How far can you see?

Close at hand and off in the distance are the spires of the mature forest where once there was cleared land for family farms, then cornfields, then tobacco patches, then grasses and scrub brush, then cedar forests. Now the cycle is completing. The forest is reclaiming itself. It is inconceivable that it will return to a yeoman's agriculture. Who today or in the tomorrows would be willing to cross the mountains to search for lands to till, homesteads to build, animals to husband? Many family farms have trickled away. Others have been swept away by the tides in a sea of debt.

From a human three-score-and-ten point of view, it's important not to have "died" without standing on the spot where Echo emerges from Mammoth Cave and enters Green River. Surely that requires no bravery. Some things are obliged to be done in the name of experience, honesty, and beauty. They hunger for the sweetness of knowledge through personal contact. Reading a word or two in a book will not be enough. A Robert Penn Warren chapter in *Cave* is a beginning. A Wendell Berry sentence from *A Timbered Choir* inspires. A Harlan Hubbard painting encourages. Davis McCombs's *Ultima Thule* sharpens the writer's passion. Roger Brucker's *Trapped!* serves as a warning against carelessness, both in caving and in writing about caving. Books are never intended as substitutes for individual participation in matters of nature.

"It is this way to the spring," says Tres. "Mind the slick spots." His voice is kind. The trail leads past giant sycamores, shallow roots spreading on the slippery surface with places for older feet to make surer purchase. The dogwood walking stick made by a friend would have been helpful, but it was forgotten in the rush to discovery. Descending to Echo Spring demands the "bear walking" crawl used by cavers when there's no other way to proceed. A two-legged creature becomes a four-legged creature with the backbone arched. Modern man becomes prehistoric.

There it is! Echo!

Crystal clear, birthing from the limestone embankment, the epidermis of Mammoth, the clarity of the water undefiled. Echo River moves toward the strand of Green River. A sapling stands there for an older man to lean against, to rest from his years, to keep from falling down the steep slope where the water is dark green, deep with reflected emerald.

Echo becomes green, the color change enforced by the larger, impounded stream. Though the waters do not usually move rapidly, the greenness does not signify stagnation. It is a place for canoes to float with ease, a time for hands to relax on paddles to guide in the flow. "The problem of meaning," wrote University of Chicago psychologist Mihaly Csikszentmihalyi, "will then be resolved as the individual's purpose merges with the universal flow."

The tiny mouth of Echo is downstream from Cave Island, upstream from Turnhole Bend and Green River ferry. The scene resembles a fabled kingdom—Camelot without kings, queens, knights, or dragons—as if a nymph unable to speak has silently left the cave to unwind a long green ribbon, curling it through the national park, decorating for pleasure, even the devilment of it. The only audible sound downstream is the small ferry's engine purring, from time to time a lone crow cawing, a hawk's screak piercing the sky.

"Shall we go to look at River Styx Spring?" asks Tres.

"Oh, yes."

Styx, one of the five rivers in Hades over which the souls of the dead are ferried, is as dubious in Greek mythology as it is buried deep at the base level of Kentucky's five-story Mammoth Cave. The image is an opposite of Thomas Merton's *Seven Storey Mountain*. Up or down is irrelevant but not irreligious; the direction, that is to say, in which the mountain is pointing is forever up or down in the cycling universe. Stephen Bishop, Roger Brucker, and Tres Seymour have discovered Merton's gift at every level of the world's longest cave.

River Styx Spring drips from a cliff of rocks near the bank of Green River, upstream from Echo. The names could be interchangeable. Echo could be Styx; Styx could be Echo. The beginning and the end. "One Ecosystem Linked by Water" is the description given by the National Park Service.

A pileated woodpecker, the size of a crow but with a different, self-directed mission, flails the stillness where River Styx joins the Green. In the distance a crow's voice is heard, cawing as if disturbed by human beings thrashing about. It is February. Songbirds are quiet. In the depths of Mammoth, eyeless cave crayfish and fish with no structure whatsoever for the blessings of vision live solitary lives with need for neither sight nor warming season. The endangered species include the Kentucky cave shrimp, the size of a human thumbnail. The mussels too—fanshell, northern riffleshell, pink mucket, ring pink mussel, clubshell, and rough pigtoe—are on the federal endangered list.

In the spring 1998 issue of *American Cave Adventures*, produced by the American Cave Conservation Association, Mammoth Cave's resident ecologist, Rick Olson, writes: "We see more clearly the relationship between a healthy economy and a healthy ecosystem. Human economies are dependent upon intact ecosystems."

"Are you ready to enter the cave?" asks Tres.

"Yes. I would like to see Echo and Styx inside, at their beginnings."

"The wooden structures leading to it are no longer in use," Tres explains.

Such decay has dual aftereffects. On the one hand, disappointment that change has altered a mental image anchored in old lithographs. On the other, relief that carnival paraphernalia is gone. There are no boat "excursions" like those described by H.C. Hovey in his *One Hundred Miles in Mammoth Cave—In 1880*: "Four of these boats now await us on the banks of Echo River. Each has seats on the gunwales for twenty passengers, while the guide stands in the bow and propels the primitive craft by a long paddle, or by grasping projecting rocks. The river's width varies from twenty to two hundred feet, and its length is about three-quarters of a mile."

These "voyages" on Echo and Lake Lethe led to much fanciful writing about the waterways of Mammoth Cave. It was high entertainment in a time long before television, cinema, and the internet. The Cave became an ultimate destination. Boating on subterranean rivers was an exotic escape from parlored Currier & Ives.

Any stream of water in a cave is considered a "river." Anybody discovering one is likely to give it a name. In Mammoth Cave, rivers presently include Bretz River, named to honor American geologist J. Harlen Bretz (in the 1920s, he studied the relationship of cataclysmic flooding and the "underfit" stream), Candlelight River, Colossal River, Echo River, Eyeless Fish River, Hanson's Lost River, Hawkins River, Houchins River, Logsdon River, Mystic River, Roaring River, Stevenson's Lost River, and River Styx.

Hydrologically, there are hundreds of "rivers" in Mammoth Cave. Since there are also possibly hundreds of unexplored miles in Mammoth, there may be thousands more rivers—unseen, unnamed, unmapped, awaiting a new generation of cavers filled with the passion for unexaggerated discovery. In his newest book, *Beyond Mammoth Cave: A Tale of Obsession in the World's Longest Cave* (co-authored with James P. Borden) Roger Brucker describes the discovery of Logsdon River in the early 1980s, "a 16-million gallon per day river compared to the Echo and Styx backwater pools that are in the process of being abandoned."

Pete Hanson and his father, Carl Hanson, were Mammoth Cave guides who in the late 1930s explored and searched for lost rivers in the underground system of waterways. Hanson's Lost River flows into Echo River, the confluence confirmed September 9, 1972, by cavers Pat Crowther, Gary Eller, Cleve Pinnix, Steve Wells, John Wilcox, and Richard Zopf. This was the team that successfully connected Flint Ridge Cave and Mammoth Cave, creating the longest cave in the world—155.448 miles.

In the cave systems of Barren, Edmonson, Hart, and Warren Counties—Flint Ridge, Mammoth Cave, Unknown/Crystal Cave, Floyd

Collins Crystal Cave, Great Onyx Cave, Hidden River Cave, and Colossal Cave—water is constantly moving, creating new patterns of pathways.

A portion of Hidden River may be viewed in Hidden River Cave in downtown Horse Cave, location of the American Cave Conservation Association and the American Cave Museum. The descent into the cave includes 175 steep steps down to a point where the air is eerily cool and Hidden River flows as if with a consciousness of its own. The blind crayfish living on the sandbars stir within the beam of a flashlight as if signaling that they better understand total darkness.

Lost River Cave is located at U.S. 31 and Cave Mill Road on the south side of Bowling Green. As the new millennium began, the site of the cave opening was under construction as a tourist attraction. The history of "the world's shortest, deepest river" (*Ripley's Believe It or Not*) is as lengendary as any stream in the Commonwealth—thousands of years of Native American presence, the Civil War period, a Jesse James hideout, mill, distillery, and underground nightclub.

A slab memorial explains that "the 1874 mill was powered by a drive extended from the Lost River through a hole which was punched in the ceiling of the cave. In addition to milling, a large brandy and whiskey distillery was operated here. The mill burned in 1915, and from the 1930's a reception building for cave tours and the 'underground Nite Club' occupied this site." The sign was donated by the Center for Cave and Karst Studies at Western Kentucky University.

The Bowling Green-Warren County Tourist and Convention Commission points with pride to a Butterfly House at "Lost River Cave and Valley" with "a vast array of butterflies native to Kentucky." Town houses compete with butterflies, tall sycamores, and more than fifty other species of trees in the immediate area of the cave opening.

Houchins River, which does not appear on surface maps of Kentucky, flows beneath Houchins Valley in the Flint Ridge area of Edmonson County. This subterranean stream was given its name by a party of cavers led by Roger Brucker. The "river" was named to pay homage to the hunter Houchins, an early settler of Kentucky who, in 1797, according to tradition, "discovered" Mammoth Cave by chasing a wounded bear into what is now called Historic Entrance. Wounded bears would seem to be the last thing in the world most sensible hunters would want to chase anywhere—but into a hole in the ground?

During the "Cave War" days of the nineteenth and early twentieth centuries, when entrepreneurs connived to capture the bear's share of the tourist trade, every cave had to have a river. Pictures, illustrations, and fanciful word descriptions had the effect of bringing home a bountiful harvest in an agricultural area with marginal surface prospects. The rich elite from afar, bored and restless, traveled at great expense to be entertained and challenged—mainly entertained—by one of the Seven Wonders of the World.

The novelty, the grandeur, the magnificence of every thing around elicited unbounded admiration and wonder...The voice of song was raised on this dark, deep water, and the sound was that of the most powerful choir.

Alexander Clark Bullitt
Rambles in the Mammoth Cave

Stephen Bishop, a black slave guide, in 1838 discovered Echo River, where eyeless fish swam as they do now, as they have for eons in the wandering stream draining the north side of Jim Lee Ridge in the myriad rivulets of the Mammoth Cave system. He had taught himself to read and write. With the inventiveness of his innermost being, he became one of the world's most renowned cavers. His domain: Mammoth Cave in Kentucky.

The underworld unchained Bishop's mind. It loosened his imagination, sharpened his creativity, became his freedom, if such a thing was possible in the madness of slavery. In the unexplored darkness beneath the Edmonson County surface of scrub pine and ragged cornfields, Bishop bear walked, belly-crawled, squeezed, chimney-stemmed, rappelled, traversed, and waded the subterranean vastness. All the while he remembered each groping, clawing inch of the way, later thinking back to it, writing it down, connecting the pieces of the vast puzzle.

To be a caver is to be more than a rabbit burrowing, quivering, frightened even of one's own whiskered shadow. Stephen Bishop, like all accomplished cavers, intuitively embraced the craft of caving with a passion springing from a burning desire for discovery, and from dissatisfaction with ordinary comforts and structured predictability. A caver in life on the surface is one who also pushes onward, inquiring, refining, searching for new knowledge.

Bishop's physical body belonged for a finite time to his master, Franklin Gorin, but the mind and the being of the universal humankind of cavers belong infinitely to the cave. There in the Great Silence— except for the rhythmic ticking of drops of water from Mammoth Dome to the Bottomless Pit, the flutter of tiny, velvet soft wings maneuvering the blackness through Little Bat Avenue—Stephen Bishop mapped in his mind the connection of passageways within the depths of the earth. He chronicled his discoveries, recreating from memory the details for the 1845 "Map of the Explored Parts of the Mammoth Cave of Ky. by Stephen Bishop, One of the Guides."

Franklin Gorin, of nearby Glasgow, was a wealthy white attorney, merchant, entrepreneur, a man with a mission—to make money and to use money to make more money. In 1838 he bought original Mammoth Cave property, including the failing Inn, for $5,000. There's no record of how much he paid for Stephen Bishop well before his investment in Mammoth Cave, but it must have been hundreds of dollars, perhaps $1,000 to $2,000, a not unusual price for a slave in Kentucky at the time. Gorin brought his slave from Glasgow and put him to work as a guide in the cave. The master probably never realized in the beginning that his vassal was such a genius, wearing his mental garments with quiet distinction, belying outward appearances.

As Brucker and Watson explain in *The Longest Cave*, "Stephen wore a chocolate-colored slouch hat, a jacket for warmth, and striped trousers. Over his shoulder on a strap swung a canister of lamp oil. In one hand he carried a basket of provisions for the longer trips—fried chicken, apples, biscuits, and often a bottle of white lightning for refreshment. In the other hand he carried an oil lantern—a tin dish holding oil and a wick, with a small heat shield held above the flame by wires. Above the protector was a ring through which he slipped his index finger."

"What I look at, Stephen looked at," says the present guide, Tres Seymour, patiently leading the way down the Steps of Time at the beginning of a new century in Mammoth Cave exploration. "Nothing has changed," adds Tres, a modern white man with abiding respect and gratitude for a black slave who pioneered the development of one of the world's great treasures, a place unique.

"When I want stability, I come to the cave," says Tres, expressing a measure of the stability that Stephen Bishop must have discovered: steadfastness, constancy uninterrupted by honking horns and rattling chains. The cave brings for Tres, as it probably did for Stephen, a sense of inner peace. Today it is possible to pause and stand in wonder at the Ticking of Time, the sound of drops of water falling from vaulted ceilings, chiseling out new passageways for the next million years, without lightning or thunder. Even the New Madrid earthquake of 1811-1812 produced only a "whoooosh" down Houchins Narrows and Broadway to Gothic Avenue in Mammoth Cave.

A slender young man with a caver's fearless intuition for solitude and discovery, Tres Seymour discreetly and generously recalls the early nineteenth century Methodist minister George Slaughter Gatewood, who preached from The Pulpit, a giant rock jutting above the cave's floor. He and his flock did not stay. They could not have been expected to do that. After their expended time of subterranean fervor, they returned to the safer surface world of wooden churches, pews, communion tables, stained glass windows, and makeshift steeples. They, the churched, must have been swayed, at least momentarily, in the presence of the Great God Underground, but they forgiveably lacked the caver's passion. The ordinary faithful were not sustained by the natural splendor of stalactites and stalagmites. They may have been profoundly fearful of what lay around the next corner of discovery, which could have led to deeper questioning, perhaps the beginning of the renunciation of their most treasured beliefs.

There's a special hush at a huge rock called the Giant's Coffin. On the other side of the immense boulder, Stephen Bishop found evidence of the aboriginal explorers in the cave, Indians living thousands of years before the birth of Christ. Mammoth Cave is better understood with portals of thought opened wide to the possibilities of millions of years, without contrivance, superficial convenience, oversimplified calendars, and religious seasons.

In the new century of technology, Tres Seymour pushes a button. A little beyond the Giant's Coffin, a recorded voice resonates in the darkness—a representation of that day when actor Edwin Thomas Booth, brother of John Wilkes Booth, the assassin of President Abraham Lincoln, stood here in "Booth's Amphitheater" and delivered Hamlet's "To be or not to be" soliloquy:

> *To die: to sleep,*
> *To sleep—perchance to dream, Ay, there's the rub,*
> *For in that sleep of death what dreams may come*
> *When we have shuffled off this mortal coil*
> *Must give us pause.*

"May we stop for a moment and allow me to say that I experience *joy* here?"

"Of course."

"Do you understand what I mean?"

"I understand," says Tres, looking back sympathetically, sharing the beam of his flashlight for unsteady feet on the slopes leading deeper into the cave. The corridors are well lighted by unobtrusive electric circuits, but a small, focused beam is appreciated.

"I mean, there is no bureaucracy here. No pretense. There is just my brain. My own ability to think. Unfettered. How sad there are so many people who never take advantage of the opportunity to be their true selves."

"I understand," says Tres, listening patiently, as we descend to the fifth and lowest level of the longest cave in the world, down to the stratum where water finds its base. He drops a small rock into a stream far below, and the flashlight's gleam reveals the ripples—in the River

Styx.

Crossing over the Bridge of Sighs above Stephen Bishop's Bottomless Pit, Tres Seymour, the young, white, twenty-first-century guide, recalls the Greek mythology of Charon's Boatman on the River Styx. "He expected to be paid."

"Certainly."

The tradition in the mythology was to place a coin in the mouth of the dead which the Boatman would retrieve as his fee for ferrying souls to the underworld. It became the fashion in Kentucky's Mammoth Cave to invoke classical images, a favorite nineteenth-century convention. Stephen Bishop, the black man for whom slavery could have been a River Styx, instead taught himself not only to be an extraordinary caver but also to read world literature with its allusions to the Latin and Greek classics. Bishop's 1845 map includes Hebe's Spring (goddess of youth, cupbearer to the gods), Dismal Hollow, Dead Sea, St. Cecilia's Grotto, and Purgatory. He discovered the Great Dome, which rightly should have been named Bishop's Dome. The slave's master took the name, and it became Gorin's Dome. If the slave complained, there is no record of it. Bishop wanted freedom, yes. He wanted that more than having a rock formation like Doric columns named for him in Mammoth Cave.

The complete story of Stephen Bishop's life has not been published. It awaits more research, a passion for exploration and imagination. Such a project is worthy of the efforts of young African American students today, but it shouldn't preclude the possibility of a white scholar. Mammoth cave makes neither ethnic nor racial distinctions.

"I have finished the manuscript," says Tres Seymour.

"And?"

"I believe they want something else."

"Why?"

"I've written it in the form of a diary, and they [the editor] would rather have it written in third person. I don't think I can do that."

"I see."

Roger Brucker so far has written eight chapters for a historical novel about Stephen Bishop (as of May 2000). "Any good book about Stephen must be written by a caver," says Roger. As used by Brucker, "caver" means he or she who patiently and professionally conducts new, scientific exploration of underground areas. Therefore, a guide in a cave is not necessarily a caver. Likewise, a scholar who conducts basic research may consider herself or himself to be an intellectual "caver." It is not the same thing as crawling into a hole and pushing forward to discover new caverns and their possible connections.

Although there's relatively little known about the great caver Stephen Bishop, much more is known about him than about Houchins the hunter, who "chased a bear" into the cave. Bishop's likeness appears on the Official Map and Guide of Mammoth Cave, alongside Floyd Collins's. Both men have the caver's relentless look of determination, the caver's eyes of wanting to know. A somewhat larger picture is in *The Longest Cave*. In this volume, Roger W. Brucker and Richard A. Watson have sketched the life of Franklin Gorin's obedient slave:

>*Stephen Bishop (1821-1857) was a young man of enormous curiosity. He was...lean and hard, with the build of an athlete. In Mammoth Cave, he moved effortlessly across the tumbled rocks. He was quite intelligent. He was a slave who had a quiet pride that did not offend his master. The dimension Stephen added was that of risk in narrow passages and across deep pits. His discoveries and the publicity given to them were the starting point of a kind of tenacious modern exploration. He pushed relentlessly through every passage that was in any way passable, in hopes of finding big discoveries beyond.*

Brucker and Watson speculate that Stephen Bishop may have maneuvered H.C. Stevenson into believing that he (Stephenson) was the first to cross "Bottomless Pit." Such a possibility made no one unhappy, and if a slave could take for a harmless ride anybody on the face of the earth or underneath it, it surely was a sin to be forgiven. Stephen Bishop married a maid who worked at the Mammoth Cave Hotel, and they had a son, but there's no known record of what became of the child, who later died a young man without heirs. Although his master provided for his emancipation, Bishop planned to buy his freedom and move to Liberia. It was not to be. The freedom was granted in 1856. It lasted one year. Stephen Bishop died in 1857. He was thirty-six years old. "Stephen Bishop is buried in the old Guides Cemetery at Mammoth Cave, beneath a Civil War surplus tombstone bearing the wrong date of death," writes Brucker.

Then there was the tragedy of Floyd Collins in Sand Cave, now a part of Mammoth Cave National Park. From the time of his entrapment on January 30, 1925, until his body was reached on April 17, the Floyd Collins story captivated the morbid curiosity of the nation. William Burke "Skeets" Miller, a reporter for the *Courier-Journal*, won a Pulitzer Prize for his coverage of the bizarre event. His extraordinary reporting was front-page news in hundreds of newspapers. He became almost as much a hero as the victim.

In *Trapped! The Story of Floyd Collins*, Murray and Brucker describe the religious interpretation of the tragedy at the time: "Floyd's entrapment was seen as punishment for his sins, his travail in Sand Cave as his Gethsemane, and his prayers for deliverance as guaranteeing him eternal life. Floyd Collins—sin-cursed man—was trapped by the rock of evil, but was finally freed in spirit if not in body by the liberating influence of prayer."

Most cavers today will agree that Floyd Collins, no matter how "sin-cursed" he may have been, committed at least three basic caving sacrileges: he went alone, he carried only one source of light, and he did not give an estimate of when he would return.

Morbid curiosity did not end when Collins's body was finally brought to the surface on April 23, 1925. Nor did it end after he was buried near his home on Flint Ridge. Murray and Brucker have given an account of what happened—"Then, on June 13, 1927, with suitable publicity, Floyd's new casket was plunked down in the middle of the tourist trail in Crystal's main concourse where visitors could pass by and look in at him. Placed at his head was a large red granite tombstone which read:

WILLIAM FLOYD COLLINS
born July 20, 1887
buried April 26, 1925
Trapped in Sand Cave Jan. 30, 1925
Discovered Crystal Cave Jan. 18, 1917
Greatest Cave Explorer Ever Known.

The Floyd Collins spectacle continued with the theft of his corpse from the coffin, the discovery of the body with one leg missing on the edge of Green River, and again the placement of the remains on public display. All that's left of the Greatest Cave Explorer Ever Known is now buried in the Mammoth Cave Baptist Church Cemetery on Flint Ridge, beside the graves of his mother and some relatives.

The cave, in all its interwoven complexity, waterways, and air passages, is infinite. At the end of a warm winter day in February, the drive down to the Green River ferry is an occasion to roll down the windows of the car. The road sign at the top of the hill has the ring of reality: "Road Ends in Water." It is a time to test brakes. There is a complete stop while the ferry operator raises the barrier arm. The short ride across the curling Green River is like nothing else in the world. The opposite barrier arm comes up, and the drive up the right bank and hill is as pleasant as a day in May. There is no necessity to look back. The way ahead leads past Buzzard's Roost and the communities of Bee, Cub Run, Winesap, Center Point, Kessinger, Mt. Beulah, and Munfordville.

No amount of wishful thinking, however innocent, can permanently alter the reality of the hydrologic cycle. Its relationship to the cycle of human experience cannot be denied. Every ground water basin has its spring; all trickles and tributaries lead to the sea. Every human being is born, dies, and puts out to sea with debatable immortality. Thoughts of discovery—beginnings and endings—are in *flow*, the essence of being and becoming.

We are told that this is the end of the cave; but it is only one of the many ends...the real end is yet unknown....We turn for a last lingering look into the wonderful, mysterious under-world, where the spirit of eternal, changeless Silence reigns supreme.

John R. Proctor
Century Magazine, 1898

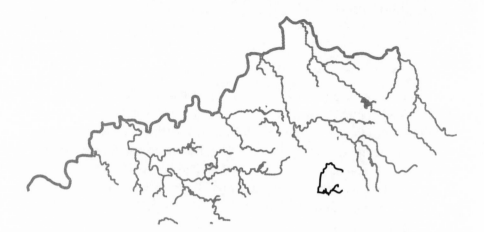

Rockcastle, Laurel, and Little Laurel

Passing the branches of Rockcastle River on our journey we saw the rock whence the river derives its name; it is amazing, and curious, with appearances the most artificial I have ever seen—it is not unlike an old church or castle in Europe.

Bishop Francis Asbury
Journal, circa 1784

You couldn't see the rock noted in Bishop Asbury's journal from KY 490 this past summer because the foliage blocked the view. But sixty-two-year-old Roy McKinney put down his varnish brush and said to be sure to come back in the fall when the leaves are good and gone. Roy's home is perched on the side of the road a stone's throw from the twisting Rockcastle River in eastern Rockcastle County. KY 490 follows the tumbling stream of water from Livingston up to Lamero.

Roy's arthritis and two strokes have cut back on his coon hunting, so he spends his day making furniture—kitchen cabinets, things like that—for a used furniture store in Mt. Vernon. Roy's three-year-old, full-blooded red bone coonhound, Reddy, is stretched out asleep, dreaming dreams of planting another raccoon up in a red oak or a white oak, it wouldn't make any difference what kind of tree it was. "You spell that Re-d-d-y?" So help us, that dog's eyes opened and closed.

"She's pretty smart, but I'm pretty sure she can't spell," says Roy. "But we had a dog before her, chow named Perkey, and that dog liked to watch television, the good shows. Had her favorites, 'Lassie' being one of them. If you turned off the television, Perkey would bite you."

Reddy's tits were swelling like ripe plums. "She got a litter?"

"Going to. Daddy's a 'red bone'".

"Sell the pups?"

"No. Give 'em away."

"How come?"

"Don't believe it's right to sell dogs," says Roy, who walks with a crutch, his toes aching with out-of-jointedness, and there's no mistaking a forefinger missing on one of his steel-grip hands. "How did you lose your finger?"

"Spring broke in a miter box saw. Cut off all four fingers. They reattached them all, but this one here," he indicated the missing member, "It lived only twenty-two days. Then it died." Roy still plays Bluegrass music when he's a mind to, but it's not easy.

His daughter, Faye Coffie, deaf since birth, picks up the brush and adds a few gentle touches to a tropical fish tank cabinet, while Roy continues the importance of a conversation with his visitor. He does not turn down the radio, which is tuned to a religious station out of Somerset. "I don't care what name they hang over the church door as long as they preach the Bible. When they get out of the Bible, I don't want any part of it," says Roy on the general subject of religion. "Don't want to put anything in [the Bible] or take anything out."

As for the presidential election: "I'll vote for Bush. We're going to pay for babies we've already killed, we'll *really* pay for it if we keep it up. Makes Hitler look like a Sunday school teacher. Clinton's morals aren't right for the job he's got. We've made a lot of progress, but in the meantime we've made slaves out of ourselves—all modern conveniences—we didn't have electricity. It costs a lot of money. Unions have ruined the country. When I couldn't fire a man who wouldn't work, I quit."

A white cat saunters up. "What's the cat's name?"

"Whitey. There's an Orangey around here too. Come over here a minute, if you have the time," says Roy to his visitor. "See that walnut tree there?"

"Yessir."

"Fourteen years old. Quite a tree to be only fourteen years old."

"You planted it?"

"Yessir."

"Tell me about Rockcastle River down there."

"Used to be twice as big—in the '30's—as it is now. Used to float logs down to Livingston. River got jammed up. Flood in '47 was bad, but so was '58. Water was six-feet, four-inches in my basement" (keeping in mind that Roy lives up on a hillside).

He mentions increased traffic since the road in front of his house has become part of a scenic highway, which is to say, traffic in drugs as well as cars, trucks, and motorcycles. "Do they bother you here, being so close to the road?"

"No sir. They know what I'll do."

"What'll you do?"

"Shoot 'em. Word gets around. Shot a feller right over there, filled him full of buckshot. He was stealing my gas. I'll give a man anything he needs, but I don't want him stealing from me."

The seventy-five-mile-long Rockcastle River begins at the meeting of the South Fork and Middle Fork about one mile above the confluence of Horse Lick Creek in southern Jackson County. Dr. Thomas Walker named the river the Lawless. Later, Isaac Lindsey gave it the name Rockcastle. Headwaters of the Middle Fork include Laurel Fork, Alum Cave Branch, Mill Creek, Buzzard Branch, Hog Branch, Peter Cave Branch, Renfro Branch, Panther Creek, and Robinson Creek in Jackson County. Laurel Fork is formed by Mill Creek and Alum Cave Branch. Indian Creek is also a tributary of the Laurel Fork in the area of a proposed dam site that was delayed in January of 1998, the delay due to concern about an endangered species of mussel known popularly as the Cumberland bean. The South Fork of the Rockcastle is formed by Sugarcamp Branch, Dixon Branch, Raccoon Creek, Little Raccoon

Creek, and Freeman Branch in northeastern Laurel County.

Elsie Gilliam Jones runs the grocery store at "Lam-row," which appears on maps as Lamero. According to Mrs. Jones, the name comes down from a Mr. Lamereaux, an early settler from Pennsylvania. Before there was a bridge, there was a ferry at the Lamero settlement. Today, there are a few houses, but the Lamero Post Office was moved down the road to the Gilliam grocery store, then moved again to Livingston.

"I love it here," says Elsie, five-feet-ten, straight up and down at seventy, at home behind the long counter making a right angle with the cooler where the tubes of baloney and wedges of cheese await their moments of truth. Down at the other end of the counter are the thirty-three post office boxes, which now hold needles, thimbles, thread, personal notes, and things. Elsie sews and quilts when she's not slicing baloney. A customer comes in and with a hundred dollar bill pays for two packs of cigarettes. Elsie makes change, and the man thinks for a moment, then says, "Did I give you a hundred dollars?"

"Believe you did." .

"I thought maybe I gave you a twenty."

"Pretty sure it was a hundred."

"Thought I might have given you a twenty, but if I had I would have come back. I wouldn't have cheated you. I'm not made that way."

The sign up on the wall is nice: "Make what you're doing today important, because you're exchanging a day of your life for it."

A timber man stops for a baloney sandwich: "Whatever you want to put on it, onions, yeah, cheese, and mayo, yes."

"What kind of trees do you harvest?"

"Red oak and white oak. Red for furniture, white for whiskey barrels."

Gilliam's Grocery Store is as unlike a supermarket as a rowboat is a battleship. Elsie has the necessities—motor oil, syrup, candy, cold cuts, beans, gloves, rubber bands, shoes, overalls, light bulbs, soap—and when customers come in they're treated like family. They all respect Rockcastle River, you might say, which is the patriarch or the matriarch, depending upon where you perch on the limb of political correctness. The river doesn't give a hoot about sexual preference. Water is water, flesh is flesh, bone is bone, dry is dry, and flood is flood. When the river roared on tides in '47 and '58, the water rose to the second floor of Gilliam's Grocery Store.

South Fork of Rockcastle (sometimes called Little Rockcastle), originating just west of the Laurel County line, forms the Laurel-Jackson County line from north of Lamero, then the Laurel-Clay County line. Martin and Mill creeks join the South Fork in Laurel County. The Middle and South forks meet on the Jackson County line near the confluence of Horse Lick Creek to form the Rockcastle River.

A visit with Ben Culbertson, postmaster at Mr. Vernon, is a step in the right direction of conservative canoeing. Ben knows eastern Kentucky rivers. He has well placed contacts who can tell him almost hourly what the level of water is, which goes to the heart and soul, not to mention the survival of a canoer. Dog Drowning Hole and Canoe Eating Rock of the Upper Gorge of Red River, Devils Jumps of the Big South Fork of the Cumberland River, and the Narrows of Lower Rockcastle River didn't get their names out of thin air. When Michael Hendrix approaches the counter at the Mt. Vernon Post Office, where Ben is selling stamps and handling mail, Michael is carrying two pictures taken a long time ago by Bill Strode of the *Courier-Journal*. It shows Michael and Ben in a canoe coming through The Narrows when they were much younger and wilder. Michael puts on a show, bending deep like an old man from far up the river.

"Mistah...cud'jew...hep-may mail...these hair pitchers...to mah frend...in Awstralia?"

Ben is fooled for all of three seconds, about the length of time it takes to judge the distance from the bow of a canoe to one of the immense boulders in the Narrows. "Why, you old son of a gun, Michael, come on in here. Where you been?" Michael and Ben haven't canoed together for years, and the homecoming is as good as any promoted by church or university alumni association. We go into the postmaster's office and spend some good time talking about Bee Rock, dangers below the mouth of Beech Creek, The Loop, The Stair Steps, and The Narrows of lower Rockcastle River.

"You've got to watch out for the 'hydraulic keeper,'" says Ben.

"What's that?"

"A recirculation pattern after you come over an obstruction. It'll keep you right there—logs, canoes, human beings. You might have to dive to the bottom and swim out. Another way is to have somebody on the bank with a rope to throw to you and to pull you out. The best way is to avoid it altogether."

"A hydraulic keeper can kill you?"

"Yessir."

In his definitive *Canoeing and Kayaking Guide to the Streams of Kentucky*, Bob Sehlinger defines *hydraulic* as: "General term for souse holes and backrollers, where there is a hydraulic jump (powerful current differential), and strong reversal current." *Keeper* is defined as: "A souse hole or hydraulic with sufficient vacuum in its trough to hold an object (paddler, boat, log, etc.) that floats into it for an undetermined time. Extremely dangerous and to be avoided." Souse hole is defined as: "A wave at the bottom of a ledge that curls back on itself. Water enters the trough of the wave from the upstream and downstream sides with reversal (upstream) current present downstream of the trough."

My God!

Ben and Michael make promises to go canoeing again, maybe in the Red River Upper Gorge, maybe even one more time down through The Narrows of Rockcastle. David and Lalie would want to be with rope in hand on the bank. Ben returns to selling stamps and writing money orders, and Michael and David head south to hike to The Narrows to *scout* it, which means to study it for future reference. Oyez!

On the edge of Mt. Vernon, we make a U-turn at a flea market, where Michael finds a bargain in a hammer, and David finds books, *twelve* for a dollar. The paperbacks include: Sister M. Judine's *Goethe to Ibsen*; a collection of *Spanish Stories; Power! How To Get It, How To Use It; The Ugly American;* and *Facing Death*. Later, we completely agree with the first thought in the book on dying: When our time comes, we want "to die with some degree of dignity, in peace and with purpose." There's no telling what you'll find in a Kentucky flea market or a hydraulic keeper, just no telling at all.

Lalie stayed home on the day Michael and David went down I-75 to

Exit 38. They went southwest on highway 192 and crossed the bridge over Rockcastle River. At the entrance to Bee Rock Campground there's a sign: "In recognition of its outstanding scenic beauty and natural quality, 15.9 miles of the Rockcastle River, from the old KY 80 bridge at Billows in Lake Cumberland, are included in the Kentucky Wild Rivers System."

Somebody forgot to mention some of the world's most serious chiggers, but that's O.K. Our advice is to dip yourself in "Off" and, like sensible beekeepers, gaffer's tape the bottom of your pants before starting up the 1.25-mile trail from Bee Rock to The Narrows. Otherwise, when you arrive back home, you'll marvel how the six-legged critters have burrowed into your skin along the shinbones, the calf, and here and there around your bellybutton. A chigger inside the umbilicus would constitute madness and would be anything but dignity, peace, and purpose.

We park the car and start up the trail, where there's not a sound. Another world. Heavenward, towering tulip poplars, ash, and oak. Moisture glistening on steep rock facings. Tiny runoffs of water rippling down to Rockcastle, which is on our right. The water is low in the river, as deceptive as Michael Korda's *Power! How To Get It, How To Use It*, but there is a strategy: "...don't make waves, move smoothly without disturbing things." That's what we do. We walk carefully, trying to avoid something as small but potentially dangerous as a turned ankle. About this time a small snake, probably a black racer, slithers across the trail and into the brush between the river and us. "Damn, I hate them."

"I love them," says Michael.

"Well, plunge in there and get a-hold of him."

Michael knows better than to "disturb things." He uses a stick and carefully moves aside the spiders' webs constructed across the trail by a corps of eight-legged master engineers. He is patient as we pause from time to time to catch a breath of the clean air wafting down Rockcastle. The one-mile marker comes and goes, and then there's the arrow pointing toward "The Narrows." The descent is no longer a trail. For older people it's a butt-scootin' slide from rock to rock, where the chiggers see the human legs coming and seat themselves for the feast.

The last gauntlet is the fingernail-grasping, toehold-groping climb up a mammoth boulder enthroned at a 60-degree projection. Once at the top, the reward is in the eye of the beholder. It calls to mind that movie *One Million B.C.*, in which the Kentuckian Victor Mature, made his debut. As we sit up there on the rocks of ages, watching the water move down from the mouth of Beech Creek, tumbling over the goolies, Ben Culbertson's words come back like a boomerang: "Yessir," it can kill you.

After Bee Rock, the Rockcastle River widens with the backwater of Lake Cumberland. The journey, which began all the way back in Jackson County, ends at Rockcastle Campground. Upper and Lower Troublesome Creeks have drained Rockcastle Springs and Hindsfield Ridges. Rock Creek, Bear Creek, Ned Branch, and Pole Bridge Branch have happily handed over their hydraulic keepers.

Laurel River empties into Cumberland River just east of the mouth of Rockcastle River. Laurel River Lake is a 5,560-acre home to largemouth, smallmouth, and spotted bass fishing. It is one of the ten major lakes in Kentucky, which basically are flood control projects. By the year 2001, all Kentucky farm owners (with ten acres or more) must complete and submit water quality plans, a step in the direction of taking individual responsibility for the 13,000 miles of streams in the Commonwealth. Yet, it's the threadlike feeders, the runoffs from the hollows, valleys, and tiny crevices, that are the primary causes of flood and the washing of topsoil from the Kentucky highlands to the Mississippi Delta, one of the many riches the Commonwealth has relinquished to other states. As the best time to plant a tree is yesterday, so is the building of small impoundments of water before it adds to one more flash flood and possibly sweeps away one more governor of the Commonwealth.

Named for the mountain flower, Laurel River gathers the waters of Adams Branch, Little Laurel River, Robinson Creek, Locke Branch, Lick Creek, Calloway Creek, Rough Creek, Lick Fork, Rocky Branch, Cane Creek, Muddygut Creek, John Creek, Blackwater Creek, Hooppole Creek, and Camp Branch in the easternmost section of Laurel County.

Little Laurel River's headwaters gather east of London between Laurel Hill and Cutoff Knob in Laurel County. Little Laurel passes beneath the Daniel Boone Parkway, then takes the waters of Sally's Branch, gathers the waters of Sampson Branch and Lick Branch, then passes beneath I-75 before it accepts Ward Branch, Horse Branch, and Campbell Branch. Little Laurel empties into Laurel River just west of Interstate 75 between London and Corbin.

North- and southbound motorists on the concrete superhighway in the new millennium are generally unaware that they are crossing over hallowed ground—the Wilderness Road blazed by Daniel Boone on his way to establish Boonesborough in 1775. More than two centuries later, relatively few take Exit 38 to Levi Jackson Wilderness Road State Park. Even fewer take Exit 49 to Hazel Patch, one of the earliest settlements in Laurel County, carved in 1825 from virgin timberlands.

The day in late May is gray, misty, and cool. From time to time a shower of rain blurs the view. Aging windshield wipers leave crescent-shaped streaks on protective glass, paling in contrast to Daniel's and his companions constant exposure to cloudbursts, water running down their faces all the way to their moccasins. The "Future Home of Hazel Patch Baptist Church" has a brave new beginning on cleared ground along U.S. 25. The natural wildness is gone, the land stripped to make room for another civilization where rock formations make way for tattoo and pawn shops and truck salvage businesses. A sign advertises "bulldog pupps" for sale, there's a welding shop, and there are manufactured homes galore, a sausage company, flea market, martial arts school, and a detail shop—gewgaws for all God's children in the new millennium.

What would happen if the lights went out and stayed out? What if wheels no longer turned on the interstates or the country roads because the oil fields went dry? How long would it take to reinvent the wheel? Who would know to go up Laurel and Little Laurel Rivers to look for millstones? What he hell are they?

A visit to McHargue's Mill at Levi Jackson State Park brings a visitor face to face with Bill York, the miller. His attitude is inviting. He's smiling and ready to answer questions. "So, tell me about this place."

"Well, a family immigrated from Scotland in 1748, and they brought that millstone with them." He points to a corner of the millhouse where the stone rests in perpetuity.

"How much does it weigh?"

"About two thousand pounds."

"How did they get it here?"

"Aboard ship and in the back of a wagon. Other millstones were quarried locally. A 1758 stone was brought from Pennsylvania to North Carolina to southeastern Kentucky. It was set up on Robinson Creek in the early 1800s and was in use until the 1920s. In the early '30s it was donated to the park. WPA [Work Projects Administration] and CCC [Civilian Conservation Corps] rebuilt the mill."

The milldam is a visual feast where Little Laurel spills over tiered rocks, the water creating white spray and a pleasant sound. The nearby mill pond is populated with ducks and geese, too many ducks and geese, which are quaint in fewer numbers, but with each new hatching, more sodden feathers and stinking feces are becoming a gagging situation. Present population at McHargue's Mill: about seventy-five ducks and geese in one small millpond. It's a lesson for human beings too who're continuing to stack themselves on top of one another in places like Calcutta, Chicago, Los Angeles, Manila, New York City, Mexico City, and São Paulo.

Bill the Miller sits on the floor of the mill house loft and begins to turn the wheel that allows water to rush in and activate the machinery. "It's harder to get open than it is to get closed," he explains to a nearby retired mathematics teacher and his companion from Seattle. She videos the operation and records a description of the creaking, belted shafts that rotate the top runner stone against the stationary *bedstone* below. "The first thing is to pour the corn into the hopper," says Bill with warm and pleasant understatement. Soon the cornmeal is filling up a wooden box from which the golden powder will be bagged and sold for the making of Kentucky cornbread in Seattle. Divinely simple, yet of what fiber is mankind made today that he would go in search of 2,000-pound millstones, dressing them with meticulously carved *furrows*, alternating with the *lands*, the flat surfaces that combine to convert corn into meal?

Keeping the stones in proper working condition requires unusual skill, the kind virtually unknown in the age of electricity and handy supermarket shelves. A good millstone may last for centuries, but it must not be treated indifferently. The shape of the *lands* and *furrows* must be as smooth as the sole of a fine Italian shoe.

In prehistoric days, Native Americans discovered the art of pounding grain with a rock to make the corn easier to eat. For the natives, a mill house would have seemed as marvelous as magic. "One of the oldest industries in the history of mankind" is preserved at Levi Jackson State Park, where ninety-nine millstones line the paths from the parking spaces to the mill—grand old stones emblematic of pioneer days, when there were hundreds of mills on the streams throughout the Commonwealth.

Little Laurel River may be considered a nuisance by some, a problem in the midst of sprawling land development. Fred Evans, one of the old timers, remembers the Little Laurel as a small river that makes up back in the eastern part of the county. "Had a farm," he says, quietly. "Kinda liked to farm. Four children. Worked and had the farm when raising kids. After they left, rented it out. Rented out tobacco. Last crop was sweet corn. People drove out to get it. Stripped coal in bottoms. Ran a steam shovel. Owned smaller one or two. People came out to get coal. And I hauled to a coal yard, lot of coal. Yeah, buddy—worked in here for years. Been all over these roads in Laurel County. Knew Colonel Sanders. He had his first fried chicken place in Corbin."

From millstones to pressure cookers, sweet corn picked from the field to a side dish smothered in franchised butter, Kentucky trails now favor roads more than rivers.

And that's a crying shame.

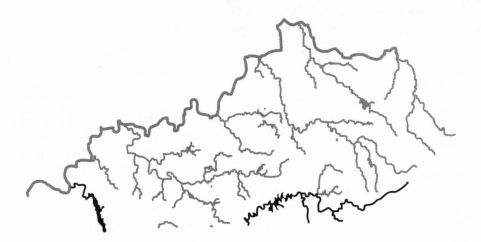

Cumberland

*Jim Helem went with his walking cane in front, punching the ground—
there wasn't any blacktop back then—and he dropped shelled corn. He
told me to stay in back and keep the ducks moving up.*

Ivan Lawless
Old Olga, Kentucky

More than two-and-a-half times longer than the Kentucky River, the
Cumberland is the only river that originates in Kentucky, flows south
from the state, reverses its direction to the north, and terminates in the
Commonwealth. The Cumberland leaves Kentucky in Vernon Bottom in
Monroe County and reenters near Linton in Trigg County, just north of
Tobaccoport, Tennessee. About seven hundred miles after its beginning,
the river named for William Augustus, Duke of Cumberland, empties
into the Ohio River near Smithland in Livingston County.

The headwaters of Cumberland descend from the eastern side of Pine
Mountain, a high, narrow span separating it from the headwaters of
North Fork of the Kentucky. Poor Fork of Cumberland arises in the Ran
Polly Gap area southeast of Whitesburg in Letcher County. The Little
Shepherd Trail follows the western side of Pine Mountain, and the zero
mile mark for the Cumberland is just south of Oven Fork.

Cumberland River enters Bell County near Cardinal, then rolls past Hulen, Tejay, Miracle, Varilla, Calvin, Ponsa, Harbell, East Pineville, Wasioto, Pineville, Wallsend, and Fourmile. The Bell County tributaries of the Cumberland include Puckett Creek, Tom Fork, Brownies Creek, Hances Creek, Yellow Creek, Little Clear Creek, Turkey Creek, Fourmile Creek, and Greasy Creek.

Clear Fork empties into the Cumberland on the eastern edge of Williamsburg, site of Cumberland College, where C.M. Dupier Jr. teaches. He and others consider Clear Fork to be a river too with its own history, character, and personality. It flows northward out of Tennessee, entering Kentucky just east of Jellico. Northbound travelers on I-75 can see Clear Fork on the right side of the highway.

Sidney Saylor Farr was born in Bell County in 1932, "as far back as it was possible to go." Her writings include a collection of poems, *Headwaters*. She is editor of *Appalachian Heritage*. In "Women Born to Be Strong," she acknowledges the importance of the place where her roots are deepest.

The twice-impounded Cumberland becomes Lake Cumberland in Clinton, Russell, Wayne, and Pulaski Counties, covering more than 50,000 acres. In Trigg, Lyon, and Livingston Counties the Cumberland becomes Lake Barkley, which includes more than 42,000 acres of water.

The South Fork of the Cumberland gathers its force in McCreary County in the Big South Fork National River and Recreation Area near the Tennessee State line. Several streams form this major fork: another Troublesome Creek and Watson Branch to the west, Line Fork and Bear Creek to the south.

Sitting on stage in the VIP seats at the *Grand Ole Opry* in that state to the south is not much of a substitute for getting into a car and heading down to McCreary County, Kentucky. The talent may be a mite less professional and not nearly as well paid, but that's all right and don't think twice. Besides, almost everything is better outside than inside.

Donna LaVaughn sets her mind to her guitar and lets loose with the old Loretta Lynn standard "I'm proud to be a coal miner's daughter." Gene Williamson sidles in with his base like the train is about to leave the old, historic tipple (which it is); Penny Perry sets his five-string banjo on fire, his fingers flashing hot as a miner's lamp searching for new places to dig.

It is the end of the day, and Gene "Bosco" Ross is about to pull two toots on the engine of the Big South Fork Scenic Railway. He has brought his day-trippers down from the former Company Headquarters at Stearns, just south of Whitley City. Now it's time to return from the old Blue Heron Mining Camp, the end of the line, where memories of the first year of operation, 1937, still linger like the velvet "wh-whoo" of a mourning dove.

The Stearns company shut down Blue Heron in 1962, after the last of the coal played out. It was the Great Closing Time, the mine's last screeching whistle. The miners and their families moved away, but some of their stories can still be heard, whispering through *now*, bringing back *then* and *before* from a not quite forgotten time, as if *after* and *later* might be everything, the everlasting kit and caboodle.

In 1989, the National Park Service recreated the mining camp. A father's voice can be heard, calling to mind the backbreaking, down-on-the-knees work up there in Mine 18; a mother lamenting her lonesome life yet holding on stubbornly; a young person longing for escape to the outside world—a people desperately wishing for *after*.

There is no more fuel, but the main tipple is there—oxymoronically named for birds like Blue Heron and Scarlet Tanager. No more of the precisely sized grades tumble into waiting railway coal cars. Only the sound of a soft summer breeze plays through the pines and the tulip poplars. A murmur of guilt tugs from before, resentful that *after* should have to explain itself.

When Penny Perry finishes picking "Bugle Call Rag" on the five-string banjo, he steps to the front of the caboose and speaks by walkie-talkie to Bosco Ross up in the engine. Reality is about to jolt the day-trippers from their reveries.

"Ready if you are."

Two toots sound, wee starting squeals, and Bosco eases the coal-defying diesel away from the Blue Heron station. The Big South Fork of the Cumberland, snaking its way north toward Yamacraw and Yahoo

Falls, defines the view on the left side of the tracks. Harry Caudill's "pitiful remnant of cull and second-growth" satisfies modern day-trippers who've never experienced the majesty of virgin timber, or witnessed the old-growth glory of Blanton Forest to the east in Harlan County, where a campaign is underway to save "a living legacy."

In McCreary County, the train switches just the other side of Roaring Creek and heads caboose—first to the Barthell Mining Camp, restored by Harold and Marilyn Koger. Their goal has been to make the camp look as much as possible the way it did around 1910. The train stops to pick up tourists who have stayed a while, remembering the past.

It's a past that sometimes pains. Giant coal operators, such as Michigan industrialist Justus S. Stearns, for whom Stearns, Kentucky, is named, has been castigated for taking out the timber, then the coal, then leaving the area and "yesterday's people" to their own naive imaginations. He has also been praised for entrepreneurship, the building of the great national machine, the dawning of "progress."

With vision, the follow-up has been as favorable as human ingenuity can devise. Tourism plays a prominent role in the new life of McCreary, Kentucky's 120th county, formed in 1912 by combining parts of Pulaski, Wayne, and Whitley Counties. Approximately 85 percent of McCreary is now owned and managed by the federal government: the Big South Fork National River and Recreation Area and the Daniel Boone National Forest.

There are 427 square miles in McCreary with a 1990 population of about 15,600. That's only about 37 people for each square mile, compared to Jefferson County's 1,723 and Fayette County's 805 people per square mile. A Kentuckian who lives a lifetime without visiting McCreary County has missed a piece of self, as important as anything any major city has to offer.

Places for hiking, camping, horseback riding, birdwatching, running the wild river, or sitting and listening for them deserve the designation of final destination. When the Big South Fork Scenic Railway backs into the station at Stearns, there are goodbyes for Donna, Gene, Penny, and Bosco. And there is a beeline for the Whistle Stop Café to sample again Sweet Kreations Fudge.

Education is the major chord, said Gov. Bert T. Combs, who graduated from Cumberland College in Williamsburg, Kentucky. He liked to recall the Chinese proverb "If you're planning for a year, sow rice. If you're plannng for a decade, plant trees. If you're planning for a lifetime, educate a child." The Kentucky Education Reform Act of 1990, with all its bumps in the road, has been a centerline stripe for the rest of the nation. Its complexity was never intended to be quick fix or instant gratification. But its benefits don't make headlines or lead stories on the nightly news unless there's scandal. School bus accidents make more news than Johnny's grades.

School consolidation in Kentucky was a necessary and positive step on the long journey toward improved education. That was part of the good news. Some of the "bad" news was a trail of broken classrooms, buckled gymnasium floors, dangerously groaning stairsteps. The ghosts of students and teachers speak softly around the corners of what used to be. What will become of old thresholds of learning? Whatever happened to dignity and respect for what once was treasured? There comes a time in the life of abandoned school buildings when a decision has to be made. Watch them go on and slowly fall apart? Condemn them, tear them down, cover them over? Or see unusual possibilities, take hold of them, and build something new and uniquely vital?

In Harlan County, at the headwaters of Cumberland, time is well spent on a little sidetrip to Benham on Looney Creek in the long shadows of Black Mountain. Looney joins Poor Fork of Cumberland River at the Cumberland community. Ask just about anyone how to find the Benham School House Inn, and they'll more than likely be pleased to point the way. Upon arrival, quietly stand there on the outside and shape the sight, mix it with memories of the days in the other, now abandoned school. The question may come: "Am I thinking what I'm thinking? Has somebody actually taken an old, ghostly school building, preserved most of the original appearance, and turned it into something that will attract visitors who'll *pay* to spend several days and nights there? Better still, a place where they'll think it's so good they'll accept it as a *final* destination, go home, and tell their friends." There you have the Benham School House Inn.

Walk in. Look around. Students' lockers still line the main corridor walls. A high school letter jacket hangs on the outside of one of the lockers, a reminder that it was earned and worn but has graduated and is needed no more. The high schoolers have been gone since the last graduation thirty-eight years ago. Elementary students have not been in school here since 1992.

Wisconsin Steel Corporation, which became International Harvester, built the Benham School in 1926. The company wanted it to be a good school, so it subsidized salaries to attract good teachers. The day would come when the school would close. Perhaps it would be said it had outlived its reason for being. Former students and teachers must have had other ideas about the place where laughter once spread across the playground, cheers rang out when the hometown team was victorious, and tears were shed at graduation time.

A group of private investors purchased the property, which now belongs to Harlan County. The structure and its new reason for being are administered by the Southeast Education Foundation in support of the Southeast Community College. "I like to call it the best-kept secret in Kentucky," says general manager Mike Hensley.

Walk into one of the former classrooms. Experience what a difference creative decor can make: thirty rooms with a summer occupancy rate of about 70 percent; conference rooms and the Great Room (the former gym) can accommodate 400. Excellent dining is available in the Apple Room. There's a Sitting Room where one may meditate beneath a 300-year-old English chandelier.

Nearby is the Kentucky Coal Mining Museum and Coal Miners Memorial Park. Within easy driving distance there's the *Trail of the Lonesome Pine* outdoor drama at Big Stone Gap, Virginia. The Benham School House Inn is only four miles from Kingdom Come State Park. It takes more than one once-was school and one forward-looking community to attract tourism dollars from as far away as Arkansas and South Carolina. It takes a multi-layered vision of pride in a region too often portrayed as impoverished.

The better news is what's happening today in one little corner of the Commonwealth. It could be happening anywhere. It's not to say every abandoned school is a sure bet, instant-success tourist attraction. Without a deeper sense of community it might be better to tear down and cover over. But a visit to the Benham School House Inn might help change some Eastern Seaboard minds.

In faded memory, Cumberland River barges come around Lawson Bottom, Irish Bottom, Rockhouse Bottom, and Wells Bottom, and they lay in at Creelsboro between Potts Branch and Millers Creek. Men and women flow in excited anticipation, seeking lusts of summer's past in the hotel bulging with business. The surrounding pastures and woodlands are just as likely as places for fields of desire. Creelsboro, situated perfectly, is poised to become home for many good old boys and good old girls of the new nineteenth century.

The year is 1809, and the town of tomorrow, in the heart of a future oil boom, has been laid out in the wildest dreams of planners. Assuredly, Creelsboro is the logical site for the courthouse for the as yet unborn Russell County. There was need of a bank, hardware store, several grocery stores, blacksmith shop, and churches where sinners might be forgiven at least until the following Sunday.

Coincidentally, 1809 is the year of the birth of Abraham Lincoln, the Larue County boy from away up the road, fated to become president of every politically-nested county courthouse and crossroads across the land from Creelsboro, Kentucky to Springfield, Illinois. "If we could first know where we are, and whither we are tending, we could better judge what to do, and how to do it," Lincoln said in the summer of 1858. "'A house divided against itself cannot stand.'"

President Abe will reach all the way down to the village on the Cumberland River to honor a child grown up beneath the firmament scudding the bottomlands. Little Reuben Creel will become U.S. consul to Mexico. Elijah and Eliza Creel have conceived Reuben, and for the pioneer parents, Creelsboro has been named and baptized in the glorious promise of muddy Cumberland River water.

Reuben's son, Enrique, will rise up to become governor of Chihuahua

State and in time he will become Mexico's ambassador to the United States. Creelsboro cannot be prouder, for it has attained international fame, but good old boys and good old girls, being both good and old in the ways of politics and planning, will decide, in 1825, when Russell County is carved out of Adair, Cumberland, and Wayne counties—Creelsboro will not be the county seat.

Damnation! How can such a destiny be denied? How can reason become so impotent? Here's how. All's fair in lust by riverside. One man's strategy is another man's counter-scheme. Local politics prevail. Jacksonville will be the first name of the new county seat of Russell to honor one of the best of the grand old boys, President Andrew Jackson. But that will last only as long as the Jacksonians occupy the courthouse steps. When the opposing forces take charge, they'll rename the child, the new county seat, Jamestown, to pay suitable respect to James Woodridge, a very prosperous good old boy, one of the very best, the one who donated the hundred acres upon which to build the town.

Creelsboro's decline into obscurity begins, sealed when, upstream, Wolf Creek Dam is built in mid-twentieth century, forming Lake Cumberland (more than fifty thousand acres, the largest lake in the Commonwealth), leaving a crossroads with scarcely any reason for being except as a rare footnote in local history. Today, three counties meet at Rockhouse Bottom, a short distance downstream from Rock House Natural Bridge, near Creelsboro, a small place with a ghost-town reputation. Edgar Allen Poe, born in the year of Creelsboro's creation, would have found many ravens here, tell-tale hearts in a red-hot town that wanted to grow up to become a full-fledged county seat. Today, the spurned village is a whispering trip through a strained affair of past and present.

The old Creelsboro Bank building is deserted and crumbling. A pickup truck is parked where the hotel used to be a haven for trysting tourists. The five doctors are gone. The skeletons of two groceries and a hardware store groan in an early May breeze. Two-story frame and paint-flaking residences lean in deepening desolation, while nearby "manufactured homes" make their own statements of the new culture of changing, make-do times when an estimated 550,000 Kentuckians today live in 233,000 manufactured homes.

The Creelsboro Church of the Nazarene has a new lease on life—a new building with a clean, bright sign, a new water spigot in the front yard. The Creelsboro Christian Church shines in the midday sun along KY 379. A man on a tractor mows rich, green winter cover crop in one of the bottoms that have nourished the Creelsboro community of farmers, lovers, and Fruit of the Loom workers.

"Hey, just a second," says Ray Oliver, counting on his fingers the number of people living today in Creelsboro proper. "Four...eight...about sixteen, all told."

"Was that the old bank building over there?"

"Hey, there was a robbery there once."

"When would that have been?"

"Hey, I was nine years old."

"So that would have been, when?"

"Just a second..."

"How old are you now?"

"Hey. I'm eighty-one. You figure it."

"Must've been seventy-two years ago, 1928."

"Yessir, and the robbers made Jim Poppelwell ride on the running board on the way out of town."

"Who was he?"

"Cashier. Hey, they had Kenneth Irvin on the running board too. He jumped off and ran up through the woods."

"How much money did they get?"

"Three thousand dollars."

"Did they ever catch the robbers?"

"Yessir. It was a local boy who grew up wanting to rob a bank."

It's only a few miles from Creelsboro to Old Olga on the south side of Crocus Creek, a few miles farther to just plain Olga at the head of Mud Lick Creek. Neither Olga nor Old Olga had any fantasies about becoming county seat. They were just being themselves with a tinge of immortality lying in the corners of collective memory. "How did Old Olga get its name?"

"I don't know," says Ivan Lawless, eighty-two years old. "But I remember one time, old Jim Helem said we ought to raise some ducks and sell the feathers."

"What kind of ducks?"

"Indian runners. About fifty of them."

"Hatch them out?"

"Yessir. But it didn't work. Jim Helem said, 'We got to sell these things. Ought to drive the ducks to Old Olga and sell them to Old Man Gaines.' He was a traveling trader."

"How old were you?"

"Ten or twelve years old. Jim Helem went with his walking cane in front, punching the ground—there wasn't any blacktop back then—and he dropped shelled corn. He told me to stay in back and keep the ducks moving up."

"Did you sell the ducks?"

"Yessir. About twenty-five to fifty cents apiece."

"You say, you don't know how Old Olga got its name?"

"No, sir."

Olga and Old Olga are good examples of what is lost when local histories, written and oral, have not become the personal responsibility of individuals. There are other place names between Lake Cumberland and the Tennessee state line—from Olga to Ota, Ribbon to Bow, Judio to Raydure. Comedy and tragedy, some of it recorded in local newspapers. But much of it has been and will be lost if the people of the rivers of Kentucky are not visited and respected.

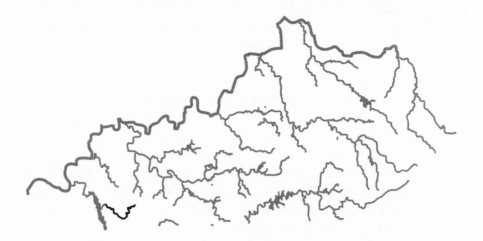

Little

Sing like you really love God. Doesn't matter how you sound. It can be as bad as a bull moose in mating season.

Glen "Chaplain Woody" Woodard
Emanuel Baptist Church, Henderson
at the Cadiz, Kentucky, Encampment

The mouth of Little River is on Lake Barkley, west of Cadiz in Trigg County. The headwaters of Little commence in Christian County. There's North Fork, South Fork, and Muddy Fork. South Fork begins near Pine Knob. Its tributaries include Warrens Fork, Rock Bridge Branch, and many streams whose names are known only locally, if at all. North Fork of Little's tributaries lie to the north of Hopkinsville, and they include White Creek, Upper Branch, Middle Branch, and Lower Branch. These waters supply Lake Blythe, Lake Morris, Lake Tandy, and Lake Boxley. The main stream of Little continues westerly past the communities of Herndon, Binns Mill, and Peedee. The tributaries of Little include Casey Creek, Potts Creek, Grigsby Creek, Belford Spring, Sinking Fork, Mill Stream Spring, Coon Cane Spring, Stillhouse Branch, Burge Creek, Kelly Branch, Dyers Creek, and Blue Spring. The tributaries of the Muddy Fork of Little River, which joins the main stream north of Cadiz, include Long Pond Branch, Dry Creek, Shelly Creek, Kenady Creek, Brushy Grove Creek, Horse Creek, Wallace Fork, and Sugar Creek.

At Cadiz, on a Saturday afternoon in late March, a crowd of people gathers in the park where Little River bends around a rocky cliff and an ancient sycamore, flaking white, almost wasted. Swirls of dark blue cloud drift against a robin's egg blue background, infinity being with the changing color above the bank of the river, where a boy, thirteen years old, soon-to-be fourteen, moseys with a fishing pole and a tackle box. He calls himself looking for a place to drop his line. It's a time in his life when hormones are playing games with him and he's seldom winning. "Any luck?"

"Caught a big catfish, once."

Nearby, a dishwater-white duck and a deep green and brown mallard waddle at the edge of Little River. Further downstream, two glistening white geese and one gray, threatening gander-long neck stretched, eyes intense, horny beak snapping—stand alert on picket duty. The air is still, but it's filled with the smoke of campfires from one of those bivouacs close by with the white tents in neat rows, pegged down for the night, bottom edges warmed by straw to keep out the wet cold. A bigger tent with a sign that says "Twin Rivers Mercantile" is doing a brisk business in buttons, Confederate bills, and colored rock candy on sticks.

"We don't like the Klan, don't like them using our flag," says a Son of Confederate Veterans, leaning his forearms on the side of the pickup truck bed. Richard P'Pool marks Confederate graves. Lying in the back of the pickup is a new marker unwrapped enough to be read:

Pvt George W. Murphy
Co B, 8th Kentucky
Mounted Infantry
Sep 28, 1821 - Apr 5, 1884

Of forty ancestors of Richard Morris P'Pool of Trigg County, "Eight were Yankees, thirty-two were Confederates."

"P'Pool?"

"Yessir, that's the way I spell it."

"All right."

"I lean to the South."

"I understand."

"We lost the war."

"Yessir."

"This is the fourth year for the encampment. Started with fifteen reenactors and fifty spectators showed up; 198 reenactors last year."

If there are doubts about this not being a racial thing, there are several African American children from Missouri who seem to be enjoying the Civil War reenactment as much as the young white campers. "We've had a memorial service for a black Yankee, a twenty-one gun salute," says Richard. "He was the oldest descendent of the U.S. Colored Heavy Artillery. We got to honor our enemy."

"I see. What can you tell me about Little River?"

"Several mills on it. Could fish in it. Took a canoe trip one time. Put in at Peedee just up the way from Binns Mill. I was fourteen years old. Could swim in it."

"The river's in bad condition today?"

"Better now than it was ten years ago. They're watching pollutants going into it—bleach bottles, tires."

"That's good. And the reenactment?"

"Indiana, Illinois, Missouri, Tennessee, Mississippi, and Kentucky all represented. Everything free." Bumper stickers abound with messages to remind visitors that not everything is sugar candy on a stick:

Secession Now
The Right thing to do

Welcome to the South
Now Go home

"Was there a battle at Cadiz?"

"No, but during 1864 Colonel Hylan B. Lyon came out of Tennessee and was burning courthouses, but not the one at Eddyville."

"Why not?"

"He lived across the street."

"Well."

"He was recruiting for the Confederacy. [He built a small brigade.] Courthouses had troops in them."

"So, this here today is...?"

"Living history demonstrations."

"All right."

"Keeping history alive. A useful educational service that doesn't cost the public a penny and costs the participants a pretty penny. How do you feel about it?" asks Richard P'Poole, leaning into the fender of the pickup truck.

"Never been to a reenactment. Came driving down that hill, and here you were. Wondered what it was. Decided to stop and see for myself."

"The battle was at one o'clock, but there'll be artillery firing tonight."

"I'll stay for it."

From mid-afternoon to the closing in of darkness there is the laughter of children in period clothing—suspenders holding up baggy linsey-woolsey trousers, bonnets sheltering young womanhood faces. A high school freshman looks much older in his Union uniform. Trees along Little River are late-winter bare, still undressed in stark wantonness. A dog yaps from time to time. It's such a stillness, otherwise marked by children scampering over bales of soggy straw. They skirmish, tightly gripping make-believe flags and popguns, acting out little *Red Badges of Courage*.

In the distance, to the south, at Fort Campbell, real world cannons are booming. Or is this sound the thunder of battles fought by Billy Yanks and Johnny Rebs? Might the blast have been a deep-seated hunger for fighting? Might the roar have been a catharsis bespeaking peace, not war? Maybe there has always been something about humanity that likes to anticipate and savor cannon fire, the anxiousness, the desperate thrill of cannon fodder, no matter what direction it's taking or the vengeance it may be wreaking. Oh, glorious bloodletting-bloodbathing, should it come to that.

Lanterns are looked to for lighting, and groups, the Blue and the Gray, lean across tables, elbows on edges, eyes inquiring, voices close in hushed conversation, sometimes whispers, then suddenly in small bursts of laughter. Night is coming to cover North and South. Campfires are kindled and drums are rolled.

The conversation with the Johnny Rebs turns to recent cuts in tobacco allotments by half, the threat of "foreign impurities," unequal and therefore unfair imposition of standards. The tobacco patch is no longer a level playing field, pathetically not worth fighting over in a glorious Civil War. Family farms, what are they? Words appearing on paper when you come to think of it. Most smokers don't even think that much about it. Family farms? Stupid-assed thing if you ask me. But you're not asking me, so what difference does it make?

At the next table, the Billy Yanks are talking, some sitting and some standing with a chilled crispness, precision of look and manner. The Billy Yanks contrast sharply with the Johnny Rebs, so much so that the codified Boys in Blue are, in fact, goddamned Yankees, intimidating in manner and appearance. "May I sit with you?"

"Why, sure."

"I grew up in Kentucky, thinking that if I'd lived back then, I would have gone with the North, even if all the rest of my family headed South. I thought I was an abolitionist. I didn't think of myself as a Johnny Reb. I knew slavery was wrong. Maybe I was a phony Yankee. Why am I thinking this way?"

"It's the blue and the tall hats and the new uniforms and the cohesive appearance," says one goddamned Yankee with a smile.

"Not ragtag, you're saying? Is that it?"

They nod, in precision, like ducks walking.

"The South was defending its homeland, and that could be the main reason why they fought as well as they did."

Billy Yank is not even a little sentimental or forgiving. He's more positive and calmly arrogant in the fateful lightning of His terrible swift sword. Billy was defending his homeland too, but he didn't talk in the manner of Johnny. The issues were the Union and the economy, and slavery was the touchstone.

"If Illinois had seceded, would it have split the North?" the young high school student in blue wants to know.

The other Billy Yanks return point-blank stares.

"I'm serious," persists little Billy.

He doesn't get an answer, not then he doesn't. Later in his tent, an officer of the 44th Illinois or the 1st Illinois Artillery Battery C could request an explanation of such a preposterous question. "If the Confederates had taken St. Louis it might have made the difference," proffers a Union private.

"No, it came down to the Confederates not fighting better in the center of the state, the heart of it," says another senior Billy, now a nuclear plant employee, who says he likes Tennessee better than Kentucky. Whoa!

"The Confederacy should have fought better in Missouri," says the first Billy with a note of strained conviction, a weakness that does not complement the correctness of his uniform.

"It's a neat hobby," says one of the reenacters, who also acknowledges that it's an expensive pastime.

"I don't meet people like this in everyday life," says a construction worker.

Sitting around a campfire, studying the flames, Captain Rick explains the battle, a seesaw affair that has been scripted out with an "overall commander." A young girl settles down to the studious business of licking a hard candy stick, and a black Missouri youth sits quietly as the idea of segregated Union troops is explained. The stretch may be smoldering beneath the youth's blank look.

"Generally young people hate to read," says Captain Rick. "Reenactments are a way of reading and teaching. It was our ancestors' involvement, and we need to lead and help children." The sky is frowning in doubt, beginning to have a Bela Lugosi look to it, clabbered clouds scudding, a full moon winking and blinking in and out like a one-eyed creature. Tree frogs are singing along Little River as cannoneers of the twenty-first century are getting ready for the 7 p.m. reenact in "dead air night." Shadows move silently back and forth along a line of three artillery pieces pointed toward the arc of Little River.

The ghosts of the 6th Wisconsin, one of the regiments in General John Gibbon's Iron Brigade, decimated at Petersburg, are there to play at war, a picture of mortal combat seen through peaceful pursuit, recapturing something of history. The studious, consummate cannoneers of the new millennium roll double-wrapped tinfoil around ten ounces of gunpowder and ten ounces of flour. "It produces more resistance and makes just as much boom," one of the gunners explains.

They ram the concoctions down into the throats of the artillery barrels and make a final check of the friction primers. The shadows are poised to pull the strings, while the spirits of the 10th Missouri (Union), 3rd U.S. Colored Cavalry, 17th Kentucky (Union), 1st Illinois Artillery Bat. C, 5th Tennessee, 10th, 15th, 46th, and 50th Tennessee (Kentucky Confederates "had to go south and amalagmate with other units"), and 1st Mississippi Regiment stand by their tents, awaiting the fiery salutes. (Reenactors sometimes take both sides.) Napoleon III, Emperor of the French from 1852 to 1871, nephew of "the Little Corporal," was responsible for the big leap forward in friction primer technology. It makes things much easier in Cadiz, Kentucky, in the year 2000.

It's 8:24 p.m. Central Standard Time.

"Number One! Ready?"

"Ready!"

"FIRE!"

BOOOMMM!!!

The grass bends over, lying low in front of the cannon, having the good sense to take cover.

"Number Two! Ready?"

"Ready!"

"FIRE!"

BOOOMMM!!!

There are a baker's dozen of rounds for each of the three weary reproduction guns. Enough smoke belches to almost satisfy the insatiable, and the horrendous sound eclipses the singing tree frogs. But they immediately resume as if it has been only crashing thunder along Little River.

"Number Three! Ready?"

"Ready!"

"FIRE!"

BOOOMMM!!!

"We're looking at it just like it was at Fort Sumter, twenty-four hours of it," says a man to his wife and children. "They won't let us use bayonets," he adds.

The following morning, in his black hat, black ribbon tie, and frock coat, Glen "Parson Woody" Woodward conducts church services. The title of his sermon is "To Learn to Love," but before he holds forth on the subject, he tells a joke about somebody threatening on Saturday night to throw a skunk into his tent.

"I don't use hundred dollar words, I use everyday language," says the parson, short of stature but compensated by conviction. Then he announces his custom of conducting a "non-denominational" service on such occasions as these, and he says it's time to "sing praises to God." A choir of six Confederate boys rises and leads the way through the first and last verses of "Rock of Ages" and "Amazing Grace." It sounds sweet and low, matching the quiet flow of Little River.

While Parson Woody preaches on "without fear of persecution" and "to show our love," a few Billy Yanks and Johnny Rebs, standing by their tents, are tamping down powder into their Springfield rifles. "We're willing to take a whuppin sometime," mutters one.

"We know we're not perfect," preaches Parson Woody.

George Colbert of Cadiz, standing outside Twin Rivers Mercantile, says a friend of his caught forty-seven crappie in January, crappie being better than bass. George, approaching the big Eight-Oh, has worked in steel mills and factories, worn the badge, been a mechanic and security guard, and for the last twenty-five years has lived in Cadiz. He and his regulars have caught river cat, "all different kinds" of catfish, Kentucky bass, large and small mouth bass, rock bass, blue gill, and redears (sometimes called shellcrackers).

"We would like sunshine, but we thank you for rain," says Parson Woody, who has a goodly sized gathering. But many others are sauntering at daybreak with cups of coffee, cigarettes, and cold, wet, groggy pride. Both the Rebs and the Yanks have the look of "The main idea was to kill you sons of bitches." Of course, it's a reenactment, but the conviction can be read on faces and deep down burning in their genetic bones and souls. "If I am killed that will be all right, because the cause is right." Some of the cups for coffee look ceramically modern, but many are tin cups, hands holding them tightly. Grim faces with lonely and stubborn expressions forlornly wait for *wahr*. The Johnny Rebs have a hangdog, downcast, guilty look about them, the look of embarrassed defeat. Some play the part of desperate but dangerous ragamuffins, wild-eyed and muley faced, long-haired bushwhackers bent on saving the Southland.

"The Bible is a holy shelter for sinners to go in," preaches Chaplain Woody. (He prefers "Chaplain" to "Parson," and it does have a more dignified ring to it.)

Howard Stokes of Todd County, partial to Confederate President Jefferson Davis, likes to pull a Billy Yank's legs, especially if he's poised with a reporter's notebook in his hand. "That racist monument over there at Fairview? Well, if it's racist and they want to tear it down, they ought to tear down the Washington Monument too. He had slaves."

"How about the Jefferson Memorial?" says another Johnny Reb, close by. "He had slaves."

"Tear it down, too."

The Jefferson Davis Memorial, soaring 351 feet above nearby Todd County farmland, is undergoing repairs. In the second week in June, there's a Jefferson Davis Memorial celebration of the defeated president's birthday, June 3, 1808. Robert Penn Warren (1905-1989) was also born in Todd County.

"Have you read his book honoring Jeff Davis?" Howard Stokes wants to know.

"Yes, I have it at home. What did you think of it?"

"I liked it," says Stokes. "Warren was an agrarian, part of that Nashville bunch," he adds, proudly.

Pride is evident throughout the encampment, beginning with

excitement, eagerness, and the joy of rebirth. Though the weekend concludes with cold and soggy conditions, the participants appear ready for another "next time." They carry on in the flow of living history.

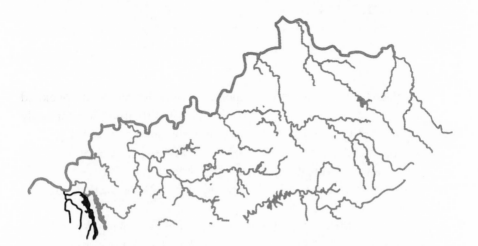

Blood, Clarks, and Tennessee

"We'd swing out into the river and play 'when the cat dies.'"

Max Bonner
Pottertown Road
March, 2000

There are two theories about the origin of Blood River's name. One is that there was a battle fought by Indians in the area, that the fighting was so fierce it was said the river ran red with blood. The other belief is that iron ore deposits gave the stream a tinge of red. There may be other convictions.

Many Kentuckians have never heard of Blood River, much less the source of its name. Some contend it's not a river but a creek. All the more reason to make a visit. You'll never know what you'll discover on rivers of Kentucky, from the mouths to the headwaters, until you've at least headed in their direction. Of course, nobody can go everywhere and please everybody. Somebody's feelings will always be hurt. Some river rats are so turned inward they'd object to glowing accounts.

The Kentucky part of Blood River, which is the last leg of it, is entirely in Calloway County in the southeastern corner of the Jackson

239

Purchase. Blood spills out of Tennessee, east of Freeland, and circulates more or less northward past New Concord, then empties into the Tennessee River, which at that point is Kentucky Lake. Blood River is the largest embayment on Kentucky Lake. So is it a stream, a creek, a river, or an embayment? It's some of all three, but in *Rivers of Kentucky* the Blood is a river and takes its rightful place with the best of them.

Today, in March, Max Bonner is the guide for looking at Blood. For listening to it, too. Max was born near the edge of the stream, and he prefers the Indian massacre story because hereabouts he doesn't know of enough iron ore to make the river any more than a muddy brown, which it mostly always is after a heavy rain. At other times it's reasonably clear, depending upon how the word is defined. No river in Kentucky at the present time comes close to resembling Caribbean waters and that's just the way it is. Max Bonner is seventy-two years old, and he doesn't ever remember Blood being red. That settles that until somebody comes up with a better idea.

From his pickup truck, Mr. Bonner points out several of the Kentucky veins pouring toward Blood: Little Sugar Creek near Buzzard Roost, Wildcat Creek, Grindstone Creek, Tan Branch, Beechy Creek, Panther Creek, Goose Creek, Lax Creek, McCullough Fork, Coleman Branch, and Dog Creek.

Dog Creek calls to Max's mind the story about the doctor who threw a party down around New Concord, which is no more than two or three drops in the bucket to the east side of Blood River. The gathering, which was well before Max was born, was the occasion of a big barbecue given for lots of the doctor's patients and friends. Most doctors aren't known for treating their patients to parties, so the crowd enjoyed the feast exceedingly, not knowing when they'd enjoyed themselves so much, and they went home with stuffed stomachs and hardy dispositions.

There may have been a burp that resembled a bark. Unbeknownst to the unsuspecting, what the good doctor had barbecued was a big fat dog.

Well, that just did it. When the word got out, which it inevitably would in a community as small as New Concord, the doctor's friends put up a howl that would have put a frown on a full moon's face. They convulsed into a collective conniption fit. New Concord became New Discord. The doggoned guests forced the doctor to leave the community altogether. There's no telling how many went on a diet after that, or had their stomachs pumped. Stands to reason, the next time there was a barbecue, everybody wanted to see the critter before it was cooked.

Mark Twain's "Celebrated Jumping Frog of Calaveras County" in California doesn't have a thing on what is remembered on Blood River in Kentucky as the "Famous Dog Dinner of Calloway County."

Then there was Max Bonner's story about the skinny-dipping boys of Blood River. Birthday suits have a rich, well-deserved tradition along almost all rivers of Kentucky. There's hardly anything as innocent as a birthday suit. When you look at it, everything seems to be in about the right place. There may be a difference here and there, but for the most part it is what it is. When artful fantasy is stripped away, all that's left is a collection of functional parts, plumbing that takes care of business. Well, according to the gospel of Max Bonner, "We didn't have any bathing suits and the boys were so rank, being onery, some old mean boys, they were swinging their things."

"Swinging their things?"

"You know. Their privates."

"Well, now."

"Yessir. Pap put a stop to it."

"That's good."

Why, there's no telling where this kind of behavior might have led to if Pap hadn't stepped in and straightened out things. Human sexuality definitely ought to be, so to speak, nipped in the bud. Or covered with a leaf. It's one thing to have a thing. It's another thing to swing it. Lord have mercy. It's the last thing thought about on the nude beach at Club-Med on Guadaloupe. Mercy. You'd think nudity by now would have earned its rightful place in the sun.

"In the spring, it was popular to have revival baptizings, and there was another swimming hole below one of the dams on Blood, but we wouldn't go in after a baptizing."

"Why not, for Heaven's sake?"

"Because we were told that the sins might wash down on us," said

Max, handing over a crusted piece of iron that looks like it has been permanently keelhauled.

"What's this?"

"A toy truck, a 1914 replica. It was fished out of Blood River."

"Well." It must have been a child's wonderment. Somebody may have saved milk and egg money to buy it for a birthday, or maybe it was a Christmas gift, probably not just for the heck of it. Times were too tough back then. It was the year after the great floods on the Ohio River, when nearly five hundred lives were lost. Flood or drought, Max Bonner says, "People had to hustle to make ends meet."

He offers another water-worn object heavy with age. It's flat, about tip-of-fingernail- to first-joint thick, square with a hole in it. Would have made a considerable paperweight.

"What is it?"

"Old mill lock."

The conversation with Max Bonner begins in what has become the basement of his home, the space that used to be his grocery store. Look around and there are still traces of it, but the muddy footprints are gone, two fingers placed to thoughtful, pinched lips are no more. Up until ten years ago, it was a mom and pop business with gas pumps out front. It lasted right onto a quarter of a century. There was trade with fishermen—groceries, fish, and tackle—that sort of thing. Bait, too. "At four o'clock in the morning, people would be outside banging on their minnow buckets," says Max. "I'd have to get up and go get the bait. They'd fish all morning and come in about noon."

"Sell them baloney sandwiches?"

"Lots of baloney sandwiches. Awful busy in spring."

There are individual preferences bordering on prejudices concerning the noble baloney sandwich. One is that it ought to be disgraced with American cheese. Another is that it needs to be graffited with mustard or stained with a slice of tomato. Some radicals insist on lettuce. The best way is to consummate it between two pieces of *light bread*. If that's not handy, just fold the baloney over and work it into your mouth like a posthole digger. Bites, not nibbles.

Time was, Max had a dock, and he rented five or six boats. That is to say, until people began to have their own boats. It was before you could put in at Wildcat Creek boat ramp. After that, things began to change. Many things. Yessir, downright changed. They still call it "progress," and maybe that's what it has been—bring your own boat, your own minnows, your own baloney sandwiches. Mind your own business and do your own thing. Swing your own thing too.

Nowadays, Mr. and Mrs. Bonner have gone in the other direction. They've "retired" to become gardeners again, preservers of the fruits of the soil, "More than we can use"—green beans, kraut, pickled okra, jalapeño peppers, tomatoes, green tomato relish, ripe tomato relish, tomato juice, beets, sides of bacon, two-year-old cured hams from hogs, not dogs.

"I played in Blood when I was a kid," says Max. "Dad ran a water mill, a gristmill for corn, a sawmill, a cotton gin for quilts. People grew a little cotton for quilts. We moved there in '31. Along Blood River there were Brandon Mill, Hamlin Mill, Stubblefield Mill, and Freeland Mill. Pap ran his until TVA run us out."

"Bitterness?"

"Got fair price at the time. Some people didn't want to move. TVA bought everybody out. Started buying in '39. Flooded in '45. Took more than they needed. Some people had to move more than once, some moved three times."

Max and his wife, Anne, have accepted reality, perhaps the same way the Chickasaw Nation acceded to General Andrew Jackson and Governor Isaac Shelby in a deal to be recorded as the Jackson Purchase. It added up to about two thousand square miles of Mississippi Embayment upon which to build the new, advanced civilization of eight Kentucky counties: Ballard, Calloway, Carlisle, Fulton, Graves, Hickman, Marshall, and McCracken. Blood River and a lot of unrecorded Chickasaw history came with it.

The Chickasaw people were simply overpowered. The Five Civilized Tribes—Cherokee, Chickasaw, Choctaw, Creek, and Seminole—were forced to walk (some traveled by boat on the rivers) to a promised land, the Indian Territory, what is now Oklahoma. A fourth of those evicted from their homeland and required to resettle died on the Trail of Tears.

Stories of Blood River echo through Max and Anne Bonner's forsaken grocery store, skipping like a flat rock on a muddy, stilled surface. Memories keen past the green beans, kraut, and green tomato relish on shelves that once held that which accommodated the descendants of those who banished the Native Americans. The country grocery store is history too, but at least this one time a family garden has risen from the dead and replaced the mass-produced, advertising-driven, manufactured commodities of the "new" culture. Now there's time to savor better recollections, because bitterness pays poor wages.

"Two to three hundred yards up on that hill there was a tree-rope swing, and we'd swing out into the river and play 'when the cat dies.'"

"'When the cat dies?'"

"It was an old birch tree up on the side of the river. We'd run down the bank and swing 150 to 200 feet out into the middle, then we'd swing back. A boy who had his clothes on, he swung out, but he couldn't hold on. That's when the cat dies."

"How deep was the water?"

"Eight to ten feet."

Max doesn't say whether the cat lived to talk about it, but if he hadn't survived, Max probably would say so. Most boys of summer are born to swim. Most swing their things as best they can with what they've got. Max mentions again that he doesn't remember Blood River ever being red. He says it was muddy after rain for sure; otherwise, it was clear. If this is true, the Indian massacre legend begins to take on more likelihood. There are outlines of tribal mounds along the Blood, and Max believes there were Indian villages too. Historians have found little or no evidence to support a belief that the small Chickasaw Nation used what is now the Jackson Purchase (also called the Mississippi Embayment) for anything more than occasional hunting forays.

It is also believed that the Chickasaws and the Choctaws once were a single tribe. What is now the land bought from the Chickasaws in 1818 was then a wilderness of sloughs, a potentially contentious hunting ground that was one of the most forbidding places on the face of the earth. It could be speculated that Blood River was named as a result of the two tribes fighting over epic hunting rights. Somewhere, in either pre-Kentucky or pre-Tennessee, there may have been mortal combat on such a heroic scale that the river indeed ran red with blood.

Max Bonner didn't win a Congressional Medal of Honor, but he knows about war. He was with the infantry in Korea, 24th Infantry Division. On July 13, 1951, a piece of shrapnel hit him in the head, and he was laid up for a month in a hospital. He thought it was one of those million-dollar wounds, certainly bad enough to be ordered home with, but "They sent my ass right back where I was, on the front line. I rotated out after one year."

Max is secure in the darkening last pickup truck phase of his life. He's not out skinny-dipping, letting cats die, or barbecuing dogs. He's just plain Max Bonner from Blood River, living out as good a life as he knows how, liking his catfish and his crappie, toting his own minnow bucket. Max still remembers the times when he was sixteen or seventeen years old and cut bushes for twenty cents a day. "Hard way to make a living. We boys growed up tough as nails."

Paul Max Bonner lives three hundred feet from the spot where he was born. Jim is his seven-year-old bird dog. He's slowing down but shows life when Max appears. "You going to eat him?"

"No, but I'm not going to hunt him much. My hip is bothering me."

Max drives out to look at what's become of the neighborhood, what's happened to the farms, the timberland, the streams flowing into Blood.

"There was the two-room schoolhouse over there. See that old brick house overlooking Blood River? It was built in 1838. It has walls two and a half feet thick. My great-grandfather, Charles Brandon, dammed up the river. Lots of snakes right below the dam. There used to be a community fish trap. Blood River Baptist Church moved up on the hill when the water came up. Everybody had their own little place and stayed on it. Never was much and is less now."

Pottertown Road leads past Whiskey Ridge Road to a subdivision of slivers of real estate, little pieces of chopped up earth with a river view of Blood, everything from condominiums to mobile homes, utility sheds, carports, and fishing paraphernalia.

A Chickasaw face might have a tear on it.

New Concord, once called Humility, used to have a blacksmith shop, a general store, a hotel, and a man who barbecued a dog. Today, there's a post office (the zip code is 42076), there's a spot where the old New Concord High School used to be, and there are a Your Store (Under New Management), a beauty shop, and a bait shop. There are the New Concord Church of Christ, Bethany Baptist Church, and the old New Concord Cemetery.

"When the railroad came, New Concord died," says Max, patiently.

Panther Creek comes in where Blood River becomes "embayment." It has rained all night, the Bradford blossoms are dripping, ducks and deer are refreshed, and Panther is stalking rapidly toward muddy Blood, hungry for the chase, gathering the swelling, saturated sloughs of cypress, oak, beech, and pine. Max parks the pickup and walks across a footbridge to take a closer look.

He stands on the edge of the bubbling confluence, where there's evidence of a campfire, probably built the night before.

"Who do you think it was?"

"People come down here and mess around. It's hard to tell, could have been anybody."

The Chickasaw face won't go away. The tearstain won't fade.

Clarks River (not Clark's or Clarks' or Clarks's) takes its name from two brothers, George Rogers Clark (1752-1818) and William Clark (1770-1838). In the winter of 1777-78, Lieutenant Colonel George Rogers Clark, with new marching orders in hand, descended the lower Ohio River. At the Falls of the Ohio he had explored the sites that would become Louisville on the south bank and Clarksville on the northern side. On January 27, 1778, Clark and his "army" of about two hundred men landed on Owen's Island near the mouth of the Tennessee River. It had taken the party four days to make the southwesterly journey from Corn Island at the troublesome Falls of the Ohio.

At Benton, in Marshall County, near the East Fork of Clarks River, revered Kentucky journalist Joe Cross Creason (1918-1974) was born. He wrote *Joe Creason's Kentucky* and *Crossroads and Coffee Trees*. Joe was born and bred a western Kentuckian, but he spoke for the entire Commonwealth. He is buried in a cemetery by the side of the road on the edge of Bethel, in Bath County. A coffee tree was planted on top of his grave; each year, it stands taller, giving wider shade to those who stop long enough to read the historical marker.

The mouth of Clarks River is on the eastern edge of Paducah on the Tennessee River, a short distance upstream from the confluence of the Tennessee and the Ohio. The Clarks River boat ramp, accessible from U.S. 60 on the east side of Paducah, is ample proof that most "$500 Fine for Littering" signs don't work worth a damn. The area looks like a garbage dump complete with obscene graffiti written on the concrete pilings supporting the highway above. It might have made as much sense to put up a sign that said "$500 Prize for Littering." Chief Paduke, Irvin S. Cobb, Joe Creason, and Alben W. Barkley may be in heaven, all singing the chorus for reform of bad habits. But then, some cultural depravities may be irreversible even in four extraordinary lifetimes.

A drive along the roads leading south from Paducah toward the forks of Clarks River is a rich study in ceramic geese and concrete lions, body shops and beauty shops, body piercing and tattoo parlors. Signs of the consumerism-driven times, these landmarks may become in two or three more centuries as powdery as the bones and artifacts of the Chickasaw tribe that once hunted the area. Clarks River continues its muddy way, and other civilizations will arise, destined to crumble and fall in the fullness of their time. There's increasingly less farmland to be abandoned, sold, and chopped up into ragged pieces.

The area called home by the Paducah International Raceway is also sprinkled with churches of assorted beliefs. One additional denomination, which with God's help might take hold and spread across the Commonwealth, could be the United Apostolic Believers in Cleaning up Mankind's Mess. Its mission would be to 1) adopt a waterway, 2) then adopt a highway, 3) adopt a culture, 4) adopt a self. Clarks River was surely pristine in the time of Chief Paduke and the Chickasaw Nation. In late winter the stream, whose headwaters reach deep into McCracken, Marshall, and Graves Counties, was fast moving, churning, and muddy after heavy rain.

East and Middle Forks of Clarks River begin in Tennessee, crossing northward into Kentucky like capillaries emerging from the tips of long fingers, spreading inward toward the palm of the hand—the Jackson Purchase of 1818, formerly the hunting grounds of the proud Indian tribes of the Chickasaw Nation.

In exchange for $300,000, the Indians gave up all claim to lands east of the Mississippi River and north of the Mississippi state line. Kentucky grew by two thousand square miles and Tennessee by six thousand square miles

The Tennessee River is 652 miles long and begins at the confluence of the Holston and French Broad Rivers on the eastern edge of Knoxville. The Tennessee, stretching as far south as northern Alabama, drains an area of almost forty-one thousand square miles, an area larger than the entire Commonwealth of Kentucky. Tennessee enters Kentucky just south of Fort Heiman at approximately latitude 36.39 and forms Kentucky Lake, believed to be one of the largest manmade lakes in the world—84 miles long with a shoreline of more than 2,300 miles, and covering a surface of nearly 50,000 acres in the Commonwealth. (The rest is in Tennessee.) Arthur B. Lander Jr. calls Kentucky Lake "arguably the state's top reservoir, both in quality of fish and species diversity." Fishermen will find it worth their bait to consult Lander's *Fishing Guide to Kentucky's Major Lakes.*

The Tennessee Valley Authority was established in 1933. One of the nine main TVA dams on the Tennessee is Kentucky River Dam, built in 1944 near the juncture of Livingston, Lyon, and Marshall Counties. Despite the enormous benefits of its activities—flood control, reduced electric power rates, and increased recreational and commercial opportunities—TVA has been controversial from the outset.

There is a "Land Between the Rivers" and there is a "Land Between the Lakes," sometimes called "LBR" and "LBL." There's a world of difference. The formation of Kentucky Lake on the Tennessee River and nearby Lake Barkley, constructed by the Army Corps of Engineers in 1965 on the Cumberland, created the Land Between the Lakes (170,000 acres.) For every new boat dock, there was an obliterated home, barn, church, or hitching post. The people who had lived in the area (about 2,500) had always called it the Land Between the Rivers. To outsiders unfamiliar with local history, the Land Between the Lakes is a place to hunt, fish, and bask in sunsets. For the thousands of homesteaders who were displaced from the Land Between the Rivers, there are remembrances deepening into bitterness.

The Jackson Purchase tributaries of the Tennessee River include Blood River, Snipe Creek, Anderson Creek, Cool Creek, Jonathan Creek, Bear Creek, Cap Spring Creek, King Creek, Malcolm Creek, Little Bear Creek, Cypress Creek, and Clark's River. One of the tributaries of the West Fork of Clark's River is Panther Creek, near the Clear Springs community. Two years after the 1818 treaty with the Chickasaw Nation, the ancestors of Kentucky author Bobbie Ann Mason (born1940) settled in this area. Five generations later, she has achieved national fame with her novels *In Country*, *Feather Crowns*, and *Clear Springs*, a finalist for a Pulitzer Prize.

Mississippi

The Mississippi is a just and equitable river; it never tumbles one man's farm overboard without building a new farm just like it for that man's neighbor. This keeps down hard feelings.

Mark Twain
Life on the Mississippi

All rivers of Kentucky find their way to the "Father of Waters." Not one escapes it. The smallest rivulet is pulled to it. The mightiest river, the most peevish wet weather runoff, the most placid of pools has a destiny with Big River. As it is with moving water, so it is with humankind. The Mississippi is a main stream that collects who we are, what we've been, who we hope to become, bearing us onward inexorably—children, adults, tree limbs, plastic bottles, and other objects subject to gravity. No turning back. No excuses. No re-voting. All postponements are short-lived. Ego-driven explanations are as rock and moss clinging stubbornly—in time, detached, borne downstream. We may be swept away at flood crest, we may flow more smoothly and willingly, but leave we must. The hydrologic cycle banks on the good-natured Huck Finn of our best of selves.

Isolation, deadly as greed, is unnatural in a watershed. Cycling

251

moisture is a gift; stagnant ponds produce rot. When Huck left his drunken Pap and shoved off down Big River, he chanced upon Jim and in that meeting there was implicit faith that it was the best chance for freedom.

The Mississippi River's rounding off of Kentucky is a final reminder of certain mortality, possible immortality, and behooving mortals in their innocence, recklessness, or stupidity neither to presume nor to persuade too much. Innocence on Big River is often rewarded with misery, but arrogance on it is certain to incur disaster. There's *flow*, and it must be felt to be understood. The Hucks and Harlan Hubbards of earthly rivers will dare to dream, allowing for doubt with questioning minds, studying human and watery conditions, wary through fog, around islands and over sandbars, giving space to passing towboats, fellow rafters, and shantyboaters.

Huck and Jim had missed Cairo in the fog, but there was no turning back on the raft. They were at the beginning of the lower Mississippi, the broad sweep from Wickliffe, Kentucky, to New Madrid, Missouri, and Kentucky Point Bar in westernmost Fulton County. The Confluence of America—the meeting of the Ohio and Mississippi Rivers—is a coming together of the rivers of Kentucky and streams as far away as Montana and Minnesota. Harlan Hubbard described it in *Shantyboat: A River Way of Life*. "The Ohio did not end, nor did the Mississippi, at first, seem to be different. It was all water merging and making its way down to the sea, carrying us along with it."

The volume of water at Cairo, Illinois, and Wickliffe, Kentucky, is measured in hundreds of thousands of cubic feet per second. From this point to the Kentucky Bend, Old Man River has engorged to become more than a mile wide, with a solemn, fat, old man's attitude to match.

From Fort Defiance with Civil War nightmares ingrained at Cairo, its downtown desolated by more recent river flood and racial discord, past the Native American Wickliffe Mounds, A.D. 1000 to 1300, the Mississippi rolls past the towering, shining Fort Jefferson Memorial Cross at the Confluence, a statement for egocentric Christianity and ecumenical longing. The controversial manmade symbol is vulnerable to lightning bolts and non-Christian conviction, while the Mississippi is watertight in timelessness.

"The Gibraltar of the West" stands approximately halfway between Wickliffe and Hickman. The late Joe Creason, a journalism jewel in the *Courier-Journal* crown, explained, in *The Best of Joe Creason*, how Hickman County, Kentucky, came "close" to being the District of Columbia of the United States. Takes some explaining.

First of all, Hickman, the town, is the county seat of Fulton. Hickman, the county (adjoining Fulton County), has Clinton for its county seat, but there's also a Clinton County, which is in south central Kentucky, and Albany is its county seat. Joe Creason always had a lot of fun with these Kentucky oddities. It's useful knowledge when trying to be sure you're where you think you are, and more important, where you want to be.

In 1812, some willfully visionary land developers came up with the grand design, the whoopee notion that since the British had burned the Capitol in Washington, it made all kinds of patriotic sense to move the capital of these new United States to the farthest western point in the new nation. Why not Red Banks on the Mississippi River between Wickliffe and Hickman? The name would be changed from the run-of-the-mill "Red Banks" to the flag-waving "Columbus," even though it was still part of the Chickasaw Nation and six years away from being part of the Jackson Purchase. What did Indians know about manifest destiny or the entrepreneurial voodoo involved in conjuring up appropriate new white men's names? What did Indians know about platting new towns, establishing Godly values, orchestrating public relations campaigns, building a new civilization, and all that jazz?

A resolution to accomplish the location of the new capital with a population of thousands and plenty of room to grow was duly introduced in Congress, according to Creason, but the grand scheme was mercifully scuttled and that was the end of that. The real estate bonanza bombed with a thud.

Columbus, Kentucky, slept peacefully for another fifty years, until 1861, when the Confederate General Leonidas Polk looked northward from the high bluff, the Gibraltar of the West, and decided to rig a huge chain across the river, a barrier that could be raised and lowered to block damn Yankees. Each link in the chain weighed twenty pounds, and the grand scheme collapsed of its own weight. The huge anchor and chain are now a tourist attraction.

Columbus, Kentucky, had a population of 252 (1990 census). Today, it has the Great River Road State Scenic Byway and a lot fewer headaches. On the other hand, Washington, D.C., has at least been more secure on the banks of the smaller Potomac and hasn't had the perils of Columbus, Hickman, and other Mississippi River towns, where people arise each morning and wonder where Old Man River has sleepwalked during the night.

The 1937 flood forced the relocation of Columbus from the river's edge, two hundred feet up to the top of the bluff, where the view is as breathtaking as any in the Commonwealth of Kentucky.

The Jackson Purchase is an area of 2,141 square miles entirely drained by the Tennessee, Ohio, and Mississippi rivers. The Kentucky counties with a Mississippi River shoreline are Ballard, Carlisle, Fulton, and Hickman.

Bayou du Chien and Obion Creek converge at Hickman, then enter the Mississippi River. Bayou du Chien and its South Fork originate in Graves County in the vicinity of Water Valley. Little Bayou du Chien enters the main stream just west of Moscow, Kentucky. Its headwaters lie on the western side of Fulton, Kentucky, and South Fulton, Tennessee.

The Purchase tributaries of the Mississippi also include Mayfield Creek, Back Slough, Mud Creek, Little Mud Creek, Running Slough, Sutton Slough, and Pond Slough. (Beaver Slough and Long Slough cross into Tennessee before emptying into the Mississippi.) The small patches of water in the Kentucky Bend are Beaver Slough, Long Slough, Stonewall Lake, and Watson Lake.

Seismologists predict that another earthquake with a magnitude of 6.0 or higher will strike the New Madrid seismic zone. The consequences will be exceedingly greater than those in 1811-12, when an earthquake, moving as stealthily as a snake handler, seized Old Man River, squeezed it by the throat, and slung it back to the ground. The Mississippi recoiled, rerouted itself, slithered away, and created Reelfoot Lake as a tiny portion of its prideful hurt. Today, a fringe of Reelfoot

National Wildlife refuge extends from Tennessee into Fulton County, Kentucky, and includes a slender finger of Upper Blue Basin.

Kenneth Lynn, tall, broad-shouldered, fifty-four years old, has lived and farmed, raised a family, and fought the river for fifty years in the Kentucky Bend section of Fulton County, the little toenail piece of Kentucky that can't be reached by land from Kentucky. Kenneth's pickup truck moves south out of the Bend toward the Tennessee state line. It's the only way out unless he's traveling by boat. Kenneth may be headed toward Tiptonville on a trip that may include the farmer's supply store, the grocery, or the doctor.

When he was a boy, Kenneth Lynn helped to clear the land in the Kentucky Bend. When he wasn't in school he picked up chunks, sprouts, and pieces of roots. By hand and by axe he and his family cleared the land, the final piece of rich soil called "Kentucky." He sees the strange car parked by the side of the road, close to the small, square cemetery graveled and enclosed with a chain link fence. Most of the eighteenth- and nineteenth-century headstones are upright and legible.

> *His body is here*
> *His spirit has gone*
> *To heaven*
> *from whence it came*
>
> *Rest Mother,*
> *rest in quiet sleep*
> *while friends in sorrow*
> *o'er thee weep*

Kenneth possibly figures the man waving his arm is lost or out of gas. There are no gas stations in the Kentucky Bend, no motels, no billboards, no KFCs, no Welcome Centers. Kenneth, who possesses openness and at the same time appears to thrive on solitude, is not unkind or impatient when an outsider flags him down. He has little to fear, except the river. Even for it, respect surpasses fear. Kenneth Lynn knows what to do. Knows it in his bones. Lives with it. Flows with it.

Has no desire to be conquered by it.

"Hello. How are you?" the stranger begins.

"All right."

"I've found that cemetery over there, but I was wondering, where's the church that's marked on my map?"

"Burned down thirty years ago."

"Did?"

"Used to be a cemetery there too, black and white cemetery."

"Well, now."

"It's gone, headstones gone, trees gone," says Kenneth, ruefully looking in the direction from which he's come, back up the two-lane road, due north. He turns again to the stranger, probably to judge for an additional time whether there's a possible threat. Seeing none, he continues, "This is the Whitson Graveyard. Hard to remember where the church was."

"Baptist?"

"Maybe Church of Christ. Two schools gone too."

"Mississippi River comes in?"

"Floods whole thing. In and out by boat."

"Not worried about being washed away?"

"No. Peace and quiet. Summer nights, nice and quiet."

"What are the winters like?"

"Not too bad."

Kenneth Lynn does not take long to say what he thinks. Like most rural Kentuckians, he does not talk in paragraphs or chapters. Punctuation depends upon circumstance. Grammar is a man named Billy, who used to sing "Deetroit City" at the Grand Ole Opry, and he spells it "Grammer." A few words are usually sufficient. Sometimes even words are too much. A smile or a troubled look will speak volumes. But it would be wrong to generalize. Some Kentuckians have been known to get up a full head of steam and talk until the dogs start howling.

The *Atlas of Kentucky* calls this area "New Madrid Bend." Some Tennesseans call it "Bessie Bend." The few, like Kenneth Lynn, who actually live in the isolated curve of the river, prefer "Kentucky Bend." Whatever it's named, it's where the Mississippi River drops into

Tennessee, then curls back up into Kentucky, as if having forgotten something or somebody, then loops past New Madrid, Missouri, then falls south again between Missouri and Tennessee. Noosed in the middle are 15,000 acres owned and operated by about twelve people, farming on a leaky waterbed requiring imagination, strength, courage, and conviction. Maybe habit, too. Flotation devices probably wouldn't hurt either.

When the floods arrive, most farmers temporarily depart, but Kenneth stays put to protect the property from looters.

"No, now. You'd think not."

"Oh, yes," says Kenneth, standing tall and straight beside his pickup truck near the old graveyard, where the bones of pioneers progress to pieces in their watery graves—safe, free, untroubled, finally. One of the epitaphs speaks to the hydrologic cycle and its relationship to humanity..

Safely anchored in the harbor of eternity.

A historical marker stands where the road turns from pavement to gravel. The words recall Kentucky's claim of land to the "westernmost middle" of the Mississippi River, the squabble with Tennessee over the boundary line, the Cox Peebles Survey of 1858-59, resulting in compromise and a nearby village named Compromise. It "prospered during steamboat era but was eroded by the river ca 1880." "Erode" is one of the more polite words in the Kentucky Bend—the Mississippi River daily serves warning that it accommodates neither compromise nor Compromise.

The only land route to Kentucky Bend, the stubby little toe, most western out-of-joint point of Kentucky, is by highway 22 from Tennessee, threading through what's left of the remnants of the community of Bessie. Local residents figure that the original Bessie, such as she was, such as she may have been, such as she ever hoped to become, lies buried somewhere in the fiery muck of the 1811-12 New Madrid earthquakes. "Bessie" today is scattered houses, beer cans in the ditch beneath the sign "Welcome to Kentucky where Education pays."

James Lal Penick Jr.'s revised edition of *The New Madrid Earthquakes* contains "An Essay on Sources," a starting point for study of North

America's "Day of Judgment" and "Indian Armageddon." The quakes were centered in this area, December 16, 1811 to February 7, 1812— 1,874 shocks recorded by a Louisville engineer and surveyor. Careful consideration of the New Madrid fault goes beyond the academic. The sobering reality is rooted in the scientific prediction that a New Madrid earthquake will occur again in approximately four hundred years. But remember, children, neither earthquakes nor Mississippi Rivers conform to human prognostications. By the year 2411 the 1811-12 quakes in New Madrid, which rang bells in Boston and stopped clocks in Philadelphia, will be minuscule compared to the next probable mass devastation from Paducah through Henderson, Owensboro, and Louisville, to Covington-Newport. There's a strong likelihood that the next earthquake will occur at almost any time.

Gravel road to the north...end of a piece of the world...the Kentucky world...no hunting...no trespassing...posted...no cattle...no fences...no billboards...no double arches...lone dog barking...a hawk...no subculture...no counterculture...cry of a killdeer...winter kudzu skeletons on the levee...the damnedest biggest tree trunk...then, no houses...no barns...not anything.

There are just two roads—Kentucky Bend Road and Stepp Road (spelled Steppe on some maps)—in Kentucky Bend. The only other sign of Commonwealth earth is an island named Madrid Bar, which at the beginning of the twenty-first century is the most western sliver of anything calling itself Kentucky—this, too, subject to change without prior notice, like a High Sheriff's warrant served at sunrise or sunset or dead of night, it doesn't make a drop of difference.

The Kentucky Bend Road leads north toward "Kentucky Point." There's barely enough room for one car on the levee. It's not exactly the kind of place anybody would want to drop over the side. It looks like the end of creation. A disappearance here would stand a good chance of being deadly. Untold numbers from the time of de Soto and before have gone down into the water, never to be found. Should the end be here and now? A lover's leap? When a puddled depression with a hint of quicksand appears ahead, it's time to hope the car's reverse gear still works and the driver's eye is steady enough to back up to a tight turnaround. No time for heroics.

Stepp Road cuts west, to the right, if you're heading south. The Dead End sign is riddled with bullet holes, as good a time as any to stop and pick a blue-headed henbit, funky nuisance weed that looks like a Lilliputian bunny rabbit more than it does a baby chick. It's a good time to place it on the top of the dashboard for good luck, a white flag, a talisman to ward off trouble. On the right—a deep washpan crevice, where water drains down to the netherworld; on the left, a falling-in shed barely covering sorely-used farm equipment. At the end of the public road the "Do Not Enter" sign appears to mean what it says. The turnaround is easier and seems the proper thing to do. Respect private property. Don't go looking for trouble. Step back. Backtrack.

"I went across Stepp Road to the dead end."

"That's where I live," says Kenneth Lynn, proudly, steeped in the lore of rights and prerogatives of ownership.

"Well. Is Stepp Road named for somebody?"

"Alfred Stepp. He died in 1987. I work for his widow, Adrienne. She's eighty-six years old."

"I'd like to talk to her. Do you suppose I could?"

"Go to the end of the public road and drive on in. I live in the red house. She lives in the green house."

"Dogs?"

"I don't keep bitin' dogs. Just tell 'em to git down. Else they'll jump up on you."

"Thank you."

"You're welcome," says Kenneth, climbing back into his pickup and heading on his way south out of the Bend toward Tiptonville. Good to have friends in out-of-the-way places. No strings attached. No promises. No deceptions. No unreasonable expectations. No agendas. Only the flow of the river bringing water to a meeting place, not on human terms but mandated by himself, Old Man Mississippi. If it be flood, then flood it be. If it be float, then float it be. If it be drown, then drown it be.

These don't look like the farms on the Kentucky mainland. The Bend is space, silence, sloughs, and washpans. At one house, two dogs

259

sleeping, two dogs barking, several cars and pickup trucks, but no people in sight. Two TV antennas for one trailer. Deserted house with the red flag on the mailbox left in the up position. The mail carrier must know nobody's home. The red flag is a reminder that a family once lived on this place. A graveyard for heavy farm equipment, rusted beyond resurrection. Mongrel pups tumble teacups over saucers, clambering for any likely attention. Food would be appreciated.

For a human being, it's a better feeling crossing into "No Trespassing" territory when management says it's all right. The dogs come out to greet, ears up, tails taut, shoulder hairs bristling on the off chance that extra courage is required. The knowledge that they're not "bitin' dogs" is immensely useful. "Git down."

It works.

A knock on the door of the red house produces no stirring inside. The dogs may be thinking, we could have told you so, Pal, but you were so proud of yourself with that "Git down" business, you probably wouldn't have believed us if we had explained it to you in simple language you should have been able to understand. Damn two-leggers to hell and back, anyway. Sometimes, feel sorry for them.

The dogs are waiting at the green house and hear "Git down" again, so unnecessary, so trite, so like pompous Dog Lords. A knock on the door brings instant sounds of moving feet. "You want to talk to *her*," says a young man, Kenneth's son, more than likely on his way to chores. In March, farmers in the Bend are getting ready to plant corn and fertilize wheat. A constant worry is wind blowing across the Bend, bowling over the stems, making the harvest less bountiful. The women know this too, but they don't allow themselves the luxury of fretting aloud. They are tough because they know their men must be tough. All God's children goin' to be tough together.

Adrienne Stepp walks to the front door with confidence born and bred by the river. She needs only to be told that Kenneth said a visit would be in order, for when Kenneth Lynn says something, she'll bank on it. An eighty-six-year old matriarch has her fond reminiscences, her earned privileges, but she needs a sidekick with a strong arm, a straight back, and an honest disposition. That spells Kenneth. "Come in," says

Adrienne, taking the center place on a comfortable couch. She faces north, her back to the homeland built upon a deep sense of place, generations of heritage to be defended, values to be cherished. All of that is enough for any one mortal coming to the conclusion of a lifetime full of dreams and the work that makes them real.

"Thank you, ma'am. I've come to talk about rivers of Kentucky, especially the Mississippi, because, well, here it is."

"I've lived on the Mississippi all my life," says Adrienne, widow of Alfred, who once vowed he'd spend every penny he had to keep the State of Tennessee from petitioning the Bend away from Kentucky. Things were bad enough without that atrocity. In the beginning, there were 4,000 acres, but over the years Alfred and Adrienne saw the acreage reduced by necessity born of capricious, mainly declining, then vanishing markets. Four silos stand empty—the cattle operation has ceased because it wasn't making a profit. The hogs are gone—they weren't paying their way. There's no livestock in the Kentucky Bend in the year 2000—only corn, wheat, and beans. No need for fences, no need at all. There are about a half-dozen houses in the Bend and some of those are deserted. In spring, when the floods usually come, the houses are forsaken, except for the one or two people, like Kenneth, who ride it out in boats to protect property against looting.

Adrienne explains it in an even tone, muted by a go-round last year with pneumonia and a recurring bronchial condition. She calls out, friendly like, to the other room: "Barbara and Lucy, you all come on in here."

Two younger steel magnolias appear—Barbara, the wife of Kenneth, and "Lucy" (Mary Catherine), their daughter. Sentinels, they've been invited into Captain's quarters to relax from housekeeping jobs. They take places, protectively, on either side of Adrienne. They are long-suffering as the conversation returns to water.

"Wished the flood wouldn't get us about every year," says Mary Catherine, perpetual apprehension checked for the moment.

"When does it come?"

She has the look of a deer anticipating bright lights. She cautiously nibbles at the sprigs and stems of conversation.

"' Bout now," she says, looking up, as if reminded that the time for

261

the annual threat and its searing pain, the moving out, is near. Staying ahead of the floods, outwitting them, refusing to be vanquished by them—such has been the burden of generations of men, women, children, and four-legged creatures in the cutoff called Kentucky Bend. The hawks and the eagles circle above the distress, and they claim superiority.

Mary Catherine Reynolds, twenty-seven years old, wife of Michael, mother of two sons, Hunter and Joshua, sits resolutely on one end of the couch on the downstream side. She's in Adrienne's homestead at the end of the line, as far west as you can go in Kentucky and still be in Kentucky. You might be in a boat or slogging around on the Mississippi River side of the levee, but that's not recommended for the tenderfoot or the faint of heart. Out there, by the levee, oh yes, great God Almighty, it's a tangle of mammoth trees and mats of scrub brush harassed by the river coming around like a noose twirled by a pursuing posse. Coiled, constantly changing, the Mississippi River shoreline doesn't care one snag for definite tracing, doesn't respect convenient lines drawn on deeded plats, a fact of Big River life that Huck and Jim understood. They had a healthy respect for godforsaken havens populated by venomous water moccasins with stoney-hearted pits beneath their glassy eyes, mouths gaping in sticky, frothy whiteness.

Mary Catherine's mother, Barbara Lynn, sits on the other end of the couch beneath the window overlooking Watson Lake, usually a pleasant finger of water. But each year the arm and the shoulder grow restless, they flex, and the finger points accusingly. The Mississippi River floods come from that direction, backwater encroaching from Kentucky Point Bar. Before the last two houses are encircled and the lane leading in from Stepp Road begins to disappear, families know it's best to get out—just get the hell out.

In the center of the couch, the benefactress, Adrienne, owns more than 2,000 acres of the total 15,000 acres in the Kentucky Bend. Proud of her life's work, she wouldn't want to be any place else. Alfred had come there in the late ' 20s, and he and Adrienne were married in 1954. Today, in late summer, thunder booms—*bumpbumpbumppp, bumpbumpbumppp*—in the bend and the hoot owls are riled on their roosts, but the rain has still not come to break the drought. The corn is drying and the wind is blowing it over, and the harvest has come sooner than Adrienne would like.

Kenneth and his two sons, David and Donald, have come to grips with managing and farming Adrienne's land, flatter than a hard sponged pancake, sometimes aggravatingly saturated with water, other times dry as a bone, requiring double-dipped native intelligence to know when wet is too wet and when wet is about to become wetter, or dry is too dry and soon to become dryer. Of Adrienne's approximately 1,000 cultivated acres, 400 are in corn, 100 in wheat, and 600 are in beans, more or less. Knowing when to plant, when to fertilize, when to harvest are things not learned readily from books or Colleges of Agriculture. It takes a personal, watchful eye on the levee, the river, and the sky. "Straight rows—Kenneth doesn't like crooked rows," says Adrienne with a mellifluous southern accent.

Born upriver at Hickman the year President Wilson pledged neutrality before World War I, the Panama Canal opened, and Robert Frost wrote his first volume of poems, *North of Boston*, Adrienne spends her solitude, reading. "Don't care about TV, rather read," she says, looking forward to the regular arrival of the bookmobile from Hickman. She confesses that she does turn on television when the Mississippi begins to rise and another flood is headed around the bend. "I go by the river gauge at New Madrid. When the water comes and begins to cross the road, I watch television from Paducah and Cape Girardeau."

"What do you read?"

"Novels. Danielle Steele. The new writers. Phyllis Whitney. I like romance and suspense." Sometimes Adrienne puts aside fiction and holds a meeting of the Kentucky Bend Levee Board. She is vice-president and Barbara Lynn is secretary treasurer. "We mow the levee, grade it, pick up chunks after high water," says Adrienne.

"What kind of trees are here?"

"Cypress, cottonwood, pecan—sixty-six acre pecan woods," says Adrienne.

"What do you do for entertainment?"

"We stay home, don't give anybody any trouble. We play a lot of cards," says the matriarch with a sense of calm contentment. The Mississippi River conjures a mood of peace and quiet, playful at recess time, full of fury when the water swells and roars like a bully punching noses.

"The church bus was a form of entertainment," says Mary Catherine.

"Bicycles. Wheelers."

"Wheelers?"

"Four-wheelers," says Barbara.

"Garden, farm, and fish. Sometimes too quiet," says Mary Catherine, like a doe with some impatience, weary with the cares of survival.

"What do you fish?"

"Crappie, catfish, some bass," says Adrienne. "Those little round fish give a fight. When I was a young girl, we'd go to Cairo and meet the Engineers' Boat. We'd ride down around the Kentucky Bend, get off at Tiptonville, and have dinner at Reelfoot."

"And today, peace and quiet?"

"Yes, and I'm thankful to the Good Lord," says Adrienne.

"Do you fear another New Madrid earthquake?"

"Could happen. Don't worry about it. Our soil would just crack open but not crumble." Adrienne Stepp is a matriarch who understands the Mississippi River from Cairo to the Bend. She loves it. She respects it.

It's her home.

Mid-October is a season for self-possessed hawks to loiter in tall, gnarled trees along the Mississippi levee, the predators looking now and then for wide-eyed, blinking prey. Might, one day, they be looking for us? Are they checking us out now on the off chance of weakness, the possibility of stroke or heart attack? White-hooded bald eagles pass over on short, southeasterly flights to Reelfoot Lake, their favorite place to fish and nest. Why were we not born to fly as they? Why are we rooted in dirt, floated on water? The screak of the hawk and the piercing scream of the eagle cut the moistured air, audible in the absence of honking horns, motorists shouting insults. In the Kentucky Bend there's no need for human beings to be untoward. Staying alive is job enough.

264

A notion of life sustains us, supplies us with a powerfully sweet reason for being. Rivers of Kentucky roll to the sea. We flow with the water.

Dobree Adams, Donna Atto, James Ausenbaugh, Virginia
Bennett, Wendell & Tanya Berry, James Birchfield, Betty Blake, Big
John Blankenship, Max Bonner, Francine & Tom Bonny, Joy Bale
Boone, Roger Brucker, Bobby Burge, John Carson, Edward "Buck" &
Sara Louise Carter, Anne F. Caudill, James Caudill, Connie Chambers,
Marjorie Elizabeth Clagett, Thomas D. Clark, Catesby Clay, Randy
Cochran, Nick Coleman, Sara Combs, Carol Crowe-Carraco, Ben
Culbertson, Dava & Dawn, Linda Scott DeRosier, Craig Dial, Ione
Duke, C.M. Dupier Jr., Fred Evans, Ron Felty, Frances Figart,
Mike Fletcher, Stacey Freibert, Eugene French, Bill Goodman,
Goofy, Carl K. Greene, Jonathan Greene, William Griffin,
Wade Hall, Lowell Harrison, Jean Hatfield, Doc Hawley,
Michael & Miranda Hendrix, Bill Irvin, Ron Isaac, Bonnie
Quantrell Jones, Elsie Gilliam Jones, Patricia Kelley, Col.
Arthur Kelly, Bill & Sue Kelly, Jeanne Penn Lane,
Donna LaVonne, Ivan Lawless, Sam Lawson, John
Lucas, Kenneth, Barbara, & Mary Catherine Lynn,
Jane Ellen Tye Mathis, J.C. May, Ed McClanahan,
Roy McKinney, Renee Muncy, John Jacob Niles,
Gurney Norman, Mary O'Dell, Old # 26, Ray Oliver,
John Ed Pearce, Willie Peck, Frances Peluso, Penny
Perry, Richard P'Poole, Eugenia K. Potter, Terry &
Deborah Ratliff, Gale Reece, Dorothy Richards,
Gene "Bosco" Ross, Capt. Lonnie Ryan, Tres
Seymour, Coleman Sibley, Linda Slagel, Jim &
Blanche Smith, Steve Smith, Laura Sommers,
"Squeeky," Adrienne Stepp, "Radio" & Mary
Stewart, James Still, Howard Stokes, Georgiana
Strickland, Jane Stuart, Richard Taylor, James
"Buck" & Rosalyn Terry, Barry Tonning,
Catherine Tuggle, Vernon White, Bill & Martha
Wiglesworth, A.B. Willhite, Willis & Lottie
Willyard, Glen "Parson Woody" Woodard,
Bill York, Terrie M. Young, Dave
Zegeer, Gray Zeitz...

Bibliography

Andrews, Edward Demming. *The People Called Shakers*. New York, 1953.

Aprile, Dianne. *The Abbey of Gethsemani: Place of Peace and Paradox*. Louisville, Kentucky, 1998.

Arnow, Harriette. *The Dollmaker*. New York, 1954.

—. *Flowering of the Cumberland*. New York, 1963.

Asbury, Eslie. *Both Sides of the River*. Lexington, Kentucky, 1984.

Ashworth, William. *Nor Any Drop To Drink*. New York, 1982.

Audubon, John James. *Delineations of American Scenery and Character*. New York, 1926.

Ausenbaugh, James D. *A Place to Rest*. Scottsville, Kentucky, 1992.

Baer, George A., Jr. *Ohio River Basin Navigation System: 1986 Report*. Cincinnati, Ohio, 1986.

Banta, R.E. *The Ohio*. Lexington, Kentucky, 1998.

Barker, Garry. *Notes from a Native Son: Essays on the Appalachian Experience*. Knoxville, Tennessee, 1995.

Barry, John M. *Rising Tide: The Great Mississippi Flood of 1927 and How It Changed America*. New York, 1997.

Basler, Roy P., ed. *Abraham Lincoln: His Speeches and Writings*. Franklin Center, Pennsylvania, 1979.

Bates, Captain Alan L., and Captain Clarke C. Hawley. *Moonlite at 8:30: The Excursion Boat Story*. Louisville, Kentucky, 1994.

Berry, Wendell. *Harlan Hubbard: Life and Work*. Lexington, Kentucky, 1990.

—. *A Timbered Choir*. Washington, D.C., 1998.

Billings, Dwight B.; Gurney Norman; and Katherine Ledford, eds. *Confronting Appalachian Stereotypes: Back Talk from an American Region*. Lexington, Kentucky, 1999.

Birchfield, James D. "Gnomon Press and Jonathan Greene: Two Bibliographies." *Kentucky Review* 11, no. 2 (Spring 1992): 49-82.

Bladen, Wilford. *A Geography of Kentucky: A Topical-Regional Overview*. Dubuque, Iowa, 1984. Blotner, Joseph. *Robert Penn Warren: A Biography*. New York, 1997.

Brucker, Roger, and James D. Borden. *Beyond Mammoth Cave: A Tale of*

Obsession in the World's Longest Cave. Carbondale, Illinois, 2000.

Brucker, Roger, and Richard A. Watson. *The Longest Cave*. New York, 1996.

Bullitt, Alexander Clark. *Rambles in the Mammoth Cave During the Year 1844*. Louisville, Kentucky, 1845; St. Louis, Missouri, 1985.

Burns, James Anderson. *The Crucible*. Oneida, Kentucky, 1928.

Caudill, Clifton. *Eastern Kentucky Mountain Memories*. Carcassonne, Kentucky, 1996.

Caudill, Harry M. *Dark Hills to Westward: The Saga of Jenny Wiley*. Ashland, Kentucky, 1994.

—.*The Mountain the Miner and the Lord*. Lexington, Kentucky, 1980.

—.*Night Comes to the Cumberlands: A Biography of a Depressed Area*. Boston, Massachusetts, 1963.

—.*Slender Is the Thread: Tales from a Country Law Office*. Lexington, Kentucky, 1987.

—.*Theirs Be the Power: The Moguls of Eastern Kentucky*. Urbana, Illinois, 1983.

Caudill, Rebecca. *My Appalachia*, New York, 1966.

Chinn, C.W.; Edward Godrich; Sammie W. Hardman; S.A. Wakefield. *Licking River, Kentucky*. Frankfort, Kentucky, 1950.

Clark, Billy C., *A Long Row to Hoe*. Ashland, Kentucky, 1960.

—.*Song of the River*. Ashland, Kentucky, 1994.

Clark, Thomas D. *Agrarian Kentucky*. Lexington, Kentucky, 1977.

—.*A History of Kentucky*. Lexington, Kentucky, 1960.

—.*A History of Laurel County*. London, Kentucky, 1989.

—.*The Kentucky*. New York, 1942; Lexington, Kentucky, 1992.

—.*Pleasant Hill In the Civil War*. Pleasant Hill, Kentucky, 1972.

—, and F. Gerald Ham. *Pleasant Hill and Its Shakers*. Pleasant Hill, Kentucky, 1983.

Cobb, Irvin S. *Exit Laughing*. Indianapolis, Indiana, 1941.

—.*Kentucky: The Proud State*. New York, 1924.

Coffman, Edward. *The Story of Logan County*. Nashville, Tennessee, 1962.

Coleman, J. Winston, Jr. *Famous Kentucky Duels: The Story of the Code of Honor in the Bluegrass State*. Frankfort, Kentucky, 1953.

—.*Steamboats on the Kentucky*. Lexington, Kentucky, 1960.

Coomer, Captain James. *Life on the Ohio*. Lexington, Kentucky, 1997.

Crawford, Byron. *Kentucky Stories*. Paducah, Kentucky, 1994.

Creason, Joe. *The Best of Joe Creason*. Louisville, Kentucky, 1991.

Crocker, Helen B. *The Green River of Kentucky*. Lexington, Kentucky, 1976.

Crowe-Carrico, Carol. *The Big Sandy*. Lexington, Kentucky, 1979.

Csikszentmihalyi, Mihaly. *Flow*. New York, 1990.

Davidson, Robert. *An Excursion to the Mammoth Cave and the Barrens of Kentucky*. Philadelphia, Pennsylvania, 1840.

DeRosier, Linda Scott. *Creeker*. Lexington, Kentucky, 1999.

Dick, David. *A Conversation with Peter P. Pence*. Plum Lick, Kentucky, 1995.

—. *Follow the Storm*. Plum Lick, Kentucky, 1993.

—. *Peace at the Center*. Plum Lick, Kentucky, 1994.

—. *The Quiet Kentuckians*. Plum Lick, Kentucky, 1996.

—. *The Scourges of Heaven*. Lexington, Kentucky, 1997.

—. *The View from Plum Lick*. Plum Lick, Kentucky, 1992.

—, and Lalie Dick. *Home Sweet Kentucky*. Plum Lick, Kentucky, 1999.

Dowing, Jim R. *Uncle Jim's Green River Diary*. 1894.

Dyer, Joyce, ed. *Bloodroot: Reflections on Place by Appalachian Women Writers*. Lexington, Kentucky, 1998.

Eckley, Wilton. *Harriette Arnow*. New York, 1974.

Eifert, Virginia S. *Of Men and Rivers*. New York, 1966.

Federal Writers' Project of the Work Projects Administration for the State of Kentucky. *WPA Guide to Kentucky, The*. Lexington, Kentucky, 1939, 1996.

Fetterman, John. *Stinking Creek*. Lexington, Kentucky, 1967.

Finney, Nikky. *Heartwood*. Lexington, Kentucky, 1997.

Firestone, Clark B. *Sycamore Shores*. New York, 1936.

Fox, John, Jr. *The Little Shepherd of Kingdom Come*. New York, 1903; Lexington, Kentucky, 1987.

—. *The Trail of the Lonesome Pine*. New York, 1908; Lexington, Kentucky, 1984.

Giles, Henry, and Janice Holt Giles. *A Little Better Than Plumb*. Boston, Massachusetts, 1963; Lexington, Kentucky, 1995.

Giles, Janice Holt. *The Believers*. Boston, MA, 1957; Lexington, Kentucky, 1989.

—. *Hannah Fowler*. Boston, MA, 1956; Lexington, Kentucky, 1992.

—. *The Kentuckians*. Boston, MA, 1953; Lexington, Kentucky, 1987.

Goode, Cecil E. *World Wonder Saved*. Mammoth Cave, Kentucky, 1986.

Greene, Jonathan. *Idylls*. Rocky Mount, North Carolina, 1983, 1990.

Greene, W.P. *The Green River Country from Evansville to Bowling Green*. Evansville, Indiana, 1898.

Hardin, C. Thomas, ed. *Rain and Ruin*. Louisville, Kentucky, 1997.

Harrison, Lowell H., and James C. Klotter. *A New History of Kentucky*. Lexington, Kentucky, 1997.

Henley, James P. *The Inventory and Classification of Streams in the Salt River Drainage*. Frankfort, Kentucky, 1983.

Herndon, Jerry A., and George Brosi. *Jesse Stuart: The Man & His Books*. Ashland, Kentucky, 1988.

Holbrook, Chris. *Hell and Ohio*. Frankfort, Kentucky, 1995.

Hovey, H.C. *One Hundred Miles in Mammoth Cave–in 1880*. New York, 1880; Golden, Colorado, 1982.

Hubbard, Harlan. *Payne Hollow Journal*. Lexington, Kentucky, 1996.

—. *Shantyboat: A River Way of Life*. New York, 1953; Lexington, Kentucky, 1977.

—. *Shantyboat Journal*. Lexington, Kentucky, 1994.

—. *Shantyboat on the Bayous*. Lexington, Kentucky, 1990.

Hughes, John R. *Broken-Winged Flights: Forays into the Realm of Truth, Joy, and Freedom*. Lexington, Kentucky, 1998.

Jillson, Willard Rouse. *A Bibliography of the Licking River Valley in Kentucky*. Frankfort, Kentucky, 1968.

Johnson, Leland R. *The Falls City Engineers: A History of the Louisville District Corps of Engineers*. Louisville, Kentucky, 1984.

Kelley, Patricia. *Fifty Monsoons: Ministry of Change Through Women of India*. Prospect, Kentucky, 1999.

Kentucky Division of Water. *Kentucky Rivers Assessment*. Atlanta, Georgia, 1992.

King, Warren Raymond. *The Surface Waters of Kentucky*. Frankfort, Kentucky, 1924.

Kleber, John E., ed. *The Kentucky Encyclopedia*. Lexington, Kentucky, 1992.

Klein, Benjamin F., ed. *The Ohio River: Handbook and Picture Album*. Cincinnati, Ohio, 1958.

Leahy, Ethel C. *Who's Who on the Ohio River and Its Tributaries.* Cincinnati, Ohio, 1931.

Mason, Bobbie Ann. *Clear Springs.* New York, 1999.

McClanahan, Ed. *The Natural Man.* Frankfort, Kentucky, 1983.

Merriam-Webster's Geographical Dictionary, 3d ed. Springfield, Massachusetts, 1997.

Merton, Thomas. *The Seven Storey Mountain.* New York, 1948.

Miller, Jim Wayne. *Brier: His Book.* Frankfort, Kentucky, 1988.

—. *Copperhead Cane.* Louisville, Kentucky, 1995.

Moon, William Least Heat. *Blue Highways: A Journey into America.* New York, 1982.

Murray, Robert K., and Roger W. Brucker. *Trapped! The Story of Floyd Collins.* New York, 1979; Lexington, Kentucky, 1982.

Neal, Julia. *The Kentucky Shakers.* Lexington, Kentuck, 1977.

Neuman, Fred G. *The Story of Paducah.* Paducah, Kentucky, 1927.

Norman, Gurney. *Kinfolks.* Frankfort, Kentucky, 1977.

O'Dell, Mary. *Bridesongs.* Anchorage, Kentucky, 1989.

Offutt, Chris. *The Same River Twice.* New York, 1993.

Pearce, John Ed. *Days of Darkness: The Feuds of Eastern Kentucky.* Lexington, Kentucky, 1944.

—, and Richard Nugent. *The Ohio River.* Lexington, Kentucky, 1989.

Penick, James Lal, Jr. *The New Madrid Earthquakes.* Columbia, Missouri, 1981.

Perrin, W.H.; J.H. Battle; and G.C. Kniffin. *Kentucky: A History of the State.* Louisville, Kentucky, 1886.

Potter, Eugenia K. *Kentucky Women.* Louisville, Kentucky, 1997.

Purvis, Thomas L., *Newport, Kentucky: A Bicentennial History.* Newport, Kentucky, 1966.

Raistrick, A. *Teach Yourself Geology.* London, England 1974.

Rapp, Valerie. *What the River Reveals.* Seattle, Washington, 1997.

Rennick, Robert M. *From Red Hot to Monkey's Eyebrow.* Lexington, Kentucky, 1997.

Rice, Otis K. *The Hatfields & the McCoys.* Lexington, Kentucky, 1982.

Richards, J.A. *A History of Bath County, Kentucky.* Yuma, Arizona, 1961.

Richardson, Darrell C. *Mountain Rising: The Story of James Anderson Burns and Oneida Institute.* Oneida, Kentucky, 1986.

Ridenour, Hugh A. *The Greens of Falls of Rough*. Hanson, Kentucky, 1997.

Riley, James Allan, ed. *Kentucky Voices: A Collection of Contemporary Kentucky Short Stories*. Pineville, Kentucky, 1997.

Ritch, Barbara Ford. *Coal Camp Kids*. Tallahassee, Florida, 1991.

Roberts, Elizabeth Madox. *The Great Meadow*. New York, 1930.

—. *The Time of Man*. New York, 1926; Lexington, Kentucky, 1982.

Roberts, Leonard W. *South from Hell-fer-Sartin*, Lexington, Kentucky, 1955, 1988.

—. *Up Cutshin & Down Greasy*. Lexington, Kentucky, 1959, 1988.

Robertson, John E.L. *Paducah, 1830-1980*. Paducah, Kentucky, 1980.

Robinson, Michael C. *History of Navigation in the Ohio River Basin*. Washington, D.C., 1983.

Rothert, Otto A. *The Outlaws of Cave-In-Rock*. Cleveland, Ohio, 1924.

Sandburg, Carl. *Abraham Lincoln: The Prairie and The War Years*. New York, 1954. Franklin Center, Pennsylvania, 1978.

Scalf, Henry. *Kentucky's Last Frontier*. Pikeville, Kentucky, 1966.

Schmidt, Martin F. *Kentucky Illustrated: The First Hundred Years*. Lexington, Kentucky, 1992.

Sedeen, Margaret, ed. *Great Rivers of the World*. Washington, D.C., 1984.

Sehlinger, Bob. *A Canoeing and Kayaking Guide to the Streams of Kentucky*. Birmingham, Alabama, 1978.

Simpson, George B. *Early Coal Mining on the Tradewater River*. Sturgis, Kentucky, 1987.

Slone, Verna Mae. *What My Heart Wants to Tell*. Washington, D.C., 1979; Lexington, Kentucky, 1987.

Snively, W.D., Jr., and Louanna Furbee. *Satan's Ferryman: A True Tale of the Old Frontier*. New York, 1968.

Steinbeck, John. *Travels With Charley*. New York, 1962.

Still, James. *On Troublesome Creek*. New York, 1941.

—. *River of Earth*. New York, 1940; Lexington, Kentucky, 1978.

—. *Way Down Yonder on Troublesome Creek: Appalachian Riddles and Rusties*. New York, 1974.

—. *The Wolfpen Notebooks: A Record of Appalachian Life*. Lexington, Kentucky, 1991.

—. *The Wolfpen Poems*. Berea, Kentucky, 1986.

Stuart, Dianne Watkins. *Janice Holt Giles: A Writer's Life*. Lexington, Kentucky, 1998.

Stuart, Jane. *Transparencies: Remembrances of My Father, Jesse Stuart*. Archer Editions Press, 1985.

Stuart, Jesse. *Head o' W-Hollow*. New York, 1936; Lexington, Kentucky, 1979.
—. *My World*. Lexington, Kentucky, 1975.

Summers, Hollis. *Other Concerns & Brother Clark*. Athens, Ohio, 1988.

Taylor, Richard, and Adam Jones. *The Palisades of the Kentucky River*, Englewood, Colorado, 1997.

Taylor-Hall, Mary Ann. *Come and Go, Molly Snow*. New York, 1995.

Thom, James Alexander. *Follow the River*. New York, 1981.

Thomas, Samuel W., ed. *Barry Bingham: A Man of His Word*. Lexington, Kentucky, 1993.

Thompson, Ken D. *Beyond the Double Night*. Taylorsville, Kentucky, 1996.

Thompson, Ralph S. *A Sucker's Visit to Mammoth Cave*. New York, 1970.

Townsend, John Wilson. *Kentucky in American Letters*. Cedar Rapids, Iowa, 1913.

Twain, Mark. *The Adventures of Huckleberry Finn*. New York, 1884; Franklin Center, Pennsylvania, 1983.
—. *Life on the Mississippi*. New York, 1888; Franklin Center, Pennsylvania, 1981.

Ulack, Richard; Karl Raitz; Gyula Pauer, eds. *Atlas of Kentucky*. Lexington, Kentucky, 1998.

Waller, Altina L. *Feud: Hatfields, McCoys, and Social Change in Appalachia, 1860-1900*. Chapel Hill, North Caroliana, 1988.

Wallis, Don. *Harlan Hubbard and the River: A Visionary Life*. Yellow Springs, Ohio, 1989.

Ward, William S. *The English Department, University of Kentucky*. Lexington Kentucky, 1964.
—. *A Literary History of Kentucky*. Knoxville, Tennessee, 1988.

Walker, Frank X. *Affrilachia*. Lexington, Kentucky, 2000.

Warren, Robert Penn. *Flood*. New York, 1963.
—. *Jefferson Davis Gets His Citizenship Back*. New York, 1980; Lexington, Kentucky, 1980, 1995.

Webb, W.S., and W.D. Funkhouser. *The Page Site*. Lexington, Kentucky, 1930.

Weller, Jack E. *Yesterday's People*. Lexington, Kentucky, 1966.
Weller, James Marvin. *Geology of Edmonson County*. Frankfort, Kentucky, 1927.
Wheeler, Mary. *Steamboatin' Days: Folksongs of the River Packet Era.*
  Baton Rouge, Louisiana, 1944.
White, John H., and Robert J. White, Sr. *The Island Queen: Cincinnati's
  Excursion Steamer*. Akron, Ohio, 1995.
White, Vernon. *Covered Bridges*. Berea, Kentucky, 1985.
Williams, Roger D. *The Foxhound Stud Book*, vol. 2. Lexington, Kentucky,
  1904.
Wright, John D., Jr. *Lexington: Heart of the Bluegrass*. Lexington,
  Kentucky, 1982.

Maps

C.J. Puetz, ed. *Kentucky County Maps*. Lyndon Station, Wisconsin, 1987, 1999.
Kentucky Atlas and Gazeteer. 1st ed. Yarmouth, Maine, 1997.

Aarons Run • Aces Branch • Adams Branch • Adams Creek • Alderson Branch • Alum Cave Bran̶
Run • Bald Eagle Creek • Balls Fork • Barren River • Bartlett's Fork • Barton Run • Bayou du Chi̶
Beech Creek • Beech Fork • Beechy Creek • Beginning Branch • Ben Run • Bennett Branch • Bens̶
Big Doe Creek • Big Fork • Big Paint Lick • Big Rock • Big Sandy • Big South Fork Creek • B̶
Creek • Boone Fork • Bretz River • Brier Creek • Bowman Branch • Brashears Creek • Brownies̶
Buck Run • Buffalo Creek • Bull Run • Bullskin Creek • Burge Creek • Burning Fork • Burton F̶
Candlelight River • Cane Creek • Cane Run • Cane's Run • Caney Creek • Caney Fork • Canoe ̶
Cave Run Lake • Cedar Branch • Cedar Creek • Chaplin River • Chick Creek • Clarks River • Cl̶
Branch • Coldwater Creek • Colossal River • Combs Branch • Contrary Creek • Cool Creek • C̶
Crane Branch • Crane Creek • Crocus Creek • Crooked Creek • Crystal Creek • Crystal River • C̶
River • Dixon Branch • Doctor's Branch • Dog Creek • Douglas Creek • Drakes Creek • Drenn̶
Fork Creek • Duvall Branch • Dyers Creek • Eagle Creek • Echo River • Elk Creek • Elkhorn Cree̶
Fedscreek • Fighting Fork • Finns River • Flackey Branch • Flat Creek • Fourmile Creek • Fourn̶
Gladie Creek • Glenns Creek • Goose Creek • Grapevine Creek • Grassy Branch • Grassy Creek •̶
Creek • Griers Creek • Grigsby Creek • Grindstone Creek • Gullion Run • Gun Creek • Hall Branc̶
Creek • Hidden River • Hightower Creek • Hinkston Creek • Hinton Branch • Hog Branch • Hoo̶
Lost River • Houston Creek • Howard Branch • Howard Creek • Howard Fork • Hunting Fork •̶
Fork • Jenny's Creek • Jerry Fork • Jessamine Creek • Jetts Creek • John Creek • Johns Creek • J̶
River • King Branch • Kingdom Come Creek • Knob Creek • Landing Run • Lane Branch • Larm̶
Fork • Lees Lick • Left Fork • Levisa Fork • Lick Branch • Lick Creek • Lick Fork • Licking Riv̶
Bend Creek • Little Brush Creek • Little Brushy Creek • Little Bullskin Creek • Little Carr Cree̶
Creek • Little Goose Creek • Little Indian Creek • Little Kentucky River • Little Laurel River •̶
Sandy River • Little South Fork • Little Stoner Creek • Little Sugar Creek • Little Trammel Creek̶
Branch • Long Creek • Long Fall Creek • Long Pond Branch • Long Slough • Looney Creek • Los̶
Twin Creek • Low Gap Branch • Lynam Creek • MacIntosh Creek • Maggard Branch • Majors Ru̶
McAdoo Creek • McCullough Fork • McKecknie Creek • McKnight Creek • Meetinghouse Bra̶
Millers Creek • Millstone Creek • Mississippi River • Moccasin Creek • Mocks Branch • Molly̶
Creek • Muddy Creek • Muddy Fork • Muddygut Creek • Mud Lick • Mud Lick Creek • Mud R̶
Obion Creek • Ohio River • Oil Well Branch • Old Buck Creek • Otter Branch • Otter Creek •̶
Creek • Peter Cave Branch • Peter Cave Run • Pigeonroost Branch • Pigpen Branch • Plum Lick C̶
Possumtrot Branch • Pot Ripple Creek • Pottinger Creek • Potts Creek • Pretty Run • Prices Creek̶
River • Red Bird River • Red Lick Creek • Reese Branch • Reeves Creek • Renfro Branch • River̶
Creek • Rockhouse Fork • Rocklick Fork • Rocky Branch • Rocky Fork • Rogers Creek • Rolli̶
Running Slough • Russell Fork • Sallys Branch • Salt Lick Branch • Salt Lick Creek • Salt River̶
Sebastians Branch • Severn Creek • Shaker Creek • Sharps Branch • Shawnee Run • Shelby Bran̶
Creek • Snake Branch • Snipe Creek • Somerset Creek • Spears Creek • Spout Springs Branch • S̶
Camp Creek • Steele Branch • Steeles Branch • Stillhouse Branch • Stony Fork • Station Camp ̶
Creek • Sugarcamp Branch • Sugar Creek • Sulphur Creek • Sutton Slough • Tan Branch • Tany̶
Branch • Trace Creek • Trace Fork • Tradewater River • Trammel Creek • Triplett Creek • Troublesom̶
Run • Turner's Creek • Twomile Creek • Upper Bad Creek • Upper Branch • Upper St̶
Creek • Wallace Fork • Ward Branch • Wards Branch • Warren's Fork • Watson Branch • Weir̶
Run • White Sulphur Fork • Whitley Branch • Wildcat Creek • Wilder Branch • Will Branch • W̶